P9-AQJ-474
3-
JAN 30 '01
DATE DUE
JAN 2 2 '02
BRODART, CO.
Cat. No. 23-221-003

ANTIQUES
from the
GARDEN

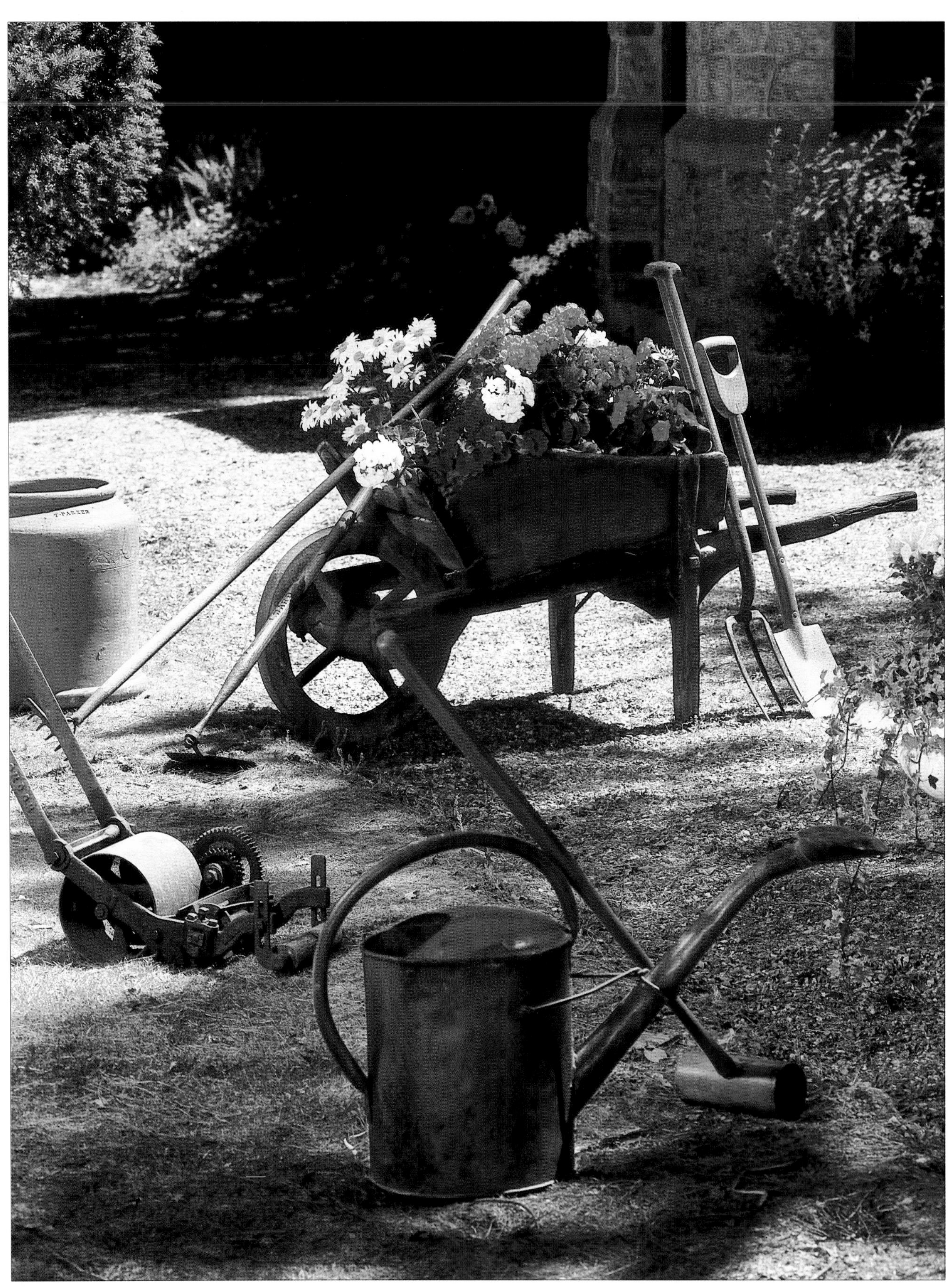
T·PARKER

ANTIQUES from the GARDEN

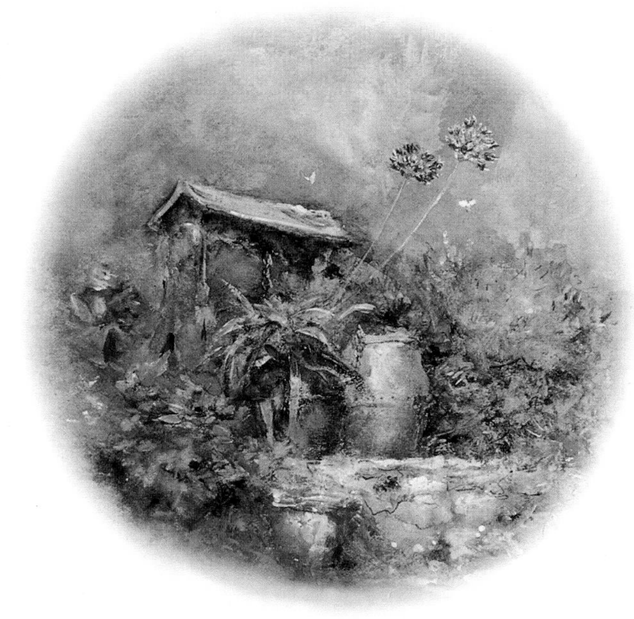

ALISTAIR MORRIS

GARDEN · ART · PRESS

First published 1996

ISBN 1 870673 17 4

British Library Cataloguing-in-Publication Data
A catalogue record for this book is available from the British Library

Published by Garden Art Press a division of Antique Collectors' Club Ltd.

Frontispiece: A selection of garden implements and accessories
Page 7: Charles Edward Wilson (fl. 1891-c. 1936), 'The Rose Bower'. (Courtesy Sotheby's)

Printed in England on Consort Royal Satin paper from Donside Mills, Aberdeen, by the Antique Collectors' Club Ltd., Woodbridge, Suffolk IP12 1DS

Contents

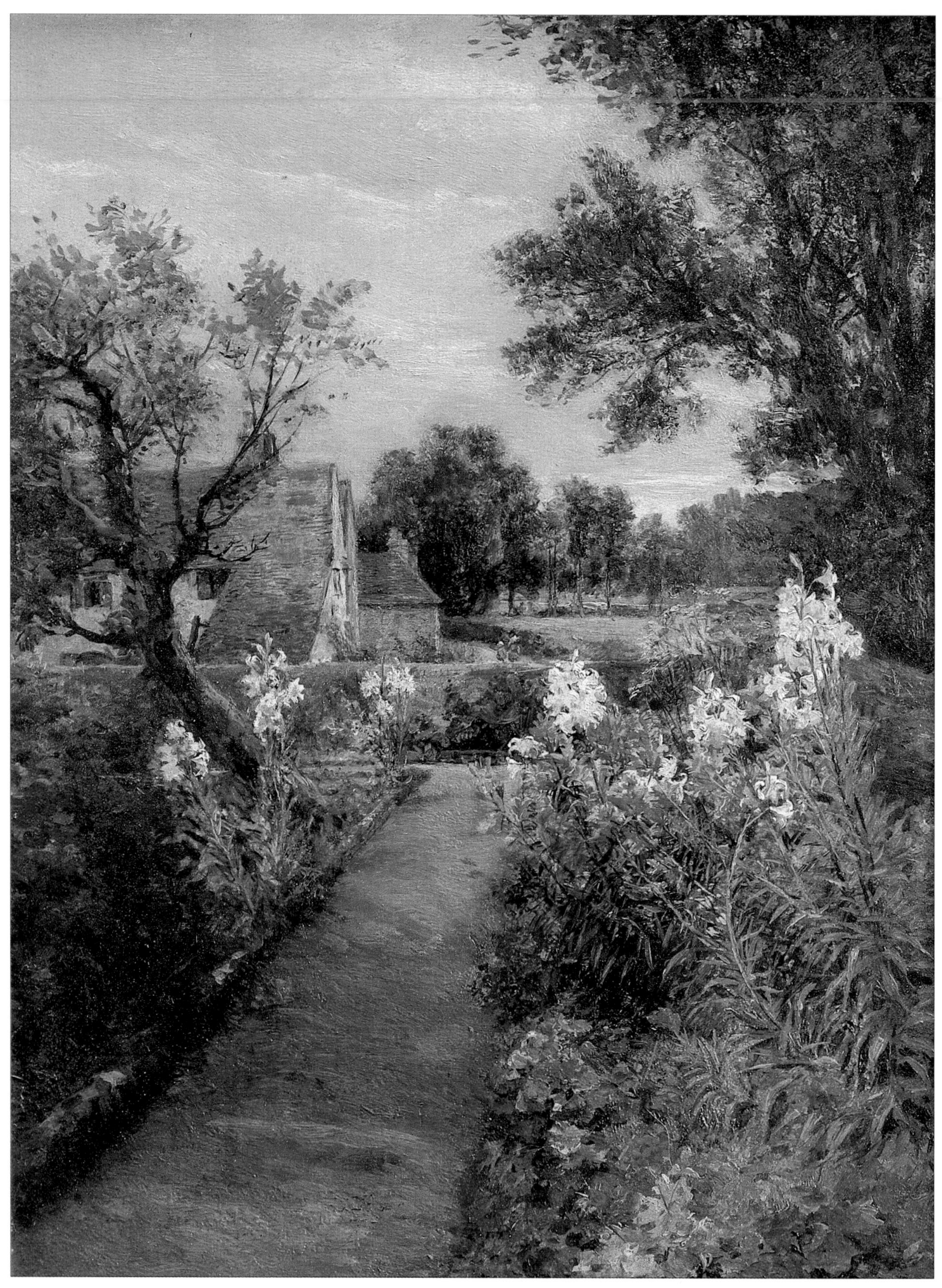

Charles James Lewis (1830-1892), 'Huxley', c.1860

For Hilary

A reader, not a weeder

Acknowledgements

I am particularly grateful to Jackie Rees and James Rylands of Sotheby's Garden Statuary Department at Summers Place, Sussex, for their interest in and generous support for this project, and to Dendy Easton for his help with the paintings and prints.

In addition my thanks to Stephen Brothwood, Bill Brown, Philip Howell, Elin Jones, Jeremy Knight, Cherry Lewis, Joanna Ling, John Massey, John Powell, Mark Stephen, Julia Yerrell, and Glynn Clarkson of Glynn Clarkson Photography, Sotheby's.

I am also indebted to The Ironbridge Gorge Museum Trust; Horsham Museum; The Mitchell Library, Glasgow; Falkirk History Research Centre; The Central Library, Edinburgh; Archives and Local History Service, Dudley; Central Library, Northampton; Derby Local Studies Library; Birmingham Central Library; Sheffield City Library; Kilmarnock and Loudoun Local Studies Library; Smethwick Library; Hawes Elliott Ltd.

Manufacturers, Suppliers and Designers

Introduction

The object of this book is to illustrate and describe a wide range of garden related ornaments, furnishings and artefacts.

It is intended to reflect items that were enjoyed or employed by garden owners or gardeners over the last two hundred years or so, and which may more regularly appear on the market. The increasing interest in practically all aspects of garden history has inevitably lead to the publication of numerous books which record the history and development of many aspects of garden decoration. Very often, though, these concentrate, understandably perhaps, on the marvellous objects that fall into the category of 'Works of Art', usually commissioned or specifically acquired for some great house or garden.

Not many of us can justify, either in economic terms or indeed garden area, the inclusion of such fine items, even if they were to appear on the market. This should not dissuade us from enjoying some practical or perhaps impractical manufactured creation in our gardens or conservatories.

There are today, as indeed there have been for at least a hundred years, manufacturers producing pleasing copies of classical ornament which in a short time may acquire an attractive tone or patina. However, this book endeavours to illustrate period products to which a date is given, although the style of the object may be traced back to antiquity. In other cases the object is so obviously of its time and fashion that it is locked firmly to perhaps a span of no more than twenty years.

In addition to seats, urns and fountains and other traditional garden furnishings, I have also included many utility and humbler items, without which a garden could not be made in the first place, as well as recreational and leisure objects which go to making up the 'life' of a garden. All these are just the sort of collectables which are becoming more and more fascinating, not only to collectors, but also to those with an interest in and appreciation of garden and social history, for they are the artefacts which tell us so much about past practice and custom.

In addition to the illustrations of items described and detailed, and in order to introduce a period atmosphere, I have included contemporary paintings and material from catalogues, books and photograph albums, to illustrate how gardens of the past looked, how they were enjoyed and how they were worked.

English School, circa 1849, 'The Gibson Children in the Garden of the House at Southall, Middlesex'. This is a charming provincial painting, in which three of the children are seen sitting in a small summer house

Garden Structures

GAZEBOS, SUMMER HOUSES, CONSERVATORIES, TRELLISWORK, PERGOLAS

The earliest garden resting place or shelter was the arbour, formed from vines or rambling plants. Wood was the most natural material to give such structures form, and apart from purpose-built stone constructions, wood, perhaps with trelliswork infill, was used for temporary garden buildings until the early nineteenth century when, due to manufacturing advancements, iron and wirework became popular.

A variety of garden structures could then be offered to a wider public who looked not just for shelter but for a romantic resting place and garden decoration.

Gazebos were originally small independent buildings with windows from which the owner and his guests could survey the estate. Today the word is more generally used to include small attractive garden structures such as arbours or rose temples. Although some of the examples illustrated in this section are 'made up', that is to say of modern construction, a number utilise nineteenth century elements and go some way to satisfying demand for a nineteenth century style structure, although this must be a matter of personal taste.

Summer houses come in all shapes and sizes, from the sophisticated to the 'rustic'. They have evolved from the simple arbour to miniature houses. They may be static or revolving, private or open. The Victorians evidently loved them, particularly the natural rustic types made of wood with a thatched roof. Time has not been kind to these buildings and they are few and far between, and perhaps the present popularity of conservatories has lead us away from expending money on such buildings, but hopefully the summer house will make a come-back in imaginative styles to complement our houses and gardens.

This section includes the ever popular trelliswork structures and pergolas which are so attractive when planted with roses or other climbers.

George Samuel Elgood (1851-1943), 'The Alcove, Arley'. From Some English Gardens *by George S. Elgood and Gertrude Jekyll, 1904*

An attractive wrought iron gazebo, French, of usual octagonal form, with trelliswork lower section beneath cylindrical uprights and arcading, domed latticework roof with ball finial. Circa 1870. Approximately 480cm.: 189ins. high

Another nineteenth century French gazebo, this time of cast and wrought iron construction; octagonal form, the lower section cast with geometric patterns and plain uprights supporting scrolling collar tied brackets with domed roof. 495cm.: 195ins. high

A wrought iron gazebo of usual octagonal form, the lower section with barley twist uprights beneath a dome and cupola pierced with scrolls and surmounted by a gilt orb. Twentieth century. 144cm.: 175ins. high

In many ways this gazebo looks more like a pagoda. Of modern wrought iron construction, usual octagonal form, the lower section set with 'Chinese' geometric patterns, the tubular uprights supporting the tapered upper section with intertwined squares and scrolling brackets beneath a ball finial. 470cm.: 185ins. high

A Regency style wrought iron arbour or rosary, the four right-angled supports pierced with segments beneath an ogee arch top cast with stylised flowerheads. 426cm.: 168ins. high. Nineteenth century catalogues depict similar arches with ornamental hanging baskets

Far left, an attractive modern Victorian-style open pavilion of cast aluminium construction with simulated copper roof. 356cm.: 140ins. high (excluding finial)

Similar to the catalogue example shown on p.15, a wirework rose temple with domed top and scroll finial, on four latticework supports. The cost of similar temples circa 1915 would have been £7 17s. 6d. (£7.87½p). Approximately 366cm.:144ins. high.

Lilian Stannard (1877-1944), 'Rose of a Summer's Day'

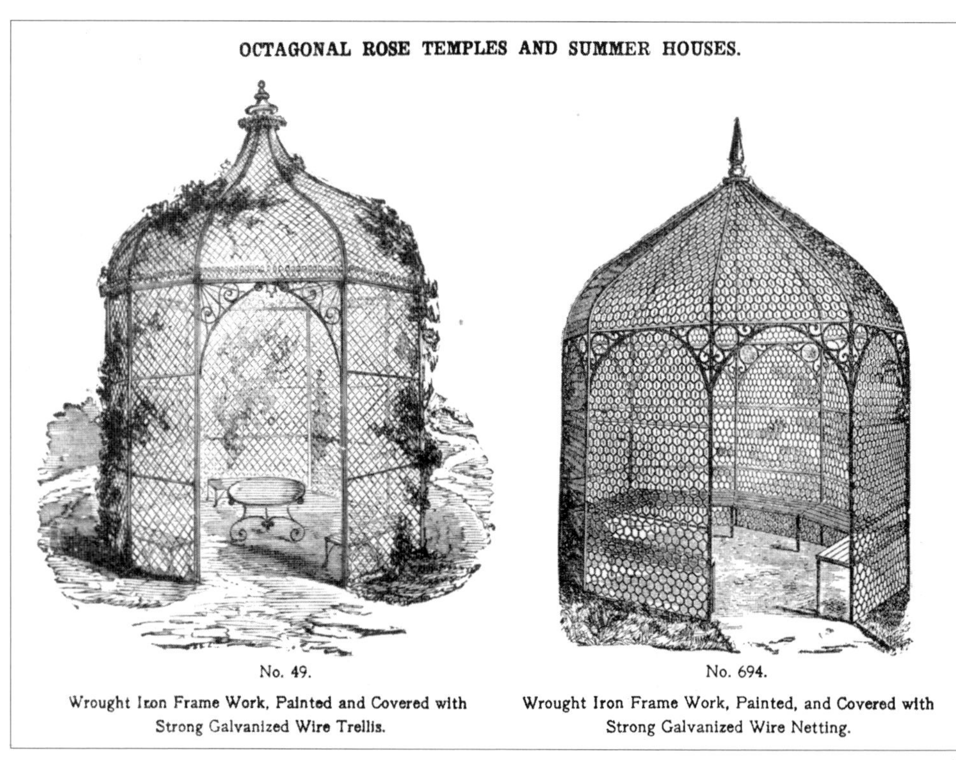

OCTAGONAL ROSE TEMPLES AND SUMMER HOUSES.

No. 49.

Wrought Iron Frame Work, Painted and Covered with Strong Galvanized Wire Trellis.

No. 694.

Wrought Iron Frame Work, Painted, and Covered with Strong Galvanized Wire Netting.

Ernest Arthur Rowe (1813-1922), 'O flowers that never will in other climate grow'

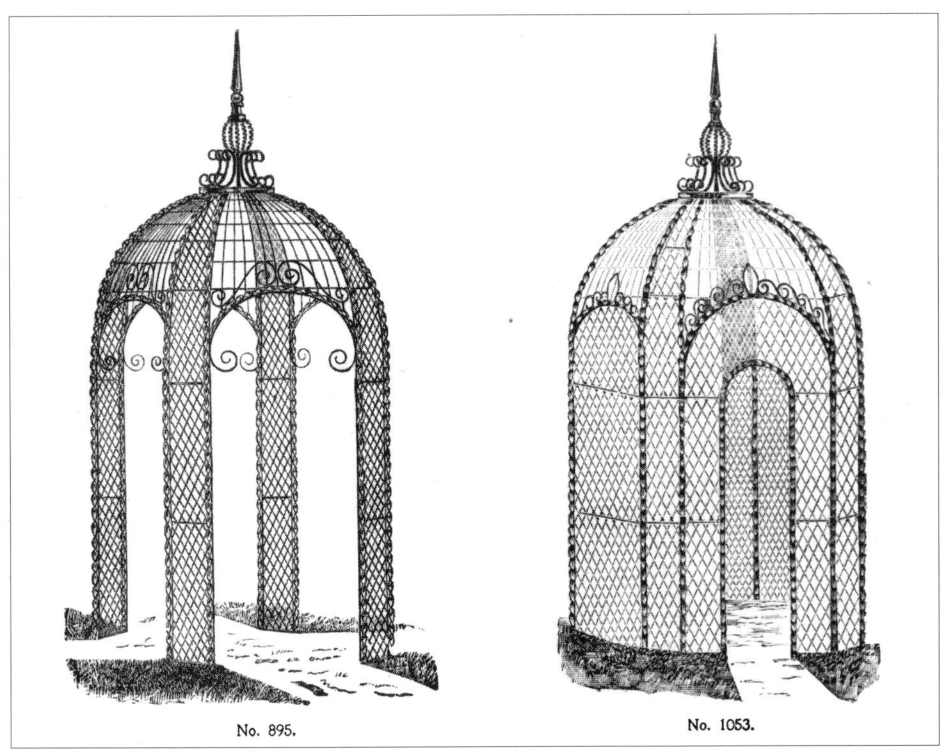

WILLIAM COOPER, Ltd., 761, Old Kent Road, London, S.E.

Portable Rustic Summer House.

No. 310.

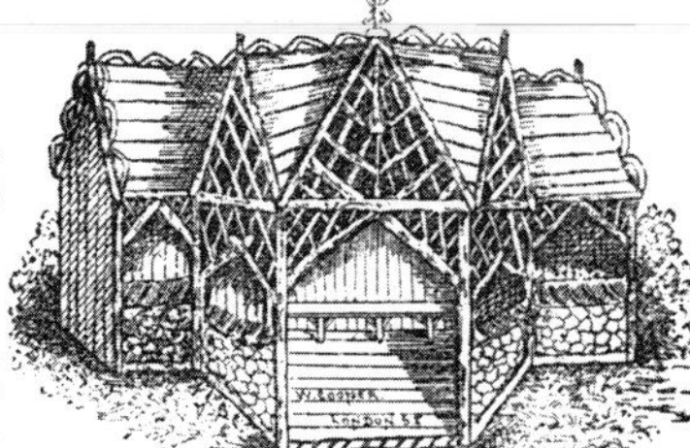

Roof weather-boarded. A handsome structure, well finished.

Size 12ft. by 10ft.

Cash Price, £22, complete. Put on rail at our Works.

Sports Rustic House.

No. 311.

Open front, span-roof house, suitable for grounds where amusements and sports are held. Soundly built of well-seasoned materials. Stained and varnished. Easily fixed and removed. Fitted with seat complete. 12ft. by 4ft.

Cash Price, £9. Carefully put on rail at our Works.

Rustic Lawn Tennis House.

No. 312.

This House is made roomy and suitable for a large party. Being made in sections, it can be fixed and refixed at will, with very little trouble.

Strongly made, stained and varnished.

10ft. long,
5ft. deep.

Complete with Seat.

Cash Price, £10, put on rail at our Works.

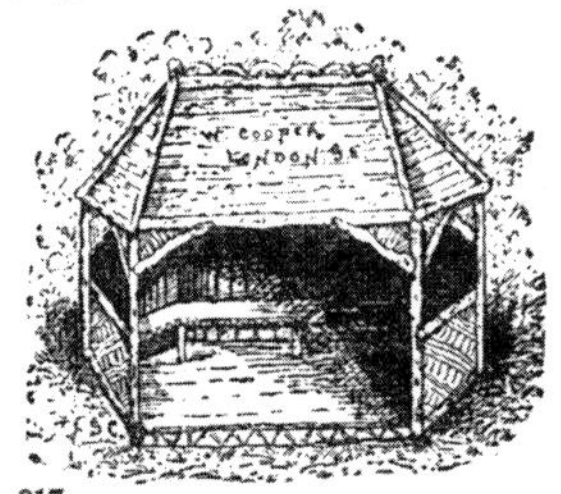

317

WILLIAM COOPER, Ltd., 761, Old Kent Road, London, S.E.

Rustic Summer House.

No. 308.

A handsome design, and finished throughout with care and skill, door and windows of cathedral glass, Swiss lined within and ornamented without. Soundly thatched, and put together in the very best manner.

Size 10ft. by 10ft. Carefully put on rail at our Works. Cash Price, £45.

Other sizes at proportionate prices.

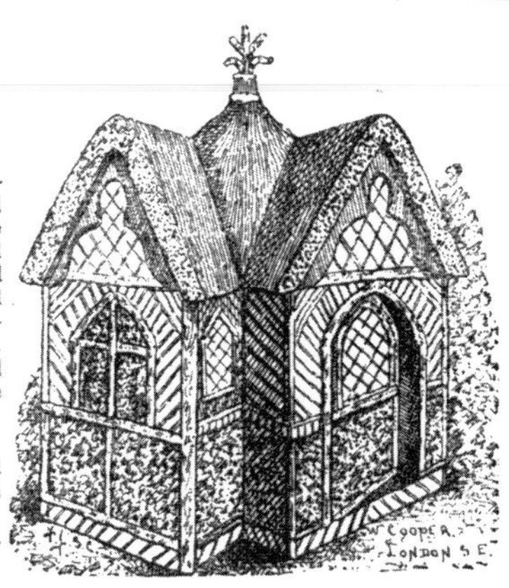

Swiss Rustic House.

No. 309.

A beautiful structure of the most elegant design, Swiss in style, and replete with finish in every detail. Its lines afford scope of an exceptional character for the purpose of illumination at night, which, effectively carried out, displays it a gem of unequalled beauty.

Size 10ft. by 10ft., 12ft. by 12ft., 20ft. high.

Carefully put on rail at our Works,

Cash Price, £55.

Other sizes at proportionate prices.

316

A number of companies produced garden buildings at the turn of the century and a wide selection of designs were on offer. The company William Cooper advised prospective buyers: 'Nothing lends a more picturesque appearance to a garden than a rustic built summer house.' The houses were made in sections: 'Any handyman can erect any size or shape in thirty minutes.' Prices started at £3 10s. (£3.50) and rose to a top of the range Swiss rustic

A thatched-roof summer house beside arches of roses. From The Century Book of Gardening *edited by E.T. Cook for* Country Life, *circa 1900*

Mrs Dempster with 'Blue' and 'Prinney', outside the garden house in My Lady's Wood. From Vale Royal Abbey, Cheshire, 1915 album

ARMY & NAVY AUXILIARY C. S., L. [April, 1913.

SEED DEPARTMENT—*contd.*

RUSTIC SUMMER HOUSES.

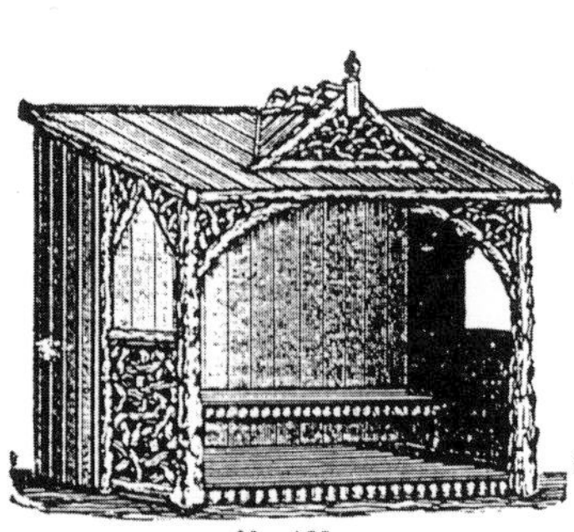

No. 129.

GARDEN SHELTER.

Improved design. Cleated over joints at sides and backs. Roof double boarded, with felt between. Size 7 ft. × 4 ft. Price £6 2 6
8 ft. × 5 ft., £9 0 0
9 ft. × 6 ft., £11 10 0

No. 116.

RUSTIC LAWN TENNIS HOUSE.

Easily erected or removed. Cleated over joints at ends and back. Size 10 ft. long, 5 ft. from back to front. Price £12 3 0

No. 157.

NEW RUSTIC SHELTER.

Regd. Design. Size 5 ft. × 3 ft. Roof match-boarded and covered outside with patent felt; a cheap and substantial shelter for suburban gardens. Price £2 12 6
Also made 6 ft. × 4 ft., £3 12 6
7 ft. × 5 ft., £4 17 6

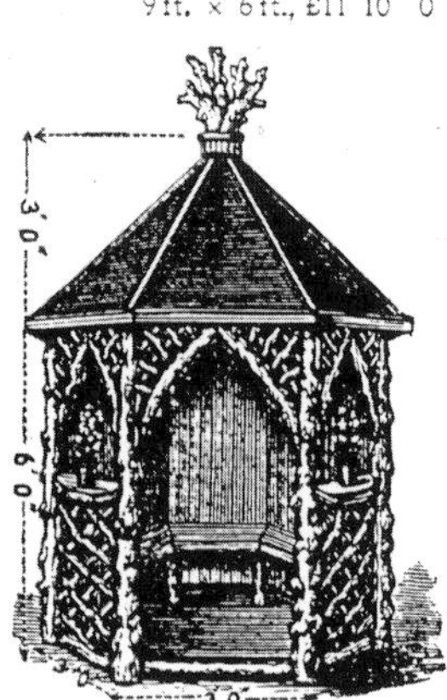

No. 233.

SPECIAL PORTABLE HEXAGONAL SUMMER HOUSE.

Very cheap and durable. Boarded roof covered with patent felt.

Angle to Angle ft. in.	Back to Front ft. in.	Height under Eaves. ft. in.	Price
6 0	5 6	6 0	.. £5 3 6
6 6	5 11	6 0	.. 6 9 6
7 0	6 5	6 6	.. 7 15 6
7 6	6 11	6 6	.. 9 18 6
8 0	7 4	6 6	.. 12 1 6

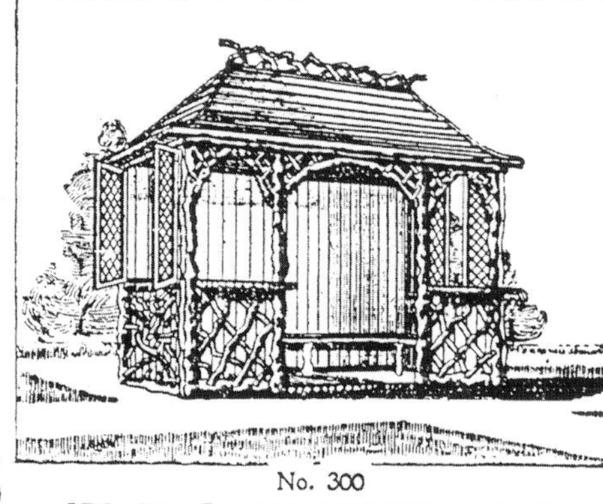

No. 300

OBLONG RUSTIC SUMMER HOUSE.

Entirely new design. Size 10 ft. × 6 ft. Rustic front and ends; back cleated; old English pattern leaded lights. Price £14 10 0.

No. 16.

SPECIAL SEXANGULAR THATCHED SUMMER HOUSE.

Boarding tongued and grooved, and cleated over joints.

Angle to Angle ft. in.	Back to Front ft. in.	Height under Eaves. ft. in.	Price
6 0	5 6	6 0	.. £9 9 0
6 6	5 11	6 6	.. 11 5 0
7 0	6 5	6 6	.. 13 1 0
7 6	6 11	6 6	.. 15 15 0
8 0	7 4	6 6	.. 17 11 0

No. 550.

SPECIAL RUSTIC LOG HUT.

With thatched roof and rustic-worked. A very effective design. Size, 12 ft. × 6 ft. Price £20 5 0

All the above, with the exception of No. 550, are stained and varnished.

These Houses are Delivered and Fixed Free in London or Suburbs, or put on Rail in London, Carriage not paid.

Summer Houses can be supplied with Revolving Gear; prices on application.
Particulars of other designs, and Estimates for Rustic Work of every description, to be had on application.
NOTE.—Procured to order only, about 10 days required. Sent direct from Works.

A page from the Army & Navy Catalogue of 1913 showing a range of garden houses available, including garden shelters, tennis houses, and thatched summer houses. No. 157 – 'New Rustic' shelter – was described as being 'a cheap and substantial shelter for suburban gardens'

John Buonarotti Papworth, 'A Woodland Seat', pencil and watercolour, circa 1820. (Courtesy Christie's)

Left, the summer house in the Quad Garden, Kelly House, Tavistock. Right, the summer house on the tennis lawn, West Dean Park, Sussex. Both from The Century Book of Gardening, *edited by E.T. Cook for* Country Life, *circa 1900*

This large late Victorian/early twentieth century wooden summer house even has an entrance porch and incorporates stained 'cathedral' glass panels to the lancet-shaped windows. The interior has tongue and groove panelling to the walls. Approximately 610cm.: 240ins. wide by 211cm.: 83ins. deep

'In the Winter, Garden', Somerleyton, Suffolk. From The Stately Homes of England *(second series) by Llewellyn Jewitt and S.C. Hall, 1881*

'The Conservatories, Alton Towers'. From The Stately Homes of England *by Llewellyn Jewitt and S.C. Hall, 1881*

Gabriel Carelli (1821-1900), 'Interior of a Gothic Style Conservatory, Hendre House, Monmouthshire', pencil and watercolour. (Courtesy Christie's)

Two conservatories shown in a 1913 catalogue. The interior view (left) is of the example at the top of the page. These conservatories were extremely well fitted with brass locks, bolts and hooks, bronze door furniture, and decorative cast iron ridge cresting

Conservatory at Vale Royal Abbey. From Vale Royal Abbey, Cheshire, 1915 album

The Orchid Houses at Burford, Dorking. From The Century Book of Gardening, *edited by E.T. Cook for* Country Life, *circa 1900*

A wonderful model miniature greenhouse, circa 1935, of wood and glass construction, hinged roof sections and opening door. The exterior has imitation stove with chimney, water-butt and tool chest, the interior is fitted with wooden stages. This greenhouse has provision for electric lighting which would naturally have generated heat so that the greenhouse may have been suitable for small cacti

Interior of the Rose House from the east, at Vale Royal Abbey. From Vale Royal Abbey, Cheshire, 1915 album.

Mildred Anne Butler (1858-1941), 'At the Conservatory Door'. (Courtesy Fine-Lines Fine Art)

John Falconer Slater (1857-1937), 'Cottage and Garden'

146 THE ARMY & NAVY AUXILIARY C. S., L. [APRIL, 1913.

SEED DEPARTMENT—*contd.*

GARDEN TRELLIS, PERGOLAS, ARCHES, APPLIANCES, &c.

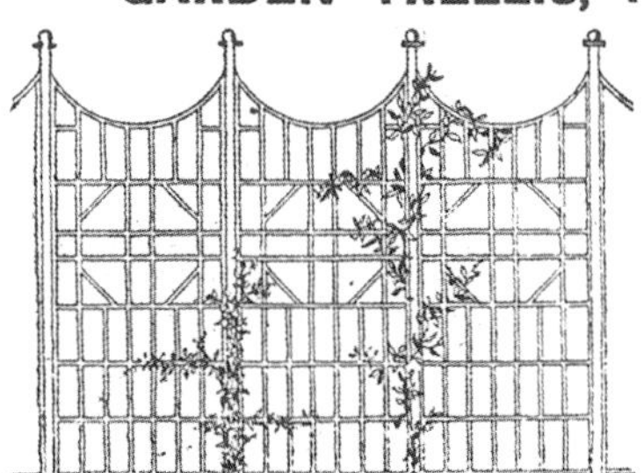

THE "GRANGE" TRELLIS.

Post and Section, 3 ft. 2 in. wide, Treated with preservative solution, 7/8. Painted, 9/1
Extra end Post. painted, 2/5; with preservative solution, 2/2. Height at lowest point, 6ft.

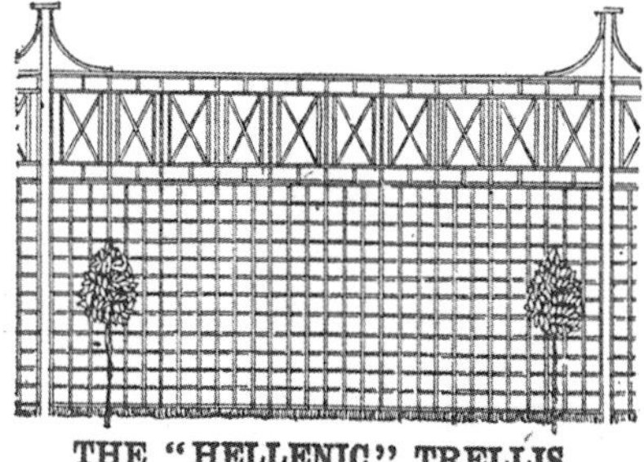

THE "HELLENIC" TRELLIS.

Post and Section, 10ft. 2in. wide, Treated with special preservative solution. 20/6; painted, 23/9.
Extra end Post, painted, 3/1; with preservative solution, 2/8. Height of top bar, 6 ft.

THE "WOODACRE" ARCH.

7 ft. 6 in. high; 4 ft. wide; 2 ft. through. Treated with preservative solution, 14/3; painted 2 coats, 16/2; unpainted, 12/10.

EXTRA STRONG ROSE PILLAR.

No. 2*a*.

Height over all 10 ft. Made with 8 ribs.
Price 6/0 each.
Made with 4 ribs, 5/9
Treated with preservative solution.

THE "CROSSFIELD" ARCH.

4 ft. wide; 1 ft. 9 in. through; 6 ft. 9 in. headroom.

Unpainted .. .. each	21/0
Treated with preservative solution .. .. "	24/3
Painted, 2 coats .. .. "	26/8

5 ft. wide; 2 ft. through; 7 ft. headroom.

Unpainted .. .. each	23/4
Treated with preservative solution .. .. "	26/2
Painted, 2 coats .. .. "	29/6

"GRAYSTOKE" TRELLIS PERGOLA.

This Pergola is made in sections, strongly constructed of best planed deal. Price for one 100 ft. long by 7 ft. 6 in. high by 7 ft. wide and uprights 7 ft. apart, painted two coats £11 0 0
Steeped in Preservative Solution 10 0 0
Or per yard, painted 7/3; steeped, 6/6.

ARCH No. 5.

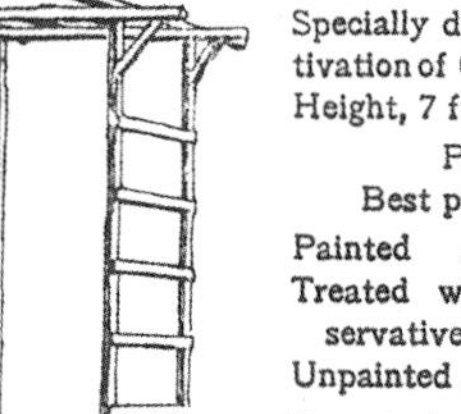

Specially designed for cultivation of Climbing Roses.
Height, 7 ft.; width, 4 ft.

Prices:
Best planed deal.

Painted	11/6
Treated with preservative solution	10/6
Unpainted	9/6

For Arches wider than 4 ft. 1/0 per foot extra.

Recommended by the National Rose Society.

Particulars of other designs for Garden Furniture may be had on application. Also estimates submitted on receipt of particulars of measurements.

NOTE.—Procured to order only, about 7 days required. Sent direct from Works, Carriage not paid.

Page from the Army & Navy Stores catalogue of April 1913 showing a range of garden trelliswork, including arches and pergola. All this trellis could be 'dressed with a wood preservative (brown colour) or painted green'

Two pergolas from the J.P. White catalogue Garden Furniture and Ornament, *circa 1910. The top example 'Southcliffe', made entirely of oak, cost £75 complete. The 'Dartmouth' below was available in a variety of treatments, the price depending on the final design*

'Rose Court, The Pergolas as seen from the Garden Room'. From Houses and Gardens *by M.H. Baillie Scott, 1906*

'Terrace House, View of Pergola showing use of water and reflected lantern'. From Houses and Gardens *by M.H. Baillie Scott, 1906*

George Samuel Elgood (1851-1943), 'Crathes; Phlox'. From Some English Gardens *by George S. Elgood and Gertrude Jekyll, 1904*

Lilian Stannard (1877-1944), 'A Glorious Summer', watercolour and bodycolour

AVIARIES AND BIRDCAGES

The use of aviaries can be traced back to ancient times when birds of various types were kept for food, song, or both.

In the seventeenth century John Evelyn, the diarist and writer, kept parrots in an aviary at his home at Sayes Court.

Peacocks were very popular in the early nineteenth century and wonderful buildings were designed for them. Smaller enclosures accommodated canaries, bullfinches and linnets. The popularity of the aviary in Regency times can be noted by the enthusiasm expressed by Papworth and Robertson in their drawings and designs of the period.

The Victorians' acknowledged interest in natural history perpetuated the concept of aviaries, though on a smaller scale.

A Regency period aviary constructed of wrought iron and wirework sections and incorporating a door and six bird hatches, the covered roof of domed cylindrical form with overscroll terminal. Circa 1820 to 1830. 287cm.: 113ins. high

An attractive Regency wirework aviary of rectangular construction with one large and one small door, under an ogee framed top. 236cm.: 93ins. high

A Victorian wrought iron aviary. This example of hexagonal form, with door, plain uprights and domed sectioned roof with finial. Late nineteenth century. 280cm.: 110ins. high

More suitable for a conservatory is this bronze birdcage dating to around 1920, of rounded rectangular form, the top decorated with two peacocks and an urn, the base is rectangular and raised on paw feet. 279cm.: 108ins. high

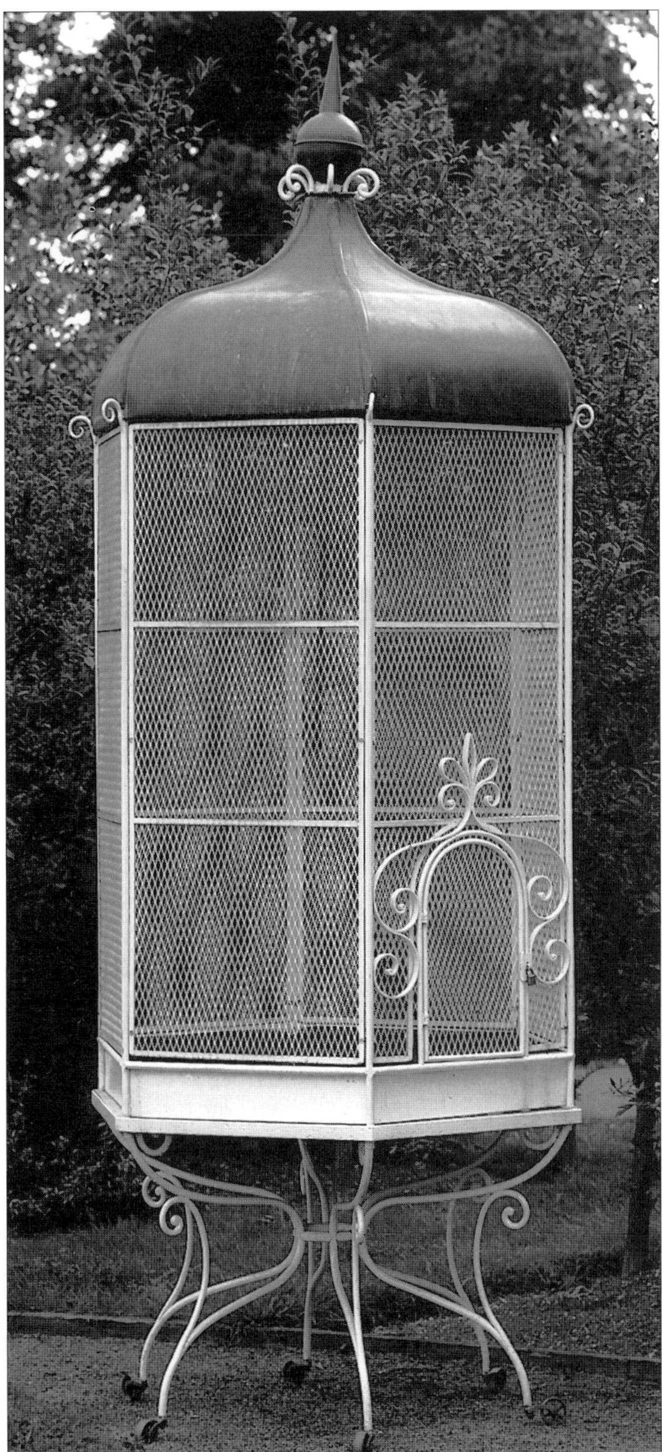

A mobile birdcage of wrought iron construction and hexagonal form. The ogee domed roof is of copper and the whole supported on a stand of scrolling legs fitted with castors. Early twentieth century. 325cm.: 128ins. high

An aviary with wrought iron frame with wirework. This example of domed rectangular form with five doors and scroll decorations to top, apron and supports. Early twentieth century. 160cm.: 63ins. high

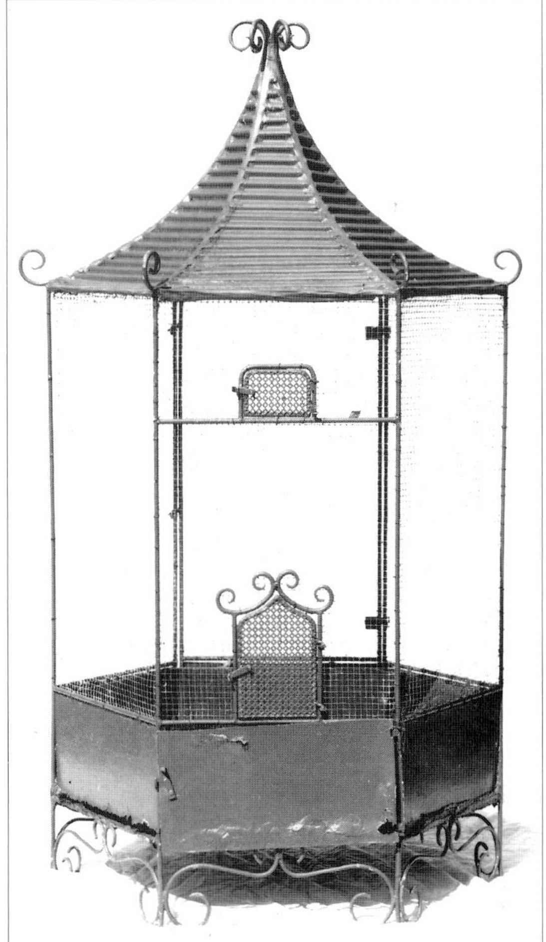

A wrought iron birdcage, twentieth century, octagonal form with pagoda-shaped roof surmounted by a scroll finial and on scroll supports. 183cms.: 72ins. high

English provincial school, circa 1840, 'A Gentleman and His Wife in Their Garden' (detail, see p.84)

Heywood Hardy (1842-1933), 'In the Aviary', oil on canvas. (Courtesy Sotheby's)

A zinc and wrought iron nineteenth century birdcage with rolling branches on bun feet. 108cm.: 82ins. high. (Courtesy Christie's)

A zinc and wrought iron dove cage, surmounted by a finial of a dove with a spreading square shaped top above the meshed cage with hinged door on turned legs. 284cm.: 112 ins. high. (Courtesy Christie's)

DOVECOTS AND PIGEON HOUSES

Although now more commonly seen as a wooden structure supported upon a pole, the dovecot or pigeon house (also known as a columbary) was formerly a more substantial small building used to attract and keep birds, particularly pigeons, as a source of food. The dove, perhaps more popular to keep in recent times, though not of course for food, has acquired a new, more slimline house.

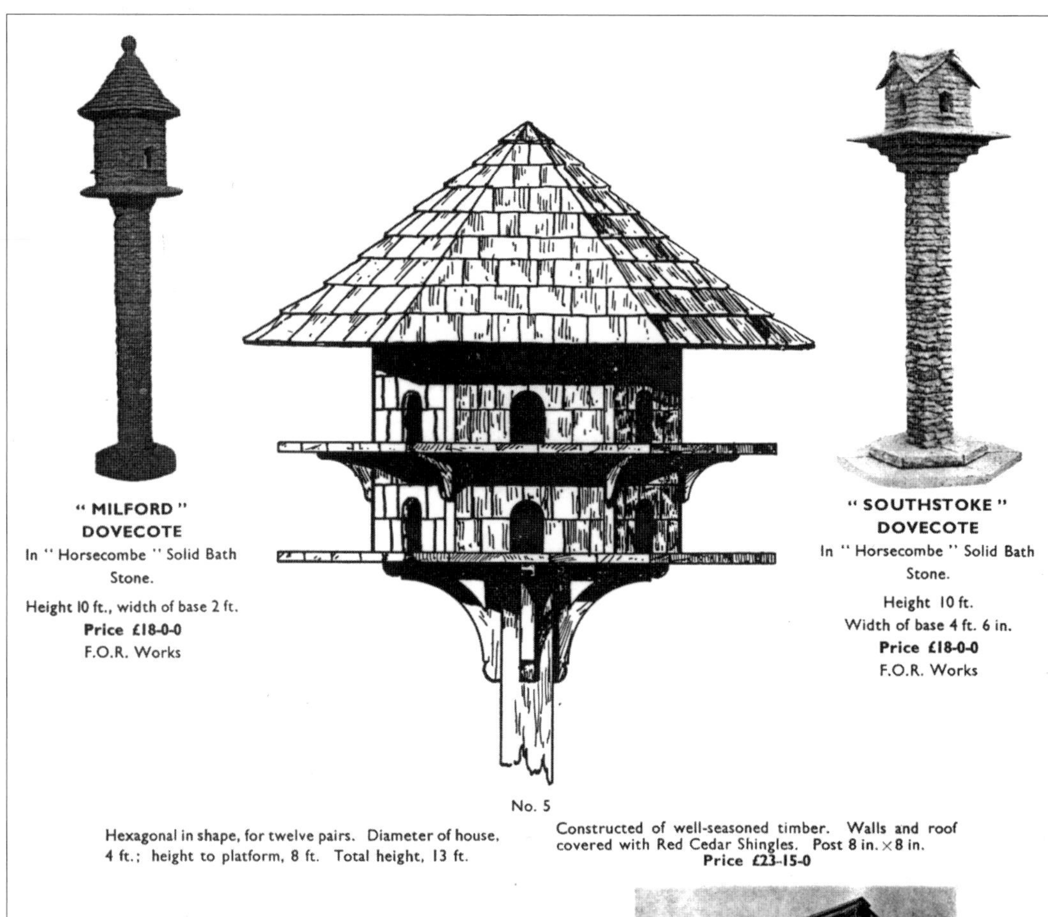

" MILFORD " DOVECOTE
In " Horsecombe " Solid Bath Stone.
Height 10 ft., width of base 2 ft.
Price £18-0-0
F.O.R. Works

" SOUTHSTOKE " DOVECOTE
In " Horsecombe " Solid Bath Stone.
Height 10 ft.
Width of base 4 ft. 6 in.
Price £18-0-0
F.O.R. Works

No. 5

Hexagonal in shape, for twelve pairs. Diameter of house, 4 ft.; height to platform, 8 ft. Total height, 13 ft.

Constructed of well-seasoned timber. Walls and roof covered with Red Cedar Shingles. Post 8 in. × 8 in.
Price £23-15-0

No. 3

For four pairs. 8 ft. high to platform. Total height, 10 ft., Constructed of well-seasoned timber, on 4 in. × 4 in. Post, and covered with Oak Tiles.
Price £6-7-6

No. 4

For six pairs. 2 ft. square. 10 ft. high to platform. Total height 12 ft. On 4 in. × 4 in. Posts, with Brackets, as shown. Constructed of well-seasoned timber, covered with Oak Tiles.
Price £8-17-6

A selection of pigeon house and dovecot designs offered by William Wood & Son, Buckinghamshire, circa 1938, including two unusual dovecot models in Bath stone, and probably quite rare if found today

Design No. 5.

Similar in design to No. 1, but for 12 pairs only.
Height ... ... 15 ft. 0 in.
Made in Deal painted, post green, cote white, roof stained carbolineum, with strong underground supports.
Price £9 12 6

Design No. 6.

Similar in design to No. 3, but for 12 pairs only.

Made in Deal painted, post green, cote white, roof stained carbolineum, with strong underground supports.

Price £6 17 6

Design No. 7.

The cote is made from a strong Oak barrel, and roofed with oak shingles.
Total Height ... ... 15 ft. 0 in.
With base formed to bolt down to concrete bed.
Price, painted complete £9 9 0

Design No. 8.

To hold 8 pairs.

Post Deal, painted green, with strong framed supports, cote white, roof covered with lead.

Price £5 18 6

Four pigeon cotes from J.P. White's catalogue Garden Furniture and Ornament, *circa 1910. White's Pyghtle works at Bedford produced an extensive range of wooden garden furnishings and the catalogue advised prospective buyers that 'All pigeon cotes . . . illustrated are supplied with posts of sufficient length to allow for fixing at least 2ft. 6ins. in the ground, and all work underground is well soaked in Carbolineum'. Design No. 8 was unusual in that it had a lead roof*

Lilian Stannard (1877-1944), 'The Garden Walk'

The pigeon cote, right, was featured in J.P. White's catalogue Garden Furniture and Ornament, *circa 1910. It is very similar to the pigeon cote on a tall wooden post, far right, which came from White's Pyghtle Works in Bedford. From* Garden Ornament *by Gertrude Jekyll, 1918*

DESIGN NO. 3.

For 20 pairs.

Height, 15 ft. 0 in. above ground, with strong framed supports under.

Deal, painted green and white. Roof stained carbolineum.

Ernest Arthur Rowe (1863-1922), 'The Dovecot, Cleve Prior Manor' (detail)

Left, a dovecot built as a finial into the end of a brick wall. In several sizes of brick, with a tiled roof, it was designed by the architect Inigo Triggs circa 1900. From Garden Ornament *by Gertrude Jekyll, 1918*

Right, in his Encyclopedia of Gardening, *J.C. Loudon wrote: 'The aviary may be made an elegant detached building . . . a curious structure of this sort was designed by Repton for the grounds of the pavilion at Brighton'*

Decorative Features

SUNDIALS

John Claudius Loudon, who wrote so extensively on all aspects of gardening in the early nineteenth century, thought that sundials were 'venerable and pleasing decorations; and should be placed in conspicuous frequented parts, as in the intersection of principal walks, where the "note which they give of time" may be readily recognised by the passenger. Elegant and cheap forms are now to be procured in cast iron, or artificial stone, which, it is to be hoped, will render their use more frequent.' However, Loudon's wish has not been totally fulfilled, for while sundials remain popular, particularly for the formal garden, they are invariably difficult to use.

The sundial is known to have been a formal garden ornament since the sixteenth century, but the majority available today will date from the end of the eighteenth century. It may comprise a dial, usually of bronze, engraved with hours and compass points together with its gnomon, and be fixed vertically to a wall or placed horizontally on a pedestal of stone, lead, cast iron or terracotta. It should be appreciated that the dial may not be of the same date as the support. Indeed it is worth noting here the extensive range of reproduction brass and lead 'antique' products manufactured by Pearson, Page & Co. of Birmingham, circa 1920. Their catalogue is a fascinating and extremely useful guide which included sundials and other garden ornaments.

Gertrude Jekyll in her book *Garden Ornament* noted that 'the general form of the sundial base in England was the baluster, round or square in section, plain or enriched with sculptured ornament. In Scotland the more usual form was a tall shaft with obelisk top, the indication of time being given by a number of faceted forms.'

Of a more astronomical nature is an armillary sphere. This is composed of a number of circles with the object of indicating the constitution of the heavens and the motions of the celestial bodies.

Most modern reproductions of sundial plates are simply made of brass or possibly lead. This Georgian plate is made of bronze with pierced gnomon and calibrated with hours, minutes and compass points. It is inscribed 'Made by Tho. Wright, Instrument maker to His Majesty'. Thomas Wright was admitted to the Clock Makers' Company in 1770. The dial is probably circa 1800. 46cm.: 18ins. diameter

A large Victorian bronze sundial, the circular plate engraved with hours, compass points, fast/slow notations and inscribed 'Made by F Barker & Son, 12 Clerkenwell Road, London', with scroll pierced gnomon. Circa 1860. 46cm.: 18ins. diameter

A material favoured for sundial plates was slate. This example is inscribed 'Richardus Melville fecit Glasgow 1848 latitude 56 8 degrees North'. It is inscribed with various countries and cities, and flanked by eight subsidiary dials calibrated with hours in other cities worldwide. Set with nine gnomons. 41cm.: 16ins. wide. Similar contemporary slate sundials are known signed 'Richard Melvin' and as the surnames are similar it is likely they were by the same maker. Another example of Melvin's work is inscribed 'Maker to the Crystal Palace'

An unusual slate sundial in a bronze frame and set with five bronze gnomons, calibrated in months, hours and cities of the world for latitude 51/30 North, together with platitudes in Latin and from the Bible and with instructions for use. The four corners with separate dials calibrated for morning New York, afternoon Alexandria, evening Isle of Borneo and night New Zealand. Mid-nineteenth century. 37cm.: 14½ins. square

An early twentieth century sandstone sundial, of square column form, the vertical dial with bronze gnomon beneath a pyramid top and on stepped square base. 230cm.: 91ins. high

An interesting nineteenth century Scottish sandstone sundial, with vertical dial calibrated with hours and with iron gnomon beneath a head, on an associated column pedestal and circular base

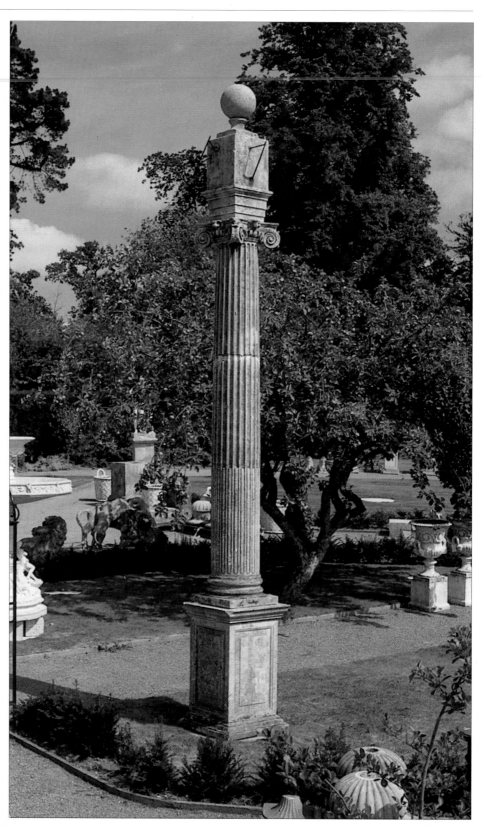

An impressive Portland stone Georgian sundial intended as a landmark at the end of a vista in a private park. The four-sided dial with iron gnomons, calibrated with hours, inscribed 'Tempus Fugit' and dated 1723, is beneath a ball finial supported on a large stop fluted Ionic column with scroll and foliate carved capital, on rectangular panelled base. Approximately 549cm.: 18ft. high

An unusual and substantial nineteenth century sandstone sundial, the top and sides calibrated with hours and set with scroll pierced gnomons, on ogee and volute carved central section carved with a 'G', on shaped square pedestal. 173cm.: 68ins. high

A composition stone sundial with seated figure of a girl pointing to a bronze gnomon on a vertical dial, and on triangular column and base. Circa 1900. 180cm.: 71ins. high

A Cotswold stone sundial, the baluster column on square base supporting a circular dial inscribed 'T Rowley, Londini Fecit' beneath an armorial shield and calibrated with hours and minutes, and with scroll pierced gnomon. Circa 1730. 150cm.: 59ins. high

A Georgian Portland stone sundial, the baluster column supporting a bronze dial inscribed 'Meredith Hughes Fecit 1765 lat. 53o 14'. 142cm.: 56ins. high

A late eighteenth century Portland stone sundial of square baluster form, the corners carved with rams' masks supporting drapes and with stiff leaf carved upper section, the later bronze dial is inscribed 'Tempus Fugit'. 115cm.: 45ins. high

A sandstone sundial, the circular bronze plate with pierced gnomon on wrythen and lobed baluster column and stepped circular plinth. Late eighteenth century. 102cm.: 72ins. high

A Portland stone sundial, the baluster column with lobed lower section and moulded circular base. The sundial plate engraved with hours, numbers and compass points and signed 'Spicer, London'. Late eighteenth/early nineteenth century. 155cm.: 61ins. high

A sandstone example following the style of earlier sundials, with circular bronze dial supported on lobed baluster column with octagonal base. Circa 1860. 120cm.: 48ins. high

Another sandstone sundial, on octagonal baluster column and square base. Circa 1880. 142cm.: 56ins. high

A more obviously Victorian sundial, again in sandstone, the cluster column pedestal with foliate carved capitals, on moulded octagonal base. 152cm.: 60ins. high

A late nineteenth century French white marble sundial, the circular top inscribed 'Les Heurs [sic] Heureuses ne se comptent pas', with bronze dial and pierced gnomon, on baluster column and stepped square base. 120cm.: 47ins. high

Displaying Gothic revivalist influence, this fossil stone sundial has hexagonal top with circular dial calibrated with hours, minutes and signed 'Berge, London, latitude 52/12', the columns carved in relief with arches and quatrefoils and inscribed 'Septr. 1825'. 150cm.: 59ins. high

An early twentieth century terracotta sundial, the bronze dial inscribed with platitudes, on square column and base with stylised floral motifs. 90cm.: 35½ins. high. (This sundial is very similar in form to the Compton Pottery birdbath, see p.46)

Henry John Yeend King (1855-1924), 'At the Sun Dial'. (Courtesy Christie's)

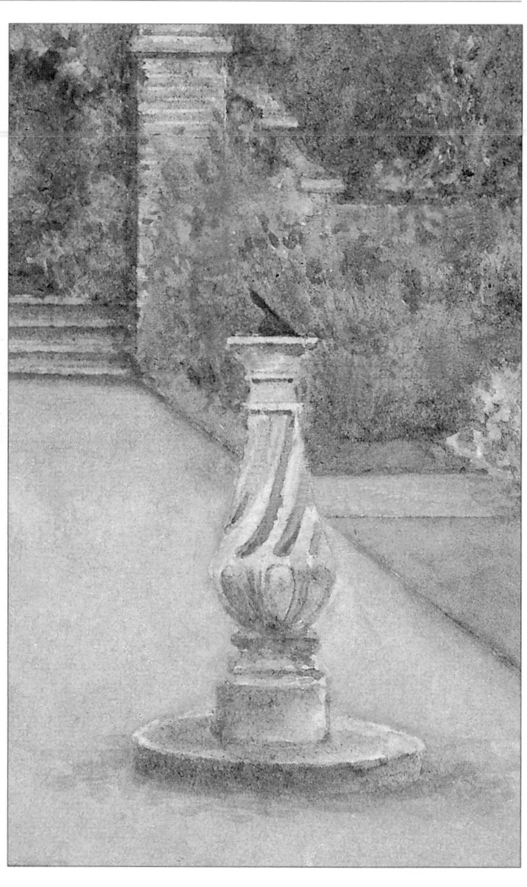

L.N. Nottage, 'The Gardens, Hatfield, detail. (Courtesy Christopher Wood Gallery)

A Cotswold stone sundial, nineteenth century, the fluted pillar of octagonal form, on a stepped octagonal base, set with an octagonal bronze dial calibrated with hours and with a pierced bronze gnomon. 113cm.: 44ins. high

A Liberty terracotta sundial with pierced gnomon, the circular bronze plate signed 'Liberty & Co, London', the surround moulded in relief with a platitude, on octagonal column decorated with foliage and amorphous decoration, stamped 'Designed and manufactured by Liberty & Co' and with registration number, on octagonal plinth. Early twentieth century. 120cm.: 47ins. high

An unusual cast iron sundial, the circular top with scroll pierced gnomon and calibrated with hours and dated 1902, on barley twist and acanthus cast column moulded with flowerheads, on square stone base. 146cm.: 57½ins. high

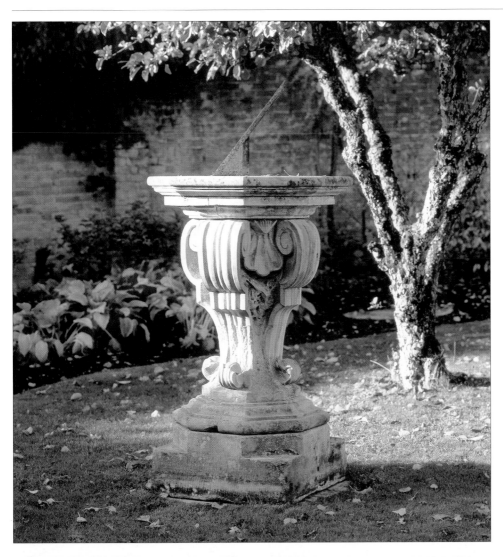

A fine and rare double horizontal brass sundial, circa 1690 signed 'Henricus Wynne Londini Fecit' and bearing the arms and motto of the Cornwallis family. The dial plate seated on three bronze bearings upon a Portland stone plinth with octagonal top and four volute supports, on moulded square base. The plinth possibly slightly later than the dial. 130cm.: 51ins. high

Far left, an armillary sundial, the sphere calibrated with hours and mounted with a flag and an arrow supported by a veined marble column on circular base. Late nineteenth century. 197cm.: 77½ins. high

Left, a bronze armillary sphere very similar to the previous example, supported on a Portland stone pedestal of wrythen baluster form. Late nineteenth century. 155cm.: 61ins. high

BIRDBATHS

As far as the British Isles are concerned, birdbaths seem to be unrecorded before the end of the nineteenth century, although urns with shallow bowls may have provided a natural alternative in earlier times, and thereby probably provided the inspiration for the birdbath.

Most nineteenth century writers understood the benefits and menace of birds in their garden and devoted quite considerable space to describing traps and deterrents. No doubt our increased knowledge and appreciation of birds has softened our outloook and, particularly in the smaller domestic garden, birds are more welcome.

After World War I the Doulton Company found there was less demand for fountains and statuary but more for birdbaths and ornamental animals.

The Compton Pottery, near Guildford, Surrey, is well known for the jardinières it produced in the early years of this century, and this must be a scarce item from the range. A terracotta birdbath with shallow circular dish on moulded tapering square pedestal with stylised tree and inscribed on one side 'He prayeth best who loveth best all things both great and small', and on the other side 'Praised be Thou my Lord of sister water for manifold is her use and humble is she and precious and pure', on moulded stepped square base. 102cm.: 40ins. high. At one point manufacturers advised purchasers that birdbaths made in grey terracotta might break up in frosty weather and therefore advised they be emptied at such times. Those made in red terracotta were not affected

Dept. Enquiries Telephone No. } 345 *No. 17, Seeds and Garden Requisites* **1061**

STONEWARE GARDEN ORNAMENTS.

Lists of other Designs in Bird Baths and Garden Ornaments will be sent on request.
A good selection is on view in the Department.

"CHELTON."
Rock Baby.
Height, 3 ft.
Price £4 4 0

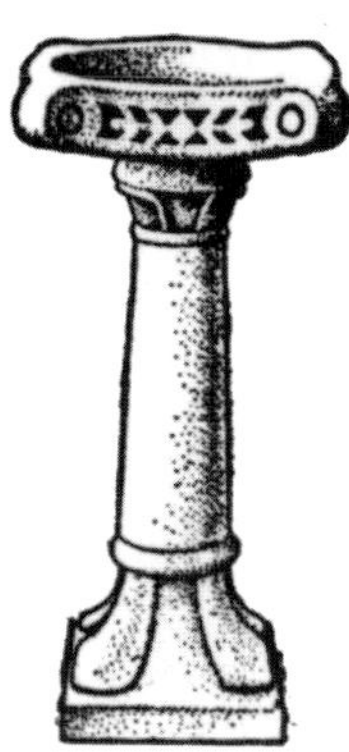

"CHELTON."
"Pam" Bird Bath.
Height 30 in.
Price 21/–

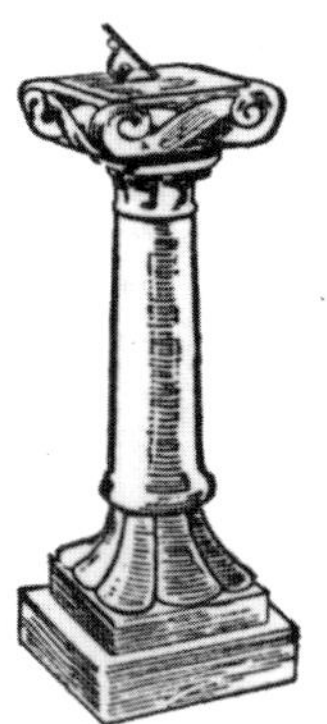

"CHELTON."
Park Sundial.
Height 2 ft. 8 in.
Price £2 10 0
without dial £1 19 6

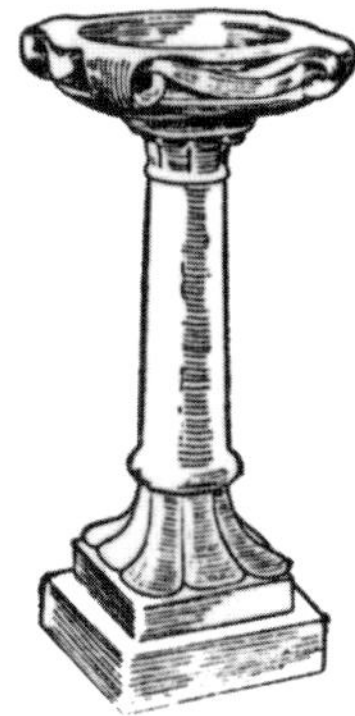

"CHELTON."
Sloane Bird Bath.
Height 2 ft. 8 in.
Price £1 19 6

"CHELTON."
Leaf and Cupid.
22 in. × 17 in.
Price £1 12 6

"CHELTON."
Holly Lawn Bird Bath.
Height 10 in.
Price £1 1 0

"CHELTON" GARDEN ORNAMENTS are guaranteed against all weather in any climate.

"CHELTON" GARDEN ORNAMENTS delivered within the Society's motor radius or sent direct from works Carriage not paid.

GARDEN ORNAMENTS.

SUNDIAL PEDESTAL
No. 206
Top 9 in. in Portland Stone.
Height 22 in. Price 25/–
" 30 in. " 45/–
Dial 7/6 extra.

SQUIRREL BIRD BATH
in Artificial Stone
No. 201
Height 14 in. Price 35/–

A Variety of both Real and Artificial Stone Ornaments are always on show in the Seed Dept.

"CHELTON."
"Wendy."
Height 4 ft. 1 in.
Price £9 19 6

"CHELTON."
Olive Bird Bath.
Height 30 in.
Price £1 4 0

List of other Designs
Free on application

42

ALL PRICES ARE SUBJECT TO MARKET FLUCTUATIONS.

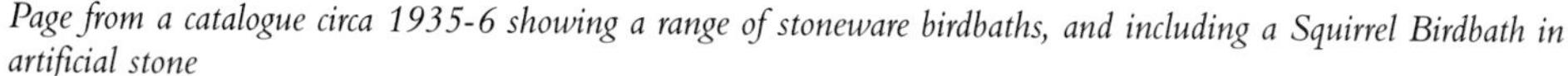

Page from a catalogue circa 1935-6 showing a range of stoneware birdbaths, and including a Squirrel Birdbath in artificial stone

George Samuel Elgood (1851-1943), 'The Garden Gate, Brockenhurst'. From Some English Gardens *by George S. Elgood and Gertrude Jekyll, 1904*

GATES

The gateway is always important since it is a foretaste to what is within. However grand or humble, gates that allow you to view beyond will be more inviting. Iron entrance gates were not generally found in England until the seventeenth century, and were no doubt influenced in manufacture and design by Huguenot refugees who brought so many skills to this country in the 1670s and 1680s. Gates of that period and of the eighteenth century will normally be of wrought iron, the decoration influenced by rococo or neo-classical styles.

In the nineteenth century the increasing popularity and relatively attractive cost of cast iron (sometimes used with wrought iron) made it a practical alternative to the lighter weight product.

Understandably not many early wooden gates will have survived and the 'Chinese Chippendale' style side gate illustrated below is a rarity. J.P. White's catalogue of circa 1910, *Garden Furniture and Ornament*, includes a wide selection of wooden gates in traditional and Edwardian designs.

A fine example of delicate and attractive French ironwork of the mid-eighteenth century. A Louis XV wrought iron gate of arched rectangular form with 'C' scrolls and flowerheads. One of a pair, each 68cm.: 27ins. wide

A rare 'Chinese Chippendale' painted wood hand gate pierced with geometric designs and with original latch and upright gate support. Late eighteenth century. 91cm.: 36ins. high This design of gate continued to be popular in Victorian times, and examples are illustrated in Beeton's gardening books (see Bibliography)

Note the rococo influence to this pair of wrought iron gates, probably continental, of rectangular form with scrolling foliate panels and cresting, the lower section with plain uprights and baluster scrolls. A good example of quality wrought iron work. Mid-eighteenth century. Each gate 136cm.: 53½ins. wide

A pair of attractive late eighteenth century wrought iron gates, of arched rectangular form with plain uprights pierced with scrolls and foliage above a dog rail with spear finials. Each gate 155cm.: 61ins. wide

An ideal way of controlling pedestrians or larger animals. A Victorian cast iron tryst gate, the 'C' shaped frame and hinged gate with plain uprights surmounted by spear finials. Circa 1870. 127cm.: 50ins. wide

Note the lightness of design to this pair of wrought iron gates of arched rectangular form pierced with scrolls. Early nineteenth century. Each gate 132cm.: 52ins. wide

A simple but attractive cast and wrought iron gate, one of a pair. Mid-nineteenth century. 147cm.: 58ins. wide

An unusual nineteenth century wrought iron gate of arched rectangular form, with waved vertical bars and scrolled decoration. 133cm.: 52½ins. high

The Coalbrookdale company offered an extensive range of entrance and side gates in their catalogues. Although associated with cast iron production they also included more delicate wrought iron work as an alternative to the more massive and heavy gates. This pair of cast iron gates incorporates pierced roundels and foliage beneath knopped plain uprights, with spear and fleur-de-lis decoration at the top. The gates are stamped 'Coalbrookdale' with registration stamp and number. Circa 1860. Each gate 130cm.: 51ins. wide

Wrought iron scrolls are used within cast iron borders on this pair of gates with plain uprights terminating in spear heads. Late nineteenth century. Each gate 152cm.: 60ins. wide

An example of early twentieth century wrought iron gates of arched rectangular form, the arches pierced with scrolls, the plain uprights with scroll and zigzag panels. Each gate 150cm.: 59ins. wide

Right, a good Victorian cast iron hand gate, the centre panel with sunflower roundel. Circa 1860. 135cm.: 53ins. wide

Far right, unusual and attractive, the design of this hand gate is highly eclectic incorporating a number of oriental and western influences. Late Victorian. 85cm.: 33½ins. wide

Example of rectangular form pierced with panels of anthemion and star motifs and incorporating a dentil frieze and spear-head terminals. Cast with maker's name 'J.W. Mare'. Circa 1840. 88cm.: 34½ins. wide. The firm T. J. & W. Mare is listed in a Plymouth directory of 1822 as Brass and Iron Founders. By 1852 the company was run by John Edmund Mare

One of a pair of early twentieth century wrought iron gates, of rectangular form pierced with foliage and scrolls centred with shields. Note the cresting in the form of a seated cat. Each gate 142cm.: 56ins. wide

OBELISKS

Obelisks originated in ancient Egypt and have been a feature of gardens since Roman times. From Renaissance Italy, they became popular in France, England and other northern continental countries. Originally they were generally raised in honour of distinguished individuals, or to mark a particular spot, for example the obelisk erected by Caesar Augustus in the Campus Martinius in Rome which served to mark the hours on a horizontal dial drawn on the pavement. The height of the obelisk's popularity in English private gardens was in the eighteenth century, and although they were less popular in the nineteenth century, they continued to be used as funerary or memorial monuments.

The trellis obelisk is currently enjoying something of a renaissance as a useful and decorative garden feature.

A white Carrara marble obelisk of tapering triangular form on similarly moulded base. Nineteenth century. 225cm.: 88½ins. high

A pair of twentieth century Vicenza stone obelisks of usual tapering form, carved with panelled decoration and surmounted by a ball, on four ball supports. 158cm.: 62ins. high, on matching square pedestals 48cm.: 19ins. high

A black marble obelisk of tapering rectangular form on four brass ball supports and with square block base. Twentieth century. 216cm.: 84½ins. high

BUILDING MATERIALS DEPARTMENT—*contd.*

ORNAMENTAL WEATHER VANES.

Wrought Iron. Well made, and specially painted in oil colours with gilt letters.

HUNTSMAN.

In scarlet. 30 in. long.

Price £2 11 0

SMALL FOX BREAKING COVER.

29 in. long from head to tail.

Price £2 11 0

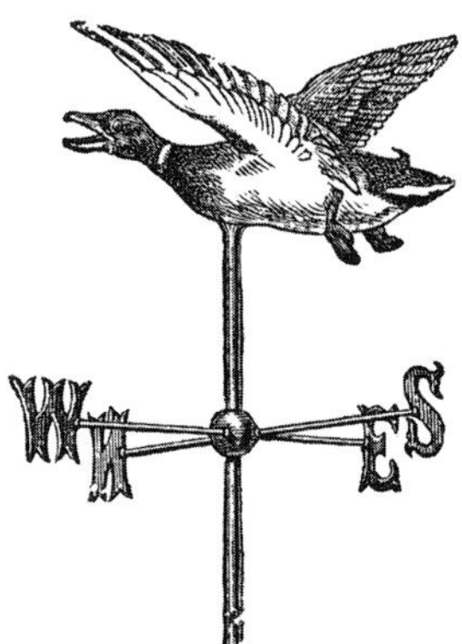

WILD DUCK.

31 in. long from head to tail.

Price £2 11 0

LARGE HUNTED FOX.

49 in. long from head to tail.

Price £3 4 0

ARROW.

Finished in best gold leaf, 31 in. long.

Price £2 5 9

Smaller size, 27 in. high, 22 in. across point, but made of copper with iron rod base.

Price £1 15 6

LION.

36 in. from head to tail.

£3 4 0

Any Favourite Animal or Prize Beast copied from photo at a small extra charge.

Tennis Racquet, Bat and Ball, Hunted Stag, Man playing Bowls, Horse Trotting, Sheep, Greyhound, Bulldog, Pike, Pointer, and several other designs not illustrated.

Apply Building Materials Department, where sample is kept on show.

PRICES THROUGHOUT THIS CATALOGUE ARE SUBJECT TO ALTERATION WITHOUT NOTICE.

A page from the Army & Navy catalogue of 1913 showing a selection of ornamental weather vanes 'well made, and specially painted in oil colours with gilt letters'

WEATHERVANES

Whilst he acknowledged them as useful, that great commentator on gardens, J.C. Loudon thought weathervanes unsuitable as garden ornament: 'The ideas to which they give rise, as connected with ships, flags, fairs, military standards etc., are all opposite to the stillness and repose of gardens'. He would probably have been horrified to see a weathervane in the form of a locomotive or a motor car!

A copper and wrought iron weathervane in the form of a Roman galley above direction indicators and scrolling brackets. Late nineteenth century. 194cm.: 76ins. high

A late eighteenth century wrought iron weathervane with pennant direction indicator above three scrolling foliate brackets. 160cm.: 63ins. wide

STADDLE STONES

Staddle stones were produced quite simply to support agricultural buildings such as granaries, raising them some two feet or so off the ground in an attempt to prevent vermin and water from reaching the stores. They have been made in a similar design for hundreds of years and, no doubt due to regional influences, come in various types of stone and slight variations of form. Staddle stones are difficult to date, though most originals will be eighteenth century. They have been popular as garden decoration since the 1920s, no doubt due to their 'toadstool' appearance.

As the illustrations here show they can acquire a rich patina, and can be used in a variety of ways – to form a garden feature in conjunction with a dry stone wall, and as the edging to a drive.

Above and opposite, staddle stones at Rodmarton Manor, Gloucestershire

A Ham stone staddle stone, domed circular top on tapering square column. 68cm.: 22ins. diameter

Two Bath stone staddle stones on tapering cylindrical supports. 76cm.: 30ins. high

A granite staddle stone with flattened circular top, tapering circular support. 71cm.: 28ins. high

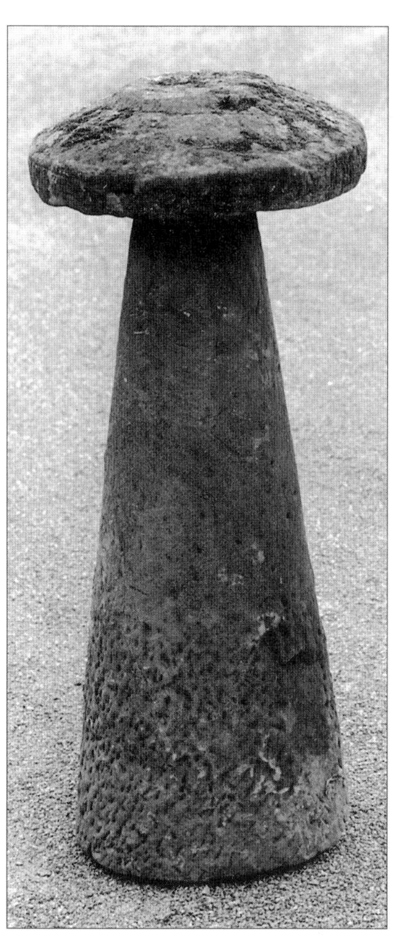

A sandstone staddle stone, circular top, tapering cylindrical column. 117cm.: 46ins. high

Two Portland stone staddle stones, domed circular tops, tapering square bases. 56cm.: 22ins. diameter

LANTERNS AND LIGHTING

Whether it be to enjoy the garden for longer than the daylight hours, or perhaps to present security lighting in a more traditional manner, lanterns, lamps and lampposts can play a useful and decorative role in a garden. Victorian cast iron lamps are popular, but other types exist for those with time to seek them out. Although they may have originally been intended for gas, most types can be converted for electricity.

A selection of Japanese lanterns in stone and in bronze is also shown. Mainly nineteenth century, they reflect the taste for Japanese style gardens in England at the end of the century. The stone types are usually formed like miniature pagodas or temples. Those in bronze may be highly decorated. Whilst in the eighteenth century far more European interest was expressed in Chinese gardens, Japanese gardens were credited with 'little of taste in design'. However, by the end of the nineteenth century Japan had opened up to foreign trade and appreciation of the Japanese garden style was far more widely received and understood. Indeed Japanese lanterns became so popular they were retailed in England by such companies as Pulhams.

A brazier is also included in this section. Although more often intended for burning coal, braziers have an alternative use, that of burning oil as a torch, the origin of which goes back to antiquity.

An attractive cast iron lamppost, fluted tapering column cast with foliage, octagonal copper and lead mounted lantern with arched chimney surmounted by foliate motifs, raised on fluted tapering column, with registration stamp. Circa 1860. 225cm.: 88½ins. high

A decorative cast iron lamp standard with domed canted tapering square top with fruit finial, on tapering square support with volutes, roundels, foliage and a shaped square base. Circa 1880. 280cm.: 110ins. high

Above, left and right, a pair of Japanese bronze lanterns, the foliate pierced centre section with hinged door beneath domed cover with flaming ogee finial and grotesque dragons' heads hung with bells, on ribbed column (entwined with a mortal dragon right hand example), the circular base cast in relief with hares and other animals amongst waves and cloud bands. Nineteenth century. 236cm.: 93ins. high. Centre left, one of a similar pair of bronze lanterns, the domed cover with stylised fish terminals hung with bells. 155cm.: 61ins. high. Centre right, one of a pair of bronze Japanese incense burners with pierced centre section, with domed roof and ogee finial, the column cast with cloud bands and entwined with a mortal dragon. Nineteenth century. 140 cm.: 55ins. high

A pair of Japanese bronze lanterns, the pierced centre section below domed roof with flaming ogee finial and hung with bells, on ribbed column. Late nineteenth century. 153cm.: 60ins. high

Cast iron braziers such as this example originally lined London Bridge and are illustrated in a picture celebrating the marriage of the Prince of Wales (later Edward VII) to Princess Alexandra in 1863. Circular bowl supported on three scrolling supports with paw feet and triform base. The base with plate marked 'W. Addis, Leicester Street, Leicester Square, London'. Circa 1860. 138cm.: 54ins. high

A shorter example than those on p.61, and perhaps more appropriate for terrace or parapet, a bronze lantern, its octagonal tapering domed top with flame finial, on four plain supports with scroll terminals, on circular base. Circa 1900. 155cm.: 61ins. high

One of a pair of wrought iron lanterns of tapering octagonal form, with frieze of stylised spear finials and with scrolling brackets. Late eighteenth/early nineteenth century. 116cm.: 46ins. high

Right, a bronze wall lamp of tapering hexagonal form with knopped finial, supported by curved wall brackets. Circa 1900. 107cm.: 42ins. high

Far right, a bronze gate pier lantern set with leaded coloured glass panels. Circa 1900. 97cm.: 38ins. high

Far left, the pagoda style influences this Japanese granite lantern arranged on three tiers with fruit finial, on four supports. Late nineteenth century. 270cm.: 106ins. high

Left, a similar Japanese granite lantern. Early twentieth century. 245cm.: 96ins. high

Far left, a Japanese carved granite Kasuge lantern with domed top above pierced apertures, ribbed column and octagonal base. Late nineteenth century. 153cm.: 60ins. high

Left, another similar nineteenth century Japanese lantern, the apertures alternating with panels of animals, on ribbed column and hexagonal base carved with stylised lotus leaves. 108cm.: 72ins. high

CANNON

It may seem a bit eccentric to have a cannon in your garden, but they have long been a decorative feature. In many cases they will have been left as remnants of earlier days when they protected the property, or perhaps some retired naval or army officer displayed them as a trophy. Most cannons offered on the market are really naval guns, and usually date from the eighteenth century.

Although bronze barrelled cannons are more desirable to collectors, and therefore more expensive, large quantities of iron cannon were made in East Sussex from the sixteenth century through to the Napoleonic wars. Often the carriage of the gun is a replacement, usually made of elm. In fact a number of guns were originally made to be stationary and therefore would not have had a wheeled carriage.

A bronze barrelled cannon of historic interest, bore diameter 3½ins., mounted on a four-wheeled carriage, the carriage bearing a brass plaque inscribed 'Captured by Sir Hugh Gouch from the Mahratta Army in Gwalior, Dec. 29th 1843', ex Tower of London

The most common type of cast iron gun, not really a cannon but a carronade. Probably dating from the late eighteenth century, this is a six pounder with cast crown and the number 6 to barrel breech; the foundry mark may sometimes be found on the trunnions. The gun is now mounted on a four-wheeled carriage, although this is unlikely to be original. Barrel 116cm.: 45½ins. long

The bronze barrel of this cannon might be French. A plaque on the wooden carriage is inscribed 'Captured from the Mahratta Army under Sindhia and the Raja of Berar by Sir Arthur Wellesley at the Battle of Arguan, November 28th 1803'. Sir Arthur Wellesley was later created Duke of Wellington. Bore diameter 5ins. Barrel 119.5cm.: 47ins. long

A large bronze barrelled cannon, bore diameter 4½ins., mounted on a four-wheeled wooden carriage, bearing brass plaque inscribed 'Captured in Bogue Forts [near Canton] by the Expedition under Sir George Bremer in 1841 in consequence of which operations the Chinese agreed to cede Hong Kong'. Barrel 294.5cm.: 116ins. long

A good example of a dated seventeenth century bronze cannon engraved at the breech 'Mountjoy Earl of Newport Mr. Generale of the Ordnance John Browne made this piece 1642' struck behind the touch hole 3.0.2., mounted on its four-wheeled hardwood (probably elm) carriage with iron furniture. Barrel 124.5cm.: 49ins. long

Left, a nineteenth century bronze cannon, bore diameter 2ins., on a non original two-wheeled carriage. Barrel 82.5cm.: 32½ins. long. Right, a nineteenth century signal cannon, bore diameter 1½ins. mounted on an associated four-wheeled wooden carriage. Barrel 61cm.: 24ins. long

Stuart Period panelled front cistern bearing the date 1666, the year of the Great Fire of London, and the initials 'I F', probably those of the original owner. The design is very simple and imitative of the decoration on some oak furniture of the mid-seventeenth century. 120cm.: 47ins. wide

Another Stuart lead cistern dated 1677, of usual rectangular form but with more elaborate strapwork panelled design cast with amorini and fruit motifs and bearing the initials 'T S M'. Although there may be variations, it is general that the flanking initials are those of the Christian names of husband and wife, the raised central motif representing the surname. 122cm.: 48ins. wide

An early Georgian lead cistern of rectangular form, the panelled front decorated with a crown, the date 1728, and flanked by scallop shells and dolphins. 74cm.: 29ins. high

This handsome cistern dated 1763 bears shields with three cannons, the arms of the Board of Ordnance, later the Royal Ordnance Corps. The cistern was probably intended for a barracks. Note the lead overflow pipe and fitted tap. 79cm.: 31ins. high

A Georgian lead cistern of rectangular form with panelled front centred with the initials 'R W L' and flanked with shell and basket motifs within wreaths, one similarly panelled side bearing the date 1767. 130cm.: 51ins. wide

At the time of the American Declaration of Independence (1776) perhaps some Englishman favoured a patriotic decoration on his cistern – St. George slaying the dragon, crowns and figures holding wreaths of victory. 92cm.: 36ins high

Water Features

CISTERNS AND BATHS

Cisterns were originally made to catch and hold rainwater for the house and garden. Usually made of lead and often decorated with the owner's initials and a date, they have been popular and practical garden features since Stuart times. They were sand cast (in a similar way to firebacks) by plumbers, formed into shape and soldered. Dated examples before 1650 are scarce. Early examples are usually simply decorated. Later, popular contemporary motifs such as crowns or coats of arms were introduced.

Although London was a centre for production, its work was not necessarily the best. Lawrence Weaver in his book *English Leadwork* wrote: 'There is not in the modelling of the applied ornament anything like the gaiety we find in the enrichment of work of similar date in the West Country'.

A revival of interest in leadwork at the end of the nineteenth century saw cisterns made and decorated with contemporary designs; these may bear dates of the last years of the nineteenth century and should not necessarily be discounted as reproductions. Today, attractively decorated cisterns in good condition are prized collectors' pieces, many being used for decorative purposes, densely planted. Early twentieth century writers such as Inigo Triggs and Gertrude Jekyll enthused over old garden leadwork and how it blended with a green background. Copies of lead cisterns are still produced, usually imitating the style and motifs of early examples and bearing spurious dates.

No doubt the wide use of cast iron in the early nineteenth century contributed to the decline of lead cisterns in favour of more robust and probably cheaper reservoirs (see p.70) For the more humble property an old barrel, tarred or painted, would suit the purpose. Towards the end of the Victorian era, mobile swing water barrows were introduced as a means of collecting rain water and transporting it within the garden as required (see p.97).

Like cisterns, baths are now rarely used for their original purpose, being usually too massive and heavy for practical use, but filled with plants they can be a decorative garden feature.

Useful for corners, this cistern is of triangular section, the bowed front with strapwork decoration cast with dolphins, dated 1788. Fitted with a bronze tap to the side. 105cm.: 41½ins. wide

A most elaborately decorated, if somewhat misshapen Georgian lead cistern, the panelled front almost completely filled with armorial crestings, putti, shells and urns of flowers, dated 1730 and bearing the initials 'R W F'. Fitted with a bronze tap. 102cm.: 40ins. wide

The use of the portcullis and coil of rope on this Stuart cistern may suggest an original connection with Customs and Excise, or possibly the East India Company who used the portcullis as their badge in the seventeenth century. This example is dated 1677 and bears the initials 'E B' with floral garlands, while only one end is decorated, with a wreath and winged cherub mask, which seems to indicate the cistern was made for a corner site. 137cm.: 54ins. wide

Although most cisterns are of rectangular form, this Georgian model is of D-form with strapwork and foliate decoration to the front and sides. The sides are modelled with cherubs, while the front has the initials 'W R' within an oval shaped cartouche and is dated 1766. Note the bronze tap set to the side. 127cm.: 50ins. wide

An attractive small lead cistern with panelled front and sides, dated 1741. Note the continuation of the panelled decoration at the corners. 89cm.: 35ins. wide

A rare early nineteenth century cast iron water tank, of rectangular bolted construction, the panels cast with stylised flowerheads and leaves. 199cm.: 78ins. wide

The Italian city of Verona is noted for its 'red' marble. This nineteenth century example of a Rosso Verona bath of rounded rectangular form is decorated in a traditional manner with ogee arches centred with masks, armorials and flowerheads beneath a dentil frieze. 180cm.: 71ins. wide

A distinguished nineteenth century white marble bath of usual rounded rectangular form, the front with carved ring handles and centred with a lion's head mask. It is is supported on paw feet. 188cm.: 74ins. wide

An interesting and unusual variation to the marble bath is this massive cast iron example, probably mid-nineteenth century, of usual rounded rectangular form, the front cast with ring handles. The bath is shown raised on associated sandstone paw supports. 330cm.: 130ins. wide

BRIDGES

Rustic Bridge.

Framed of best Deal, securely bolted together. Sides ot rustic Oak, stained and varnished.

Size, 15 ft. by 4 ft. 6 in. .. £13 0 0
,, 8 ft. by 3 ft. 6 in. .. 8 5 0

FIXING OF BRIDGE EXTRA.

The rustic bridge, above, offered in the Gamages catalogue of 1911, is similar to the bridge, right, photographed in the grounds of Vale Royal Abbey, Cheshire, in 1915

William Wood & Son of Taplow, Buckinghamshire, designed and constructed bridges to order. This example, featured in the firm's 1938 catalogue, is in roughly shaped blocks of natural stone. 6.5m.: 21ft. long

Cast iron bridge, French. Circa 1880

Two bridges illustrated in J.P. White's catalogue Garden Furniture and Ornament, *circa 1900. The Armley (top) and the Brockenhurst*

FOUNTAINS

Fountains have a magic about them, not least in how they work. Before modern devices were available, enormous effort and ingenuity were required to produce the necessary pressure. Generally the water had to come from a greater height than the fountain and even then the fountain would probably only achieve a flow of water rather than the more powerful jet we might expect. In the last century, an age of steam, Sydney Beeton, husband of the more famous Mrs. Beeton, recorded the great cost of operating fountains: 'The water to supply the fountains at the Crystal Palace is pumped up by steam power to the summit of the two lofty towers, whence it descends, producing for a short time a very magnificent display!', and he went on to note 'that this is effected at a very considerable cost, and cannot be continued for any lengthened period.' Beeton was well aware of the *jet d'eau* at Chatsworth which he felt, rather poetically, 'the most perfectly satisfactory instance we have where advantage has been taken of Nature, so as to bring it efficiently to the aid of Art!' However, there was little to encourage the owner of a private garden to consider introducing a fountain, even though fountains began to enjoy a renaissance in the late nineteenth century. Today electrically powered pumps remove the problem of finding a natural head of water.

Fountains will be found in the usual materials, stone, marble, terracotta and cast iron. Although a few exceptional examples are included here, a number of smaller cast iron fountains are still relatively affordable. However, there is something of a scarcity value for good English cast iron fountains, since many have suffered rust damage. Better examples are likely to be found in warmer old colonial areas, such as the West Indies.

Two novelties. Left, an Indian eighteenth/nineteenth century white marble water maze, of square form with inlet and outlet ducts, 60cm.: 24ins. wide. Right, an unusual eighteenth/nineteenth century Indian white marble cascade fountain, of rectangular form carved in relief with fishes and dished ellipses flanked by zigzag decoration. 85cm.: 33½ins. high

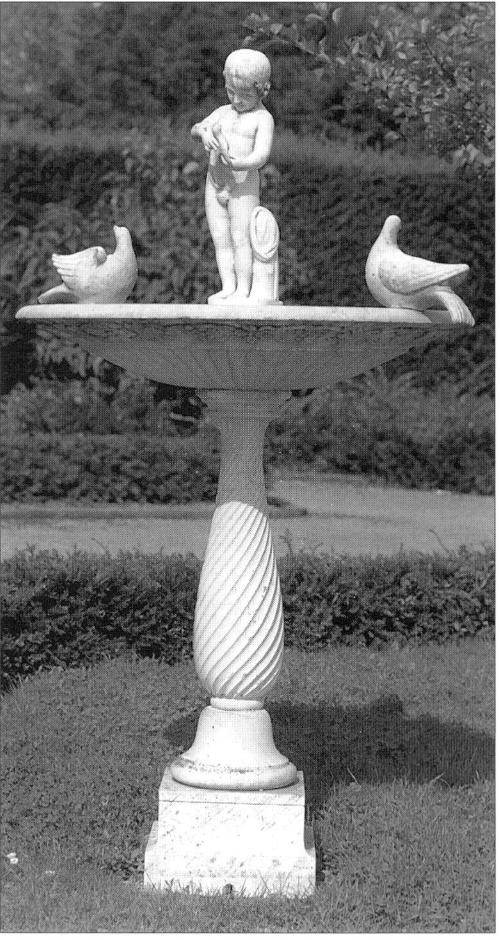

A late nineteenth century Italian white marble fountain bowl on stand, surmounted by a naked putto and with two birds nesting on the rim of the bowl. The concept of this design would also suggest it could be used as a rather superior bird bath. 180cm.: 71ins. high

The dolphin is a recurring element of fountain decoration and the concept of three entwined dolphins as seen in this French bronze and marble fountain of circa 1870 is most pleasing. The circular marble bowl is supported by three bronze putti. The dolphins' snouts are drilled for water. With traces of earlier gilding. 170cm.: 67ins. high

A Garnkirk terracotta fountain, circa 1870. The circular foliate cast bowl with leaf and scallop cast spout is supported by three standing cranes. The triform lower section, modelled with three lion's masks with mouths drilled for water, stands on a circular base stamped 'Garnkirk Fire Clay Works'. The company produced monumental statuary and salt glazed pipes, and appears to date from the 1840s and to have exhibited at the Great Exhibition of 1851. The fountain is shown with an associated pool surround

A Doulton painted stoneware fountain, circa 1900. The lobed bowls with everted stylised leaf moulded rims are supported by a tier of swans and cranes, stamped 'Doulton' on a composition stone base. 160cm.: 63ins. high

An interesting tôle fountain of octagonal form with arcaded gallery and glazed panels, the waterspout formed as a gilt flowerhead, on circular stepped base. Early nineteenth century. 99cm.: 39ins. high

A rare Victorian cast iron fountain by George Smith & Co., Sun Foundry, Glasgow. The lobed shallow bowl with egg and dart moulded rim on fluted column flanked by four griffin terms, the shaped and fluted square base with stylised flowerheads. With diamond registration mark for 22 September, 1870, and manufacturer's stamp 'George Smith Sun Foundry'. This company is recorded from the 1850s; it became a limited company in 1895 and went into voluntary liquidation in 1899. 125cm.: 49ins. high

A late eighteenth century Portland stone fountain the rectangular column supporting a quatrefoil bowl with four fountain heads. The lobed circular pool surround with four plinths and ogee sides on plinth base. 183cm.: 72ins. high

The partnership of Eleanor Coade and John Sealy was established in 1799. This is a remarkable example from the firm of a grotto fountain produced in artificial stone with realistic coral formation ingeniously moulded with grotesque masks and animal heads supporting a scallop shell dish. The base is decorated with shells, rocks and stalactites. Stamped 'Coade and Se . . . [Sealy] Lambeth 1805'. 135cm: 53ins. high

An impressive French nineteenth century Louis XVI-style carved stone wall fountain, the scallop shaped bowl surmounted by a stylised dolphin entwined with bulrushes above stalactites and scrolls. Volute breakfront base carved with acanthus and on a moulded plinth. 296cm.: 117ins. high

George Samuel Elgood (1851-1943), 'Melbourne', from Some English Gardens *by George S. Elgood and Gertrude Jekyll, 1904. The view is of the round basin with fountain jet*

George Samuel Elgood (1851-1943), a watercolour sketch for a gondola-shaped fountain

Another cast iron fountain produced by the Sun Foundry (see p.75). The fluted shallow bowl on a slender tapering column and rock base is flanked by three herons and a lily. The base stamped 'Sun Foundry, Glasgow'. Late nineteenth century. 84cm.: 33ins. high

The design of this late nineteenth century French cast iron fountain is taken from an original model by Mathuria Moreau (1821-1912) in the form of a scantily draped putto holding a paddle and seated on an upturned ewer with spout. 73cm.: 28½ins. high

A Victorian cast iron fountain, with large scalloped circular bowl with baluster spacer decorated with rockwork and overhanging stiff leaf decoration, surmounted by two further graduated bowls applied with birds and flowers. The fountain stands on an associated marble base. 371cm.: 146ins. high

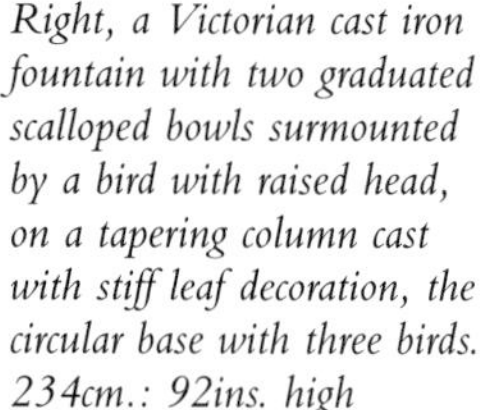

Right, a Victorian cast iron fountain with two graduated scalloped bowls surmounted by a bird with raised head, on a tapering column cast with stiff leaf decoration, the circular base with three birds. 234cm.: 92ins. high

Far right, a late nineteenth century French cast iron fountain with three putti supporting a shaped bowl cast with four lions' heads. 120cm.: 47ins. high

A Victorian cast iron fountain of three-tiered form, the lower circular bowl with leaf and rope twist moulded rim, the two graduated bowls above cast with leaves and bulrushes and with dolphins and stiff leaf spacers. Circa 1870. 203cm.: 80ins. high

A Victorian cast iron fountain, possibly by Handyside, modelled with flowerheads and stiff leaf decoration. 313cm.: 123ins. high

A highly decorative cast iron wall fountain, the arched top with urn flanked by rams' heads and centred with a female figure standing on a stylised dolphin, with an alloy water spout. The fountain stands on a rusticated base. Circa 1900. 127cm.: 50ins. high

A cast iron fountain by the Andrew Handyside Foundry, Derby. Scalloped shaped bowl surmounted by a pair of putti and supported by three intertwined dolphins. Circa 1870. 130cm.: 51ins. high

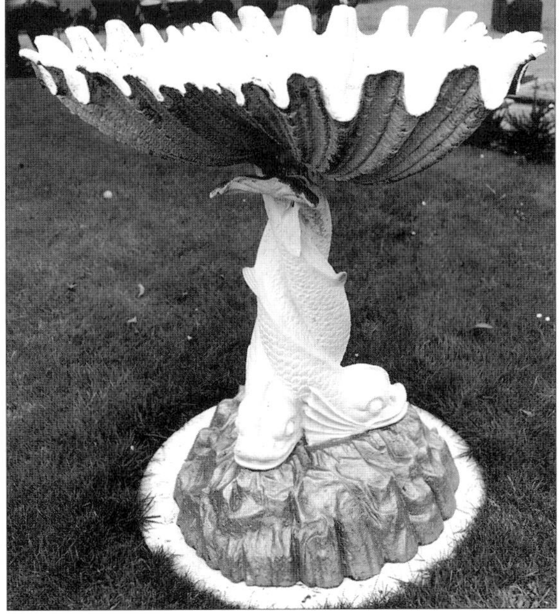

A version of the previous Handyside product, a cast iron fountain with scalloped shaped bowl supported by three intertwined dolphins on a rockwork base. 102cm.: 44ins. high

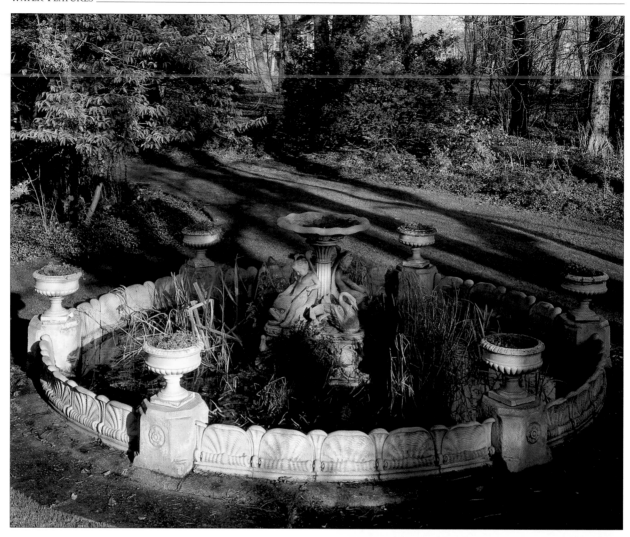

The Doulton Company manufactured a huge range of products from the middle of the nineteenth century. Although they produced drainpipes and sanitary wares, they also offered some fine and collectable decorative items and employed notable artists and designers. The company also introduced a range of garden ornaments including urns and flower pots and this was expanded to include fountains and sundials, garden seats and garden edging tiles. This impressive Doulton stoneware garden fountain of circa 1890 was probably designed by George Tinworth. The pond wall is composed of a frieze of shells interrupted by six compressed campana shaped urns raised on square plinths. The centrepiece, shown in detail, is a scalloped bowl set on a fluted column flanked by a pair of putti each astride a dolphin together with a pair of swans. The centrepiece is elevated on a quatrefoil pedestal with four wading bird supporters. Impressed mark 'Doulton, Lambeth'

An impressive Ducel cast iron fountain, French, late nineteenth century. The octagonal bowl, with serpent entwined foliage, is surmounted by a putto with feather headdress and holding a bow and dead parrot. Stamped 'J J Ducel, Paris'. 318cm.: 125ins. high. This company was founded in 1810, exhibited at the 1851 Exhibition, and in 1878 was incorporated into the Société Anonyme des Hauts Fourneaux et Fonderies du Val d'Osne

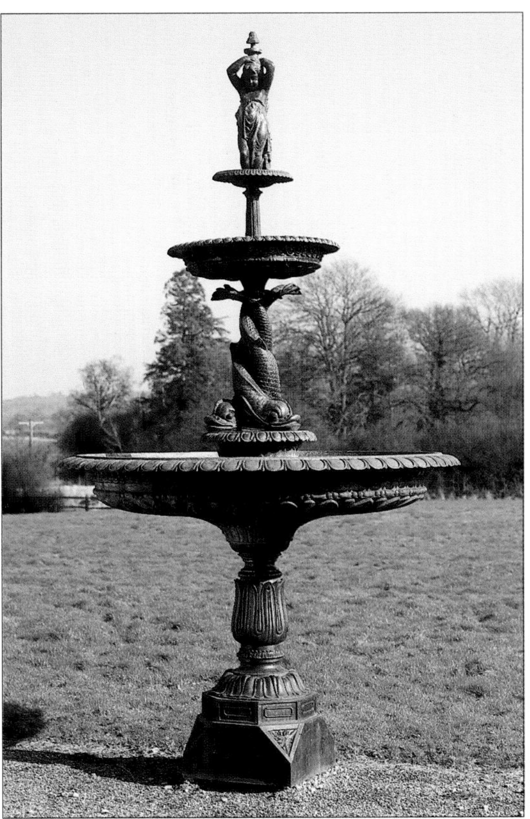

A Handyside cast iron fountain with three graduated circular leaf cast bowls, intertwined dolphins and diaphanously clad figure on an octagonal and shaped cast base. Circa 1860. 360cm.: 142ins. high. A similar fountain is illustrated in the 1873 Handyside Foundry of Derby catalogue but with two putti on top rather than a single figure. Components of the Handyside range were evidently interchangeable

Lilian Stannard (1877-1944), 'The Lily Pond, with a Cherub Fountain', signed, watercolour heightened with bodycolour

Far left, another item from Handyside's range, a cast iron fountain with a pair of putti supporting a centra.l column, on octagonal support with maker's plate stamped 'A Handyside Co. Ltd, London and Derby', with rounded tray base with egg and dart border. 117cm.: 46ins. high

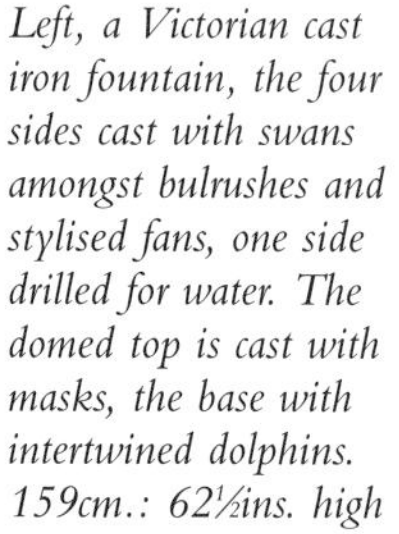

Left, a Victorian cast iron fountain, the four sides cast with swans amongst bulrushes and stylised fans, one side drilled for water. The domed top is cast with masks, the base with intertwined dolphins. 159cm.: 62½ins. high

A Handyside cast iron fountain with two graduated circular lily leaf bowls surmounted by similarly cast column surmounted by a cherub holding an urn, on octagonal base. The design is illustrated in the 1870 Andrew Handyside catalogue. 196cm.: 77ins. high

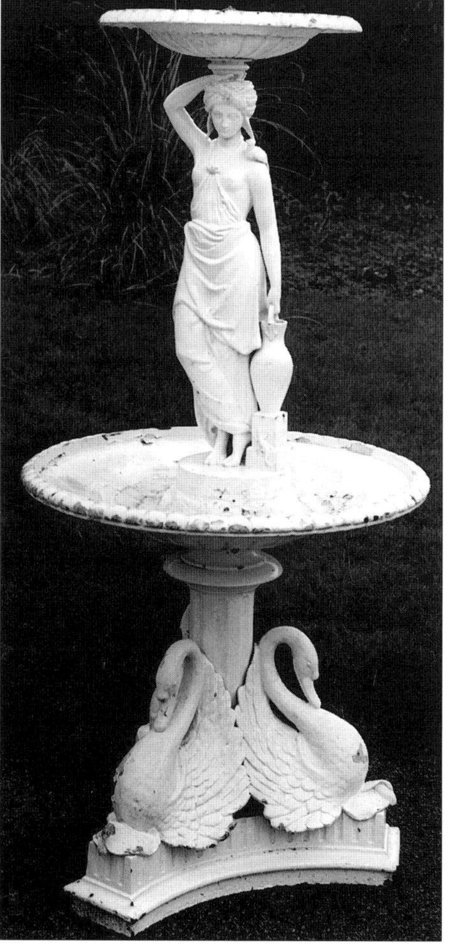

Far left, the design for this Coalbrookdale two-tier cast iron fountain is illustrated in their 1875 catalogue (Section III) and was entitled 'Boys'. The lower lobed shallow bowl is supported by three swans surrounding a shaped cylindrical column on a triform base. 122cm.: 48ins. high. Similar 'Boys' appear on Handyside fountains and a fountain offered by Boulton & Paul of Norwich

Left, the three-swan support appears again on this Coalbrookdale fountain. A bare breasted Nubian maiden carrying a water pitcher, with a bird perched on her shoulder, supports a lobed bowl. 140cm.: 55ins. high

Originally offered painted white or with a bronze finish, a rare Coalbrookdale cast iron fountain, circa 1870. The two shallow bowls supported on a foliate cast lobed column and on a circular base cast with flowerheads, stamped 'C B Dale & Co.' and with diamond registration stamp for September 1863. 112cm.: 44ins. high

A Coalbrookdale cast iron fountain, circa 1870. The lobed circular bowl supported on a tapering fluted column and triform base moulded with lily leaves. 96cm.: 38ins. high

Demonstrating the interchangeable Coalbrookdale base. Here the lily leaves of the previous fountain are replaced by the three swans (see opposite page). The two circular graduated shallow bowls have baluster supports. Originally available bronzed or with white painted finish. Circa 1875. 125cm.: 50ins. high

Far left, a cast iron Coalbrookdale fountain base with a young semi-naked girl holding an urn. The figure stands on a triangular pedestal, cast with masks and foliage, on a triform base. This figure is similar to the company design for a fountain entitled 'Slave'. Circa 1875. 142cm.: 56ins. high

Left, Coalbrookdale identified this cast iron figure as 'Young Pan' and included it on a catalogue page headed 'Figures Suitable for Fountains'. It was originally available, painted white, bronzed or electrobronzed, on an associated base. Circa 1875. 81cm.: 32ins. high

A cast iron fountain mask of a Bacchante with vine entwined hair. Circa 1870. 51cm.: 20ins. high

English provincial school, circa 1840, 'A Gentleman and His Wife in Their Garden Beside an Ornamental Fountain, with a Grotto Beyond'

SEED DEPARTMENT
—contd.

ORNAMENTAL FOUNTAINS.
(Cast Iron.)

No. 1.
52 in. diameter at the bottom basin, 79 in. high over all, and fitted with jet complete. Painted and well finished.
Each £7 1 9

No. 1a.
72 in. diameter at the bottom basin, and 79 in. high over all, and fitted with jet complete. Painted and well finished.
Each £11 6 9

No. 2.
24 in. diameter at the bottom basin, and 6 ft. 10½ in. high over all, fitted with jet complete.
Each £5 6 3
Painted and well finished.

Smaller parts of Fountains sent packed in hamper, charged 3/6

No. 1A.

No. 2.

Mail order fountains available in the early twentieth century. The example on the left continues to make use of the dolphin motif (see p. 79). These were affordable fountains for the middle classes and it is perhaps surprising, therefore, that they do not appear more often on the market nowadays

Lewis Charles Powles (1860-1942), 'The Wellhead'. (Courtesy Fine-Lines Fine Art)

WELLHEADS

Many older properties have wells, but the idea of making a feature of them by introducing a wellhead seems to have become popular in England in the second half of the nineteenth century. The types of wellhead most favoured were of marble decorated in Italy and dating back to the fifteenth or sixteenth centuries. They were brought back from Venice (a natural place for wellheads, situated as it is on a giant artesian well) by visitors on the Grand Tours of the seventeenth to nineteenth centuries.

Presumably demand exceeded supply, for before long copies were being produced, either direct imitations or reproductions of famous bronze originals at various palaces in Venice. In the early years of the twentieth century, reproductions could be ordered from the J.P. White catalogue in terracotta, Istrian stone or marble.

Wellheads sometimes come with an iron overthrow from which a bucket would be lowered.

An Istrian marble wellhead, sixteenth century, of waisted bulbous hexagonal form, the sides carved with a shield. 81cm.: 32ins. high

A Rosso Verona wellhead, Venetian, probably seventeenth century, the plain baluster body carved with oval cartouche. 70cm.: 27½ins. high

An Istrian stone wellhead of Venetian influence, the circular body with semi-circular arches with armorial shields, surmounted by animal heads below a square top. Eighteenth century. 70cm.: 27½ins. high

A fine example of an Istrian stone wellhead, carved with a lion's mask, the jaws holding swags centred with ribbon-tied armour, shields and helmets, on foliate carved foot and hexagonal base. Seventeenth century. 74cm.: 29ins. high

A simpler carved stone wellhead of hexagonal form, with wrought iron arched overthrow with scroll cresting. Eighteenth century. 213cm.: 84ins. high

An Italian wrought iron wellhead of shaped square form, the uprights flanked by collar-tied scrolls, the overthrow with barley twist uprights supporting scrolling brackets with pierced finial. Early eighteenth century. 283cm.: 111ins. high

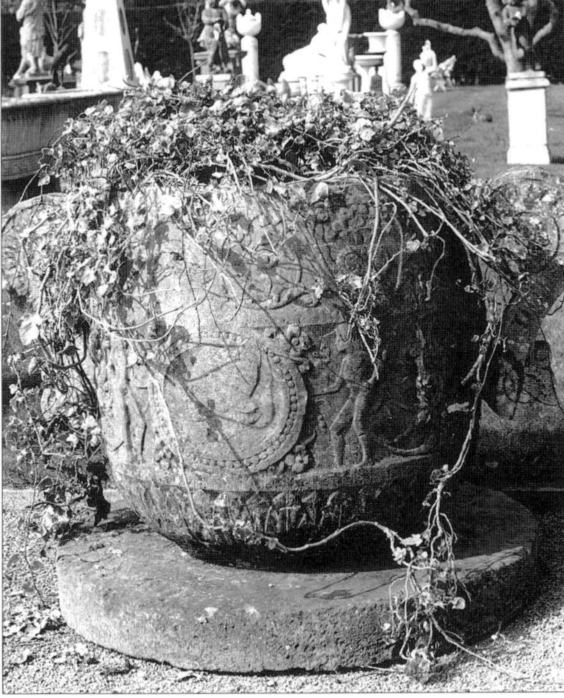

Above left, from the Low Countries, a stone wellhead of cylindrical moulded form, with aperture and step, the elaborate wrought iron overthrow with barley twist uprights comprising domed centre section with foliate and scroll finial above hanging hook. This is a large example, probably for use in a public place. Nineteenth century. 384cm.: 151ins. high

Above, an ornate wrought iron wellhead of baluster form with ogee arched overthrow with chain driven pulley. Late nineteenth/early twentieth century. 254cm.: 100ins. high

A highly decorated Istrian stone wellhead of ovoid form, carved with stylised flowers and scrolling foliage, one side centred with a shield flanked by mythological winged beasts, the other side centred with a portrait medallion flanked by standing figures, with stiff leaf lower section and associated scroll carved stone handles, on circular base. Nineteenth century. 92cm.: 36ins. high

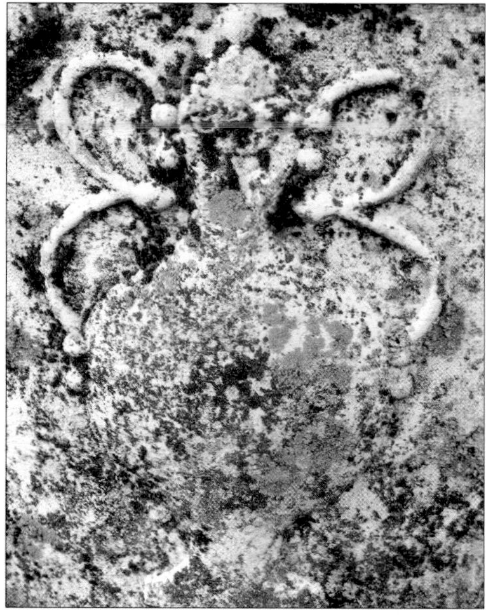

An attractive Venetian Istrian stone wellhead, seventeenth century, of tapering circular form carved on three sides with an urn (see detail) and with scroll carved corners. The wrought iron overthrow is a later addition. 230cm.: 91ins. high

Arthur Claude Strachan (1865-1932), 'By the Cottage Door', detail

Carved in high relief with a frieze of putti supporting festoons of flowers, a white marble Italian wellhead, with associated octagonal surround. Circa 1870. 79cm.: 29ins. high

Watering

WATERING POTS AND CANS

English school, circa 1810, 'Watering the Garden'

One of the earliest forms of container for watering is the earthenware thumb-operated watering pot with perforated base (p.92). In the seventeenth century this was a suitable vessel for watering young seedlings, and such pots are also identified as being used to sprinkle water to dampen rushes inside the home.

A more recognisable forerunner of the watering can is the seventeenth century earthenware example with its large perforated rose (p.92). It is believed that large numbers of these were made, possibly in south-east England.

In the eighteenth century, metal watering cans became the obvious practical successor to earthenware forms and examples are to be found in brass and copper. The Dutch were fine producers and exporters of brass metalwork in the eighteenth century and a number of cans will have come from The Netherlands. The French generally made copper cans, while the Italians continued to favour earthenware. In the mid-nineteenth century the French were credited with making the most practical watering cans, they certainly introduced the greatest variety.

In the early nineteenth century, tinplate cans were produced, often painted red or green, the red being cheaper because, at the time, red paint was cheaper than green. Tinplate cans in turn gave way to zinc cans which have continued in a similar form to present-day cans, although in competition with plastic 'cans'.

T. Mackay, 'Gardening', 1912

Early copper watering cans are very desirable. They tend to date from the eighteenth century and a number were made in France into the early nineteenth century. This attractively shaped example has a detachable rose. 46cm.: 19ins. high

A brass watering can, possibly Dutch. Late eighteenth century. 84cm.: 33ins. wide

On the left, a copper watering can with brass rose, French. Late eighteenth century. 46cm.: 18ins. high. On the right, a brass watering can dated 1769. Dutch or English. 71cm.: 28ins. long

Two French copper watering cans with French style one-piece handles. Eighteenth/nineteenth century. 49cm.: 19½ins. high and 41 cm.: 16ins. high

This type of can with its large somewhat pointed rose is depicted in a number of English gardening books published in the second half of the eighteenth century. This example in copper is stamped 1773 which may well be the date of manufacture. A rare item, probably English. Circa 1770. 38cm.: 15ins. high

Above right, an early nineteenth century copper watering can, the body of continental form but with carrying and pouring handles as favoured by the English. 56cm.: 22ins. long

This early nineteenth century French can may represent something of a transitional type since it has a body of tin and handle and spout of copper. The body retains large areas of original red paint. 38cm.: 15ins. high, with fitted rose 16cm.: 6½ins. diameter

The letters 'V R' and a crown device make this late nineteenth century can very desirable. It is probably by Haws, and the marks suggest it was intended for use in a royal or official residence. This style of can is still produced in copper and brass

A 'thumb' watering pot, which works on the principal of suction. The pot was filled with water, the thumb being used to control the flow from the perforated base. Sixteenth century. 27cm.: 10½ins. high

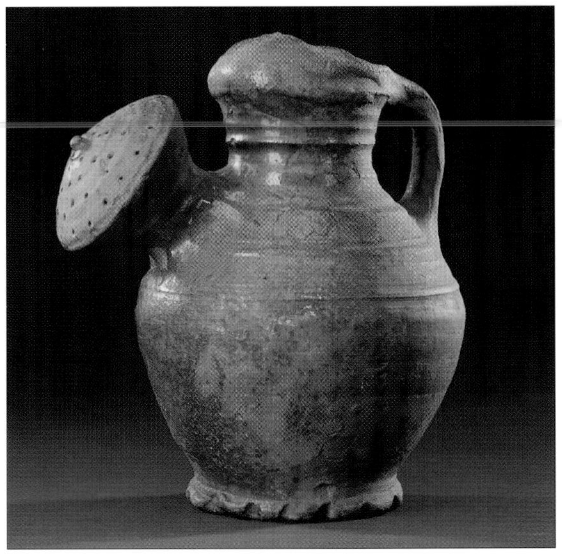

A part lead glazed earthenware watering pot. Seventeenth century. 28cm.: 11ins. high. These pots may have been made in Sussex, as a number have been found in excavations in the area. They are already of interest to collectors of early English pottery, and since about 1990 copies of varying quality have been produced

A copper watering can, probably English, with embossed scrolls and gadrooning to cover, long spout with fitted rose. Late eighteenth century. 90cm.: 35ins. long

An unusual continental, possibly Austrian, tinned copper watering can, embossed body with cast imitation horn handle. Presumably intended for conservatory or indoor use. Circa 1880. 29cm.: 11½ins. high

A selection of watering cans. On the bench, left to right, French, early twentieth century; English, late nineteenth century; English, early twentieth century; continental, circa 1900. On the ground, left to right, English estate-made can, nineteenth century; child's watering can, English, circa 1920; French, circa 1900; large can, French-style, though possibly English, circa 1860

A brass watering can, with embossed cover and stylised flowerhead punched decoration to body. Late eighteenth century. 92cm.: 36¼ins. long overall

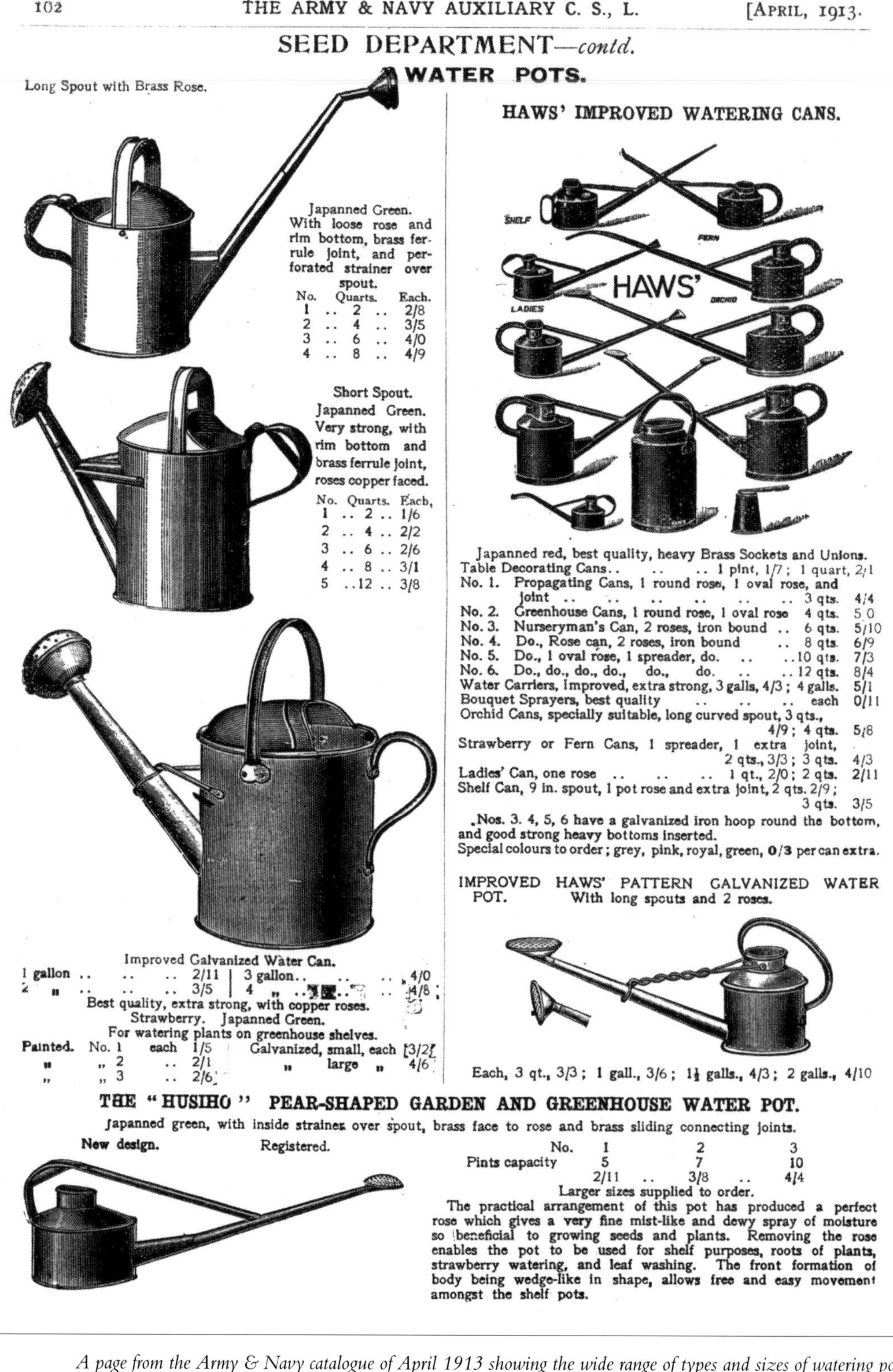

102 THE ARMY & NAVY AUXILIARY C. S., L. [APRIL, 1913.

SEED DEPARTMENT—*contd.*

WATER POTS.

Long Spout with Brass Rose.

Japanned Green. With loose rose and rim bottom, brass ferrule joint, and perforated strainer over spout.

No.	Quarts.	Each.
1	2	2/8
2	4	3/5
3	6	4/0
4	8	4/9

Short Spout. Japanned Green. Very strong, with rim bottom and brass ferrule joint, roses copper faced.

No.	Quarts.	Each.
1	2	1/6
2	4	2/2
3	6	2/6
4	8	3/1
5	12	3/8

Improved Galvanized Water Can.

1 gallon .. .. .. 2/11 | 3 gallon.. .. .. 4/0
2 „ .. .. .. 3/5 | 4 „ 4/8

Best quality, extra strong, with copper roses.

Strawberry. Japanned Green.
For watering plants on greenhouse shelves.

Painted. No. 1 each 1/5 Galvanized, small, each 3/2
„ „ 2 .. 2/1 „ large „ 4/6
„ „ 3 .. 2/6

HAWS' IMPROVED WATERING CANS.

Japanned red, best quality, heavy Brass Sockets and Unions.

Table Decorating Cans.. .. .. 1 pint, 1/7; 1 quart, 2/1
No. 1. Propagating Cans, 1 round rose, 1 oval rose, and joint .. .. 3 qts. 4/4
No. 2. Greenhouse Cans, 1 round rose, 1 oval rose 4 qts. 5/0
No. 3. Nurseryman's Can, 2 roses, iron bound .. 6 qts. 5/10
No. 4. Do., Rose can, 2 roses, iron bound .. 8 qts. 6/9
No. 5. Do., 1 oval rose, 1 spreader, do. .. ..10 qts. 7/3
No. 6. Do., do., do., do., do., do. .. .. 12 qts. 8/4
Water Carriers, Improved, extra strong, 3 galls, 4/3; 4 galls. 5/1
Bouquet Sprayers, best quality .. .. .. each 0/11
Orchid Cans, specially suitable, long curved spout, 3 qts., 4/9; 4 qts. 5/8
Strawberry or Fern Cans, 1 spreader, 1 extra joint, 2 qts., 3/3; 3 qts. 4/3
Ladies' Can, one rose .. .. .. 1 qt., 2/0; 2 qts. 2/11
Shelf Can, 9 in. spout, 1 pot rose and extra joint, 2 qts. 2/9; 3 qts. 3/5

Nos. 3, 4, 5, 6 have a galvanized iron hoop round the bottom, and good strong heavy bottoms inserted.
Special colours to order; grey, pink, royal, green, 0/3 per can extra.

IMPROVED HAWS' PATTERN GALVANIZED WATER POT. With long spouts and 2 roses.

Each, 3 qt., 3/3; 1 gall., 3/6; 1½ galls., 4/3; 2 galls., 4/10

THE "HUSIHO" PEAR-SHAPED GARDEN AND GREENHOUSE WATER POT.

Japanned green, with inside strainer over spout, brass face to rose and brass sliding connecting joints.

New design. Registered.

No.	1	2	3
Pints capacity	5	7	10
	2/11	3/8	4/4

Larger sizes supplied to order.

The practical arrangement of this pot has produced a perfect rose which gives a very fine mist-like and dewy spray of moisture so beneficial to growing seeds and plants. Removing the rose enables the pot to be used for shelf purposes, roots of plants, strawberry watering, and leaf washing. The front formation of body being wedge-like in shape, allows free and easy movement amongst the shelf pots.

A page from the Army & Navy catalogue of April 1913 showing the wide range of types and sizes of watering pots and cans offered. The Haws Company offered distinctive shapes and a range of cans that have remained popular with nurserymen throughout the century. Apparently Haws had a number of imitators, and genuine products are more easily confirmed by the presence of the Haws medallion on the breast of the can. The medallion also carries the address of the company which will assist in dating: Clapton, London, from 1885 to 1926; Bishop's Stortford from 1926 to 1953, and Stourbridge from 1953 to 1976. The company is currently at Smethwick in the West Midlands

WATERING SYSTEMS

These include garden engines, sprayers and sprinklers, syringes and back-pack sprayers. Getting water to various parts of the garden could be made easier with the use of galvanised swing water barrows to which could be fitted a semi-rotary pump. Popular in the late nineteenth and early twentieth centuries, they were also known in barrel form in the seventeenth century.

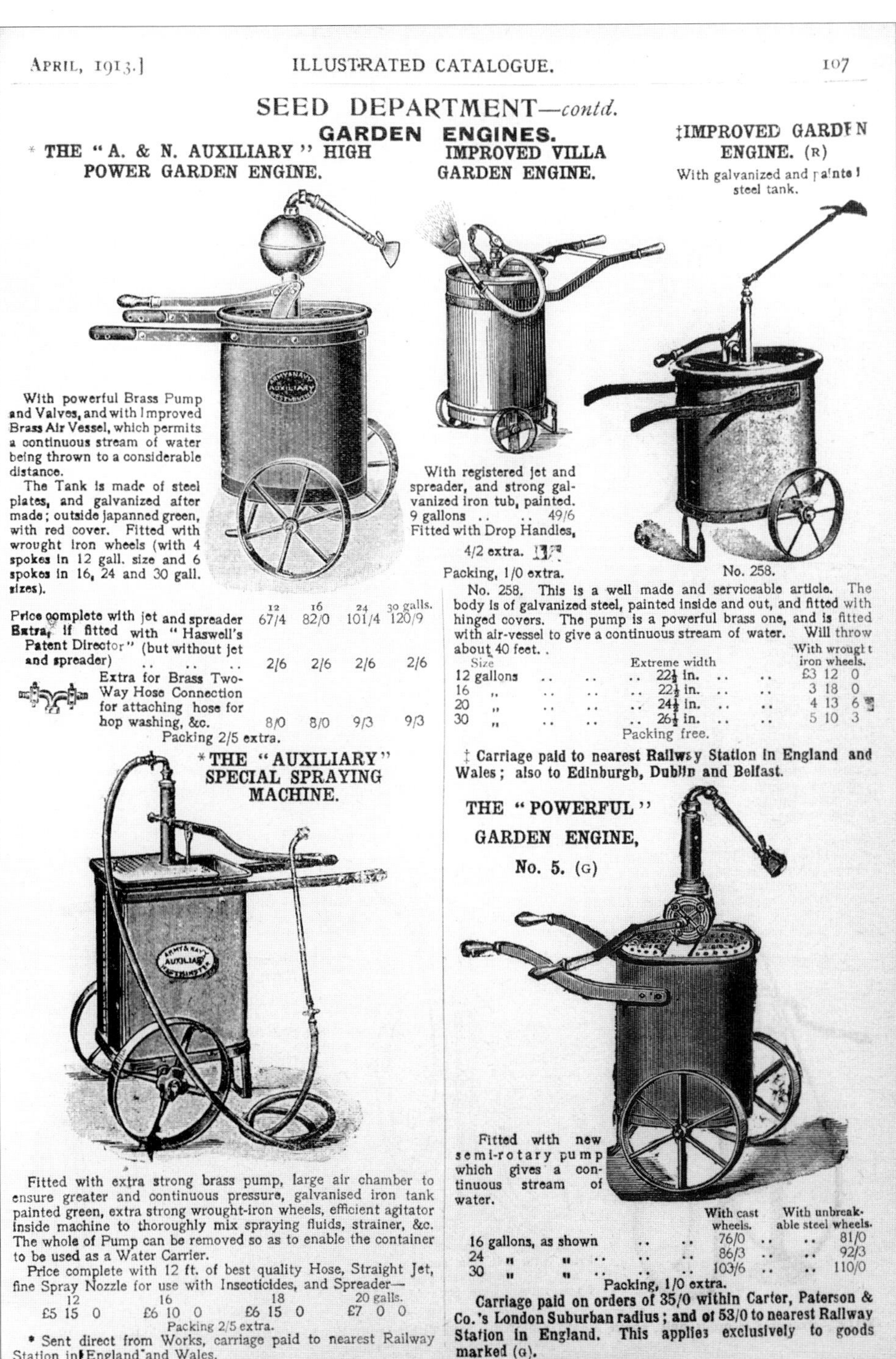

APRIL, 1913.] ILLUSTRATED CATALOGUE. 107

SEED DEPARTMENT—*contd.*

GARDEN ENGINES.

* THE "A. & N. AUXILIARY" HIGH POWER GARDEN ENGINE.

With powerful Brass Pump and Valves, and with Improved Brass Air Vessel, which permits a continuous stream of water being thrown to a considerable distance.

The Tank is made of steel plates, and galvanized after made; outside japanned green, with red cover. Fitted with wrought iron wheels (with 4 spokes in 12 gall. size and 6 spokes in 16, 24 and 30 gall. sizes).

	12	16	24	30 galls.
Price complete with jet and spreader	67/4	82/0	101/4	120/9
Extra, if fitted with "Haswell's Patent Director" (but without jet and spreader)	2/6	2/6	2/6	2/6
Extra for Brass Two-Way Hose Connection for attaching hose for hop washing, &c.	8/0	8/0	9/3	9/3

Packing 2/5 extra.

IMPROVED VILLA GARDEN ENGINE.

With registered jet and spreader, and strong galvanized iron tub, painted.
9 gallons 49/6
Fitted with Drop Handles, 4/2 extra.

Packing, 1/0 extra.

‡IMPROVED GARDEN ENGINE. (R)

With galvanized and painted steel tank.

No. 258.

No. 258. This is a well made and serviceable article. The body is of galvanized steel, painted inside and out, and fitted with hinged covers. The pump is a powerful brass one, and is fitted with air-vessel to give a continuous stream of water. Will throw about 40 feet.

Size	Extreme width	With wrought iron wheels.
12 gallons	22½ in.	£3 12 0
16 "	22½ in.	3 18 0
20 "	24½ in.	4 13 6
30 "	26½ in.	5 10 3

Packing free.

‡ Carriage paid to nearest Railway Station in England and Wales; also to Edinburgh, Dublin and Belfast.

*THE "AUXILIARY" SPECIAL SPRAYING MACHINE.

Fitted with extra strong brass pump, large air chamber to ensure greater and continuous pressure, galvanised iron tank painted green, extra strong wrought-iron wheels, efficient agitator inside machine to thoroughly mix spraying fluids, strainer, &c. The whole of Pump can be removed so as to enable the container to be used as a Water Carrier.

Price complete with 12 ft. of best quality Hose, Straight Jet, fine Spray Nozzle for use with Insecticides, and Spreader—

12	16	18	20 galls.
£5 15 0	£6 10 0	£6 15 0	£7 0 0

Packing 2/5 extra.

* Sent direct from Works, carriage paid to nearest Railway Station in England and Wales.

THE "POWERFUL" GARDEN ENGINE, No. 5. (G)

Fitted with new semi-rotary pump which gives a continuous stream of water.

	With cast wheels.	With unbreakable steel wheels.
16 gallons, as shown	76/0	81/0
24 " "	86/3	92/3
30 " "	103/6	110/0

Packing, 1/0 extra.

Carriage paid on orders of 35/0 within Carter, Paterson & Co.'s London Suburban radius; and of 53/0 to nearest Railway Station in England. This applies exclusively to goods marked (G).

NOTE.—From 5 to 7 days required. Packing not returnable.

E 4

A page from the Army & Navy catalogue of April 1913 illustrating various types of garden engine which sprayed water or fluid mixes, either in a jet or stream. Some of these designs are modifications of the swing water barrow

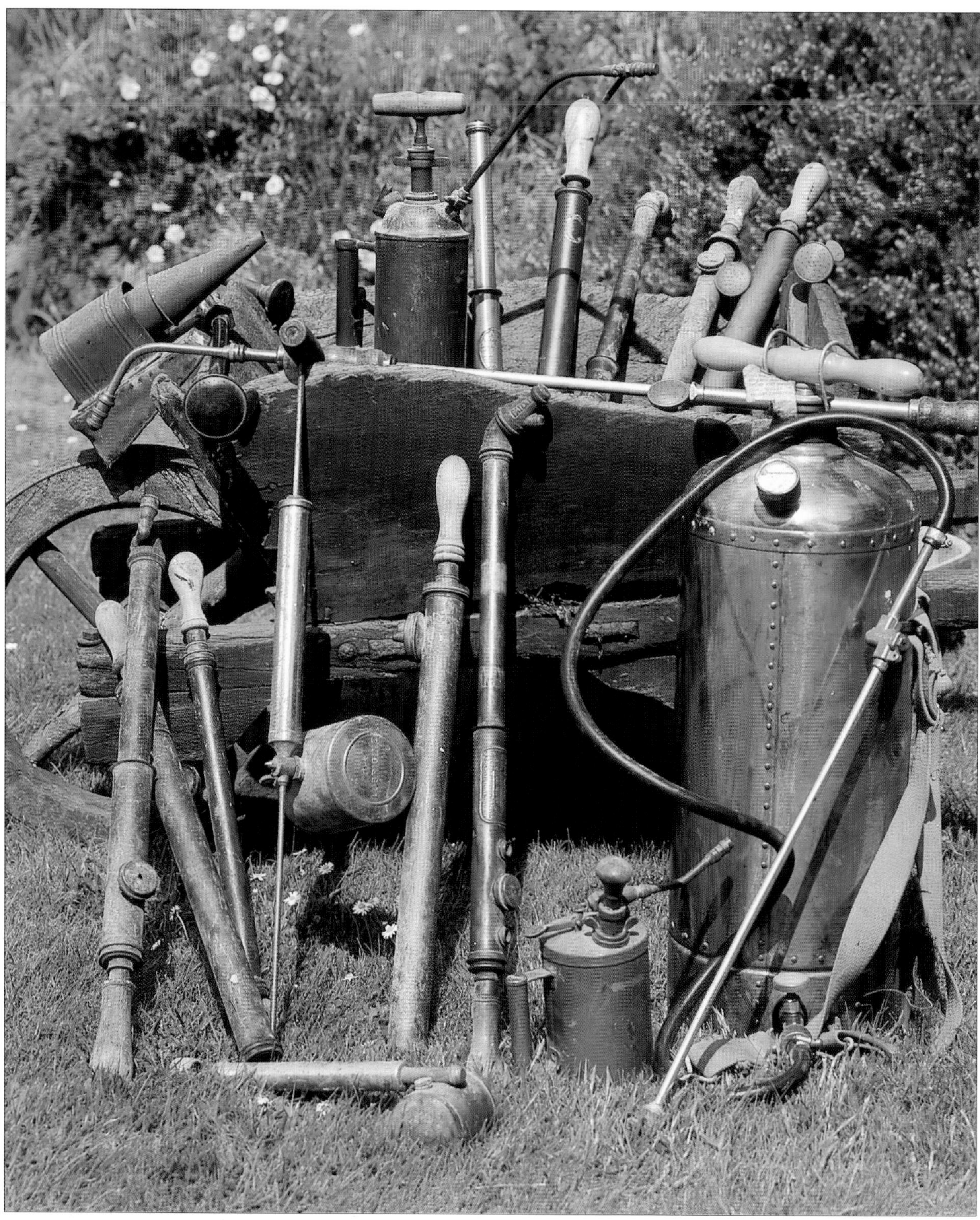

A selection of copper, brass and zinc bodied syringes, including well-known makes such as Abol and Corry. Also shown, on the right, a Four Oaks knapsack pneumatic spraying machine, similar to their 'Kent patent', usually for spraying fruit trees, vines, etc., mid-twentieth century. Beside the Four Oaks spraying machine, a copper-bodied pneumatic hand sprayer of which a contemporary advertisement stated: 'Having tubular handle it can be fitted on to a pole or bamboo lance for spraying vines, rose trees etc. which are out of our reach', circa 1935, but available from circa 1910. Leaning on top of the barrow wheel, a simple bellows to puff sulphur dust or similar fumigating substance, late nineteenth century

At the back a galvanised can, reputedly from Barcelona, mid-twentieth century; at the front two three-quarter gallon galvanised watering cans, English, circa 1915. The two water barrows in the centre are both early twentieth century, the one in front with a wrought iron frame and wheels. Although practical, nowadays water barrows are more popularly used for plants – interestingly reproductions are made today. In front of the water barrows, a wrought iron framed mobile hose reel, with galvanised drum, circa 1920

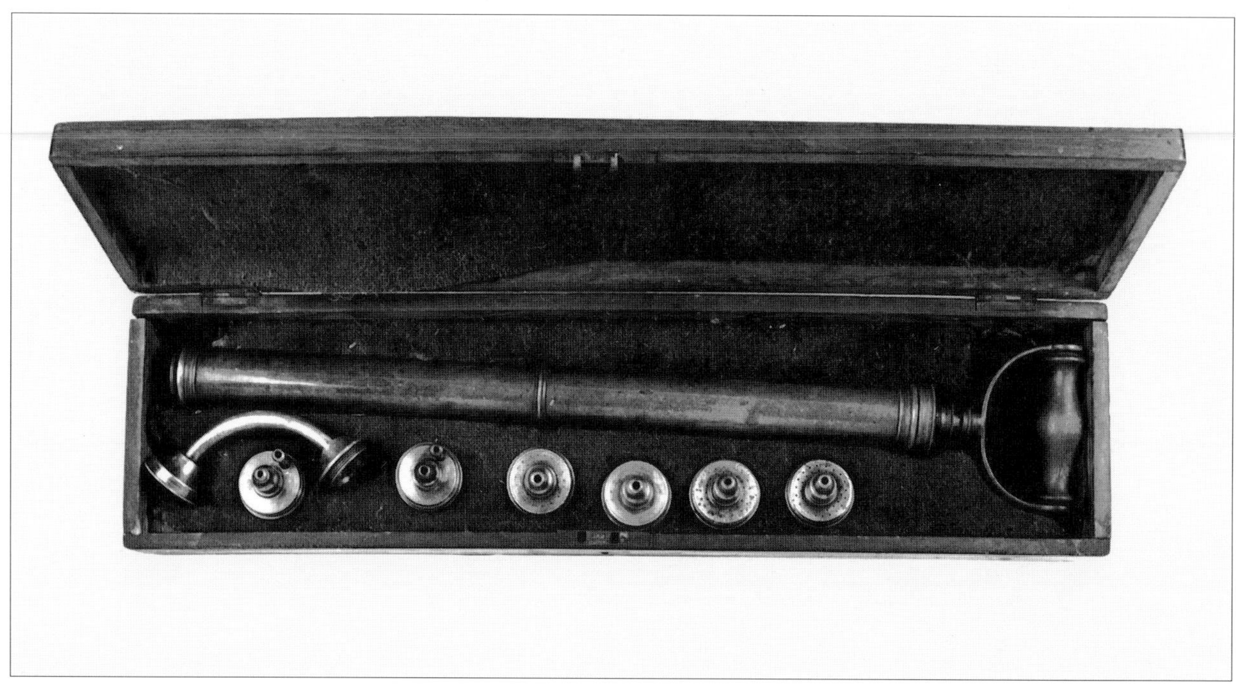

A Victorian brass spraying syringe with a set of nozzles, in original fitted mahogany case with carrying handle. Circa 1870

A large double wheel garden lawn sprinkler, the pressure rotating the spray from the two nozzles. Cast iron frame with brass fittings. Early twentieth century

Early twentieth century back pack sprayer by Four Oaks of Sutton Coldfield

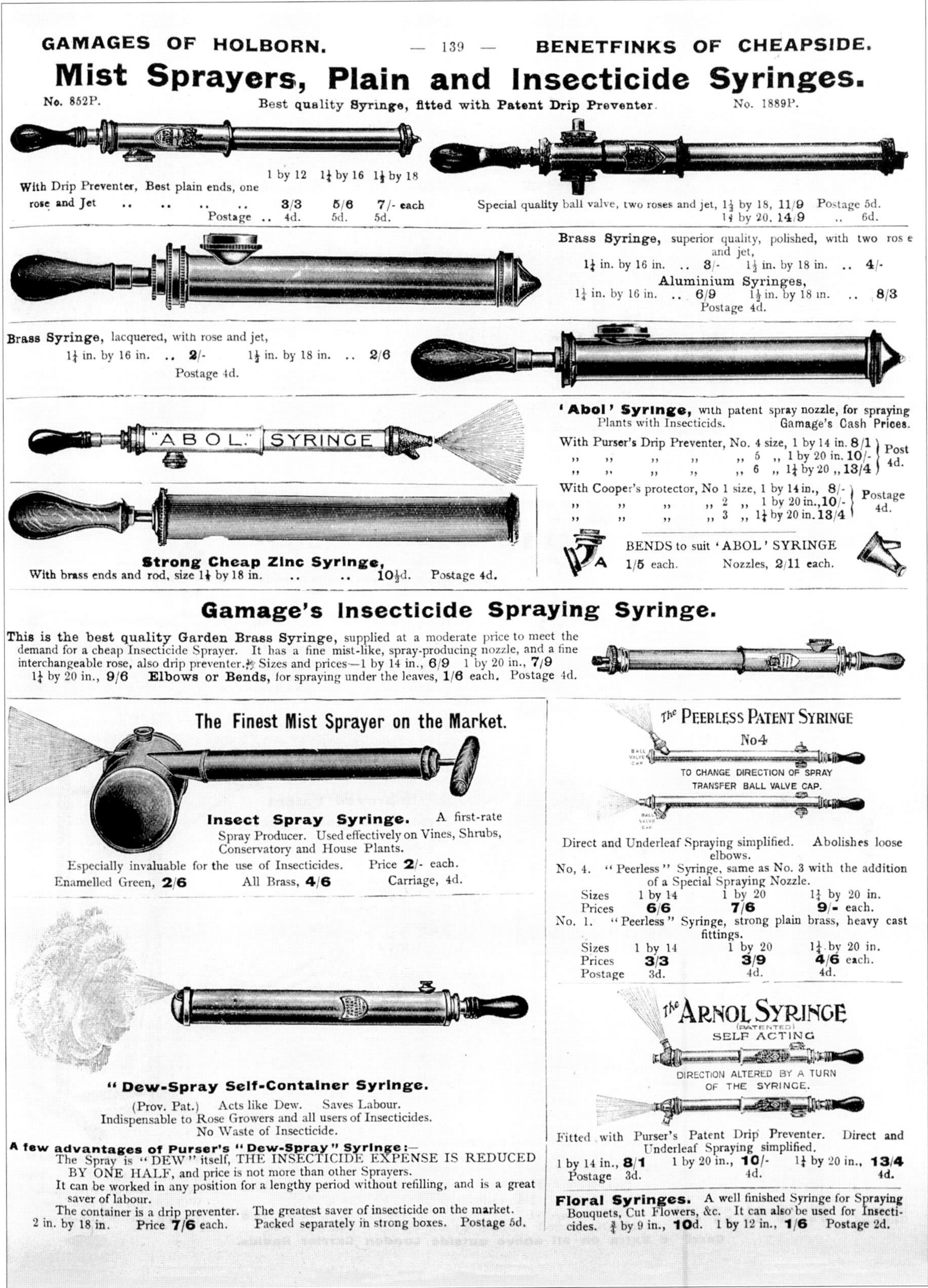

GAMAGES OF HOLBORN. — 139 — BENETFINKS OF CHEAPSIDE.

Mist Sprayers, Plain and Insecticide Syringes.

No. 852P. Best quality Syringe, fitted with Patent Drip Preventer. No. 1889P.

	1 by 12	1¼ by 16	1¼ by 18
With Drip Preventer, Best plain ends, one rose and Jet	3/3	5/6	7/- each
Postage ..	4d.	5d.	5d.

Special quality ball valve, two roses and jet, 1¼ by 18, 11/9 Postage 5d.
1¼ by 20, 14/9 .. 6d.

Brass Syringe, superior quality, polished, with two rose and jet,
1¼ in. by 16 in. .. 3/- 1½ in. by 18 in. .. 4/-
Aluminium Syringes,
1¼ in. by 16 in. .. 6/9 1½ in. by 18 in. .. 8/3
Postage 4d.

Brass Syringe, lacquered, with rose and jet,
1¼ in. by 16 in. .. 2/- 1½ in. by 18 in. .. 2/6
Postage 4d.

"ABOL." SYRINGE

'Abol' Syringe, with patent spray nozzle, for spraying Plants with Insecticids. Gamage's Cash Prices.
With Purser's Drip Preventer, No. 4 size, 1 by 14 in. 8/1
" " " " " 5 " 1 by 20 in. 10/-
" " " " " 6 " 1¼ by 20 " 13/4 } Post 4d.
With Cooper's protector, No 1 size, 1 by 14 in., 8/-
" " " " 2 " 1 by 20 in., 10/-
" " " " 3 " 1¼ by 20 in. 13/4 } Postage 4d.

BENDS to suit 'ABOL' SYRINGE 1/5 each. Nozzles, 2/11 each.

Strong Cheap Zinc Syringe,
With brass ends and rod, size 1¼ by 18 in. .. .. 10½d. Postage 4d.

Gamage's Insecticide Spraying Syringe.

This is the best quality Garden Brass Syringe, supplied at a moderate price to meet the demand for a cheap Insecticide Sprayer. It has a fine mist-like, spray-producing nozzle, and a fine interchangeable rose, also drip preventer. Sizes and prices—1 by 14 in., 6/9 1 by 20 in., 7/9 1¼ by 20 in., 9/6 **Elbows or Bends,** for spraying under the leaves, 1/6 each. Postage 4d.

The Finest Mist Sprayer on the Market.

Insect Spray Syringe. A first-rate Spray Producer. Used effectively on Vines, Shrubs, Conservatory and House Plants.
Especially invaluable for the use of Insecticides. Price 2/- each.
Enamelled Green, 2/6 All Brass, 4/6 Carriage, 4d.

"Dew-Spray Self-Container Syringe.
(Prov. Pat.) Acts like Dew. Saves Labour.
Indispensable to Rose Growers and all users of Insecticides.
No Waste of Insecticide.

A few advantages of Purser's "Dew-Spray" Syringe:—
The Spray is "DEW" itself, THE INSECTICIDE EXPENSE IS REDUCED BY ONE HALF, and price is not more than other Sprayers.
It can be worked in any position for a lengthy period without refilling, and is a great saver of labour.
The container is a drip preventer. The greatest saver of insecticide on the market.
2 in. by 18 in. Price 7/6 each. Packed separately in strong boxes. Postage 5d.

The Peerless Patent Syringe No4

BALL VALVE CAP

TO CHANGE DIRECTION OF SPRAY TRANSFER BALL VALVE CAP.

Direct and Underleaf Spraying simplified. Abolishes loose elbows.
No, 4. "Peerless" Syringe, same as No. 3 with the addition of a Special Spraying Nozzle.

Sizes	1 by 14	1 by 20	1¼ by 20 in.
Prices	6/6	7/6	9/- each.

No. 1. "Peerless" Syringe, strong plain brass, heavy cast fittings.

Sizes	1 by 14	1 by 20	1¼ by 20 in.
Prices	3/3	3/9	4/6 each.
Postage	3d.	4d.	4d.

The Arnol Syringe (Patented) Self Acting

DIRECTION ALTERED BY A TURN OF THE SYRINGE.

Fitted with Purser's Patent Drip Preventer. Direct and Underleaf Spraying simplified.

1 by 14 in., 8/1	1 by 20 in., 10/-	1¼ by 20 in., 13/4
Postage 3d.	4d.	4d.

Floral Syringes. A well finished Syringe for Spraying Bouquets, Cut Flowers, &c. It can also be used for Insecticides. ¾ by 9 in., 10d. 1 by 12 in., 1/6 Postage 2d.

Although generally available from the middle of the nineteenth century for washing and watering, syringes of the early twentieth century doubled as insecticide sprayers. Some fine quality products were produced with interchangeable nozzles. In 1913 prices ranged from 10½d. to 14s. 9d. (4p to 74p)

Stuart G. Davis (fl.1893-1904), 'The Garden Steps'

French school, 'A View from a Garden in Eveque near Vaux'. (Courtesy Sotheby's)

Decorative Containers

JARDINIERES AND PLANTERS

By the word 'jardinière' we understand a pot or container for flowers or plants, or a stand for flowers or plants (although Plant Stands have been given a separate section – see pp.110-117). Interestingly this French word does not appear to have been in general English use until the end of the nineteenth century, and today the words jardinière and planter are interchangeable. The most unusual examples are the rustic planters in the form of tree trunks, many thought to be of Scottish manufacture, from the 1860s through to the early years of the twentieth century.

The popularity of container gardening has encouraged the use of all manner of small portable containers, some of which are amusing. Increasingly popular are the Compton Pottery garden pots, some of which were favoured by Gertrude Jekyll in her designs for gardens (see pp.104 and 107). The pottery closed some forty years ago.

A large Ham stone trough of tapering rectangular form, the four side sections united by wrought iron brackets. Eighteenth century. 193cm.: 76ins. wide

One of a pair of large wrought iron jardinières, the circular bowl rising from circular base, fitted with a zinc liner. Circa 1840. 92cm.: 36ins. high

A rare Victorian jardinière of cast and wrought iron, the circular bowl with zinc liner supported by brackets cast with stylised foliage, on similarly cast triform supports, circular foot and stepped hexagonal base. Circa 1850. 127cm.: 50ins. wide

One of a similar pair of cast iron jardinières, the pierced circular body cast with stylised foliate brackets on scroll pierced triform supports and hexagonal base. A moss nest might have been used to line the interior instead of a bowl. Nineteenth century. 61cm.: 24ins. high

A French cast iron planter in the form of a latticework basket, similar to designs illustrated in the catalogue of the Société Anonyme des Hautes Fourneaux et Fonderies du Val d'Osne. Late nineteenth century. 74cm.: 29ins. diameter

Two cast iron planters, probably late nineteenth century, both of rectangular form. Left, moulded with wreaths on foliate cast supports. Right, decorated with thistles and trailing ivy, on scroll cast supports. Both 74cm.: 29ins. wide

A French cast iron planter, the body moulded with flowers and foliage and raised on acanthus feet. Circa 1870. 77cm.: 30½ins. wide

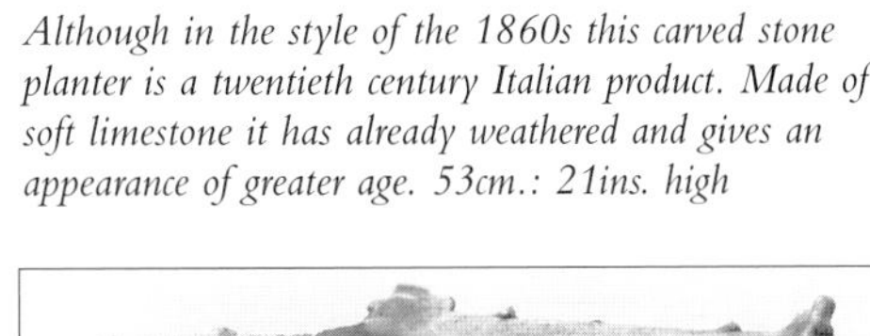

Although in the style of the 1860s this carved stone planter is a twentieth century Italian product. Made of soft limestone it has already weathered and gives an appearance of greater age. 53cm.: 21ins. high

Bearing the stamp of J.M. Blashfield, Stamford, one of a set of four fine jardinières, in the form of a latticework basket with woven handles. Circa 1860. 39cm.: 15½ins. high

One of a set of stoneware planters of canted square form, moulded in relief with oval portraits of maidens and with rustic loop handles and truncated twig borders. Circa 1870. 54cm.: 21ins. high

Two Compton Pottery scroll pots. Circa 1920

Three planters in the form of moss-encrusted tree trunks with truncated branches. Late nineteenth/early twentieth century. The glazed stoneware example on the right incorporates a trough on one side. Sizes vary from 75 to 126cm.: 29½ to 42ins. high. Smaller examples were also produced from approximately 30cm.: 12ins. high

One of a pair of Liberty terracotta jardinières, probably designed by Archibald Knox, the body moulded with interwoven Celtic inspired decoration and four handles, the inside stamped 'Designed and Manufactured by Liberty Co.' (see detail above) Early twentieth century. 52cm.: 20½ins. wide

Liberty offered a range of terracotta jardinières from the early twentieth century, some designed and manufactured by them and others made for them. This squat-bodied jardinière moulded with Celtic designs and loop handles, on moulded foot, was designed and manufactured by the firm. 44cm.: 17½ins. high

Far left, a Liberty terracotta jardinière of tapering octagonal form, moulded with panels of strapwork, the lower tapering section on octagonal base, the bowl and base stamped 'Liberty & Co.'. and registration number 422733. 123cm.: 48½ins. high

Left, a similar jardinière to the previous example but with a circular bowl. 116cm.: 45½ins. high

One of a pair of terracotta planters, possibly by Liberty & Co., of tapering cylindrical form, moulded with rectangular panels of foliage and flanked by lug handles. Circa 1900. 50cm.: 19½ins. high

A terracotta jardinière made for Liberty by Carter & Co., Poole, Dorset. Tapering circular body modelled with interwoven strapwork decoration on rising circular foot, stamped 'Carter made for Liberty & Co.'. Circa 1910. 72cm.: 28ins. high. Carter & Co. subsequently became Carter, Stabler & Adams Ltd. and was later known as the Poole Pottery

A rare Poole Pottery terracotta jardinière of octagonal form decorated with panels of birds beneath a lobed frieze and stamped 'Carter, Stabler & Adams, Poole, England'. Early twentieth century. 80cm.: 31½ins. diameter

The Compton Pottery, near Guildford, Surrey, was founded and developed by Mrs. Watts, the wife of the Victorian pre-Raphaelite painter, George Frederic Watts. The pottery (a centre for the Potters' Art Guild) designed and manufactured a range of garden pots, sundials, birdbaths, etc. in red and grey terracotta. These two large Compton Pottery jardinières are of the type favoured by Gertrude Jekyll. 58cm.:23ins. high. Sizes ranged from 41 to 66 cm.: 16 to 26ins. high and production of this type continued until at least 1938. They have become increasingly popular in recent years and prices have risen accordingly. (See also p.104)

A Compton Pottery terracotta jardinière of high shouldered form with scroll handles and pottery stamp with the motto 'Their work was as it were a wheel in the middle of a wheel, Linnerslease Compton'. Early twentieth century. 41cm.: 16ins. high. In 1938 these 'scroll pots', as they were then advertised, cost 18s.6d. (92p) for the 41cm.: 16ins. size

A similar Compton Pottery jardinière, with scrolls and intertwined serpent decoration, with pottery stamp (see below)

124 THE ARMY & NAVY AUXILIARY C. S., L. [APRIL, 1913.

SEED DEPARTMENT—*contd.*

IMPERISHABLE TERRA-COTTA GARDEN VASES, TAZZÆ, PEDESTALS, SUNDIALS, BIRD BATHS, &c.

Prices below are for **Greyish Buff Terra-Cotta.**

No. 653. Pot.
Height 13 in., width 13½ in. .. 10/0
No. 653x. Pedestal.
Height 10 in., width at foot 13¾ in. 8/3

No. 844. Palm Holder.
Height, 1 ft. 6 in., diam. 1 ft. 11 in. 26/6
No. 844x. Pedestal.
Height 8 in., width 1 ft. 6 in. .. 9/6

No. 850. Pot.
Height 9½ in., diameter 15½ in. .. 5/9
No. 850x. Pedestal.
Height 6 in., width 12 in. .. 4/9

No. 654. Flower Box.
Length 16½ in., width 9½ in., height 8 in. 7/3

No. 656. Large Pot.
Height 16½ in., diam. 25 in. £1 16 3
No. 656. Small Pot.
Height 13 in., diam. 20 in. .. £1 3 0
No. 658. Pedestal.
Height 24 in., width 14½ in. .. £1 3 9

No. 855. Vase and Pedestal.

1 ft. 10 in. diam., 3 ft. 8 in. total height.

£3 11 3

No. 632. Sundial Pedestal.

Height 3 ft. 6 in., width at top, 11 in.
£2 7 6

No. 652. Pot.
Height 13 in., width 14 in. .. 10/6
Base 4/9

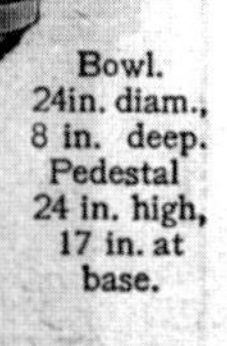

No. 928. Bird Bath. Bowl only, 28/6. Pedestal only 28/6. Also made as Flower Vase at same Price. £2 17 0.

Bowl. 24in. diam., 8 in. deep. Pedestal 24 in. high, 17 in. at base.

No. 874. Bird Bath.
2 ft. 6 in. high, 1 ft. 6 in. diam., Terra Cotta £1 6 6

No. 929. Bird Bath.
15 in. diam., 4 in. high .. 7/3

Packing Crates and Straw charged 7/6 each, Cribs 4/6 each, Hampers 1/6 or 2/0 each, which will be credited in full, if returned complete with straw, and at once, direct to Manufacturers, carriage paid.

NOTE.—Sent direct from Works, carriage not paid. Several patterns on Show in Seed Dept.

List of other Designs on application.

A 1913 catalogue selection of 'imperishable' terracotta jardinières and planters, some displaying art nouveau influence

WINDOW BOXES

There is nothing new about window boxes. They are recorded in Roman times and depicted in illustrations from the Middle Ages. Popular with the Victorians, they were produced in wood or ceramic, with zinc liners.

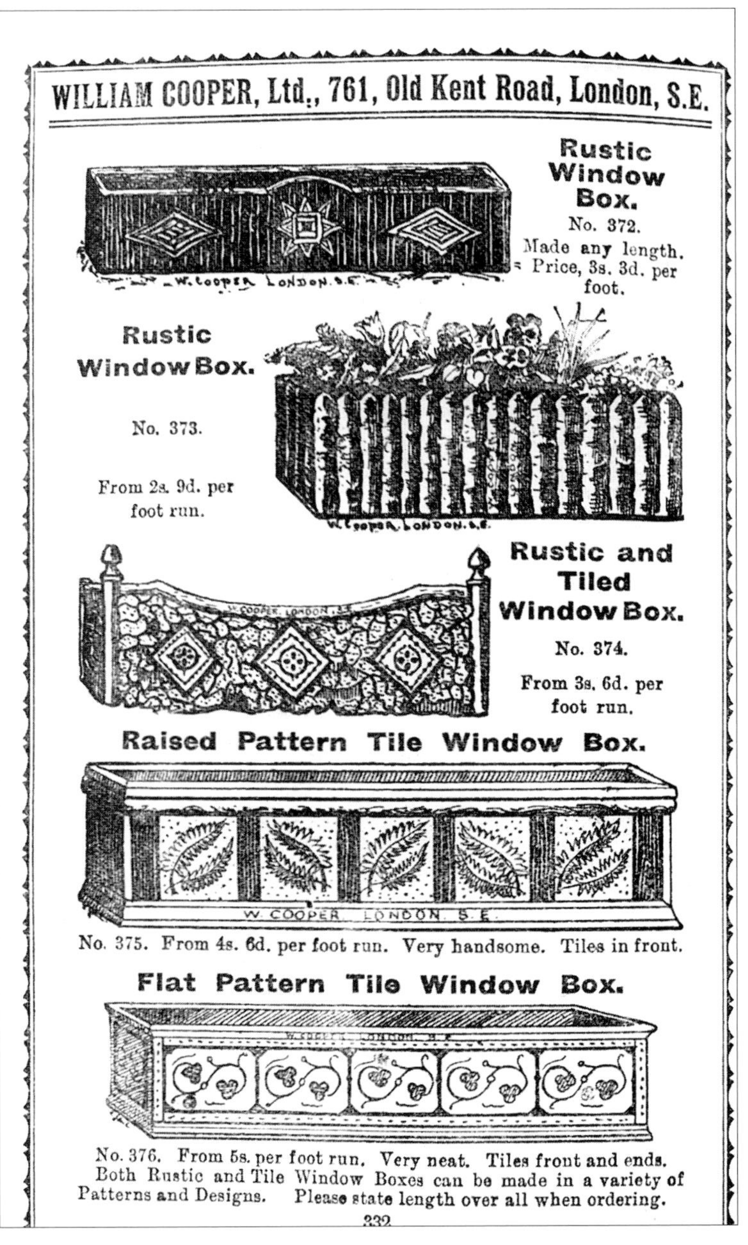

WILLIAM COOPER, Ltd., 761, Old Kent Road, London, S.E.

Rustic Window Box.
No. 372.
Made any length. Price, 3s. 3d. per foot.

Rustic Window Box.
No. 373.
From 2s. 9d. per foot run.

Rustic and Tiled Window Box.
No. 374.
From 3s. 6d. per foot run.

Raised Pattern Tile Window Box.
No. 375. From 4s. 6d. per foot run. Very handsome. Tiles in front.

Flat Pattern Tile Window Box.
No. 376. From 5s. per foot run. Very neat. Tiles front and ends.
Both Rustic and Tile Window Boxes can be made in a variety of Patterns and Designs. Please state length over all when ordering.
332

A selection of window boxes offered by William Cooper, circa 1900, including 'Rustic' and 'Tiled' forms. Compare the tiled examples with the next illustration

A most attractive late Victorian zinc plant trough or window box set with polychrome ceramic tiles, possibly by Minton, and fitted with two zinc liners. 130cm.: 47ins. wide

PLANT STANDS

The enthusiasm of nineteenth century gardeners for growing a far wider variety of plants than had hitherto been known or available created a demand for suitable presentation and display furniture. The range of cast iron and wirework plant stands reached a peak in the late Victorian era, such stands being placed in conservatories and hallways or on terraces. Whilst the cast and wrought iron examples have generally survived well, the lighter framed and more ornately decorated wire types have invariably suffered from rust and other damage. The revived popularity for such stands today and the fact that good early examples command high prices has led to a number of reproductions appearing on the market, many imported from overseas.

Right, a nineteenth century wrought iron and wirework plant stand, the oval galleried trelliswork bowl with zinc liner on quatreform scrolling base. 78cm.: 31ins. high

Far right, this nineteenth century wrought iron conservatory stand reflects a strong ecclesiastical influence. Its three graduated tiers are painted with flowerheads and supported on foliate brackets, on triform base with three plant stands and on scrolled feet. 234cm.: 92ins. high

A French wrought iron and wirework plant stand, with zinc liner and arcaded rectangular frame surround on four scrolled supports joined by stretchers. Late nineteenth century. 86cm.: 34ins. high, 120cm.: 47ins. wide. French metalwork from the early twentieth century, including garden wares, is being brought into this country at the present time

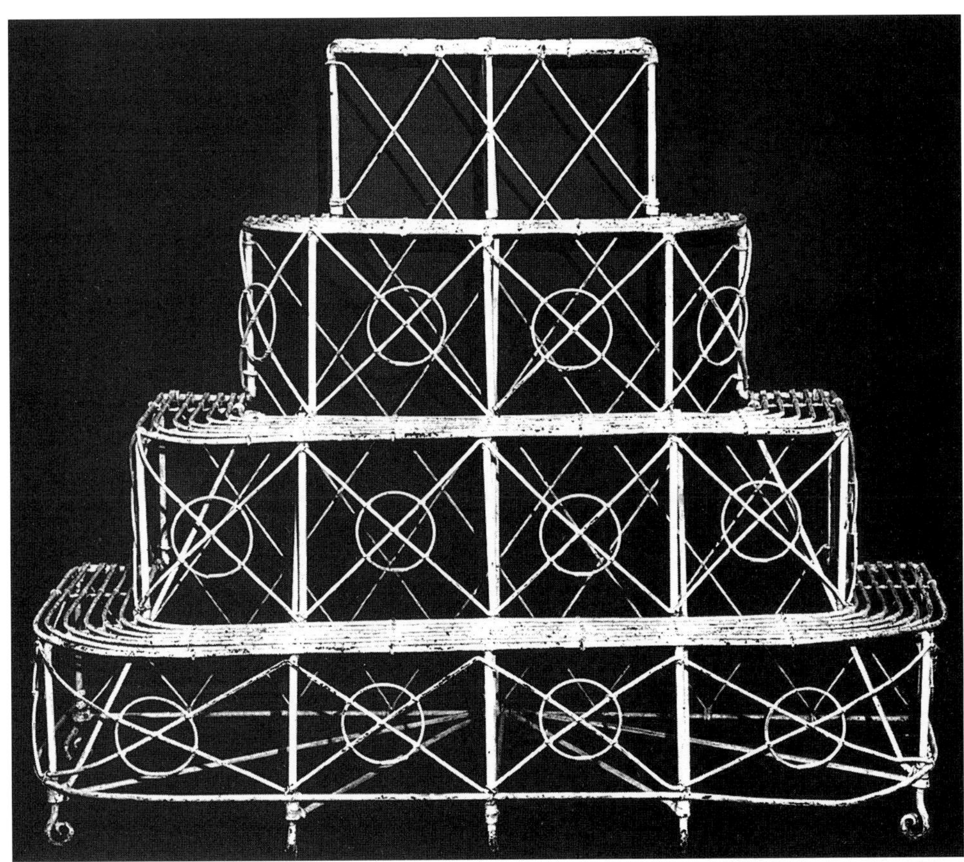

An early nineteenth century wrought iron plant stand of stepped form, the four break front shelves with upright supports joined by X-stretchers centred with circles and on scrolled feet. 155cm.: 61ins. wide

Far left, an unusual Victorian cast and wrought iron planter stand, of square form, with trellis sides centred with flowerheads, barley twist corners surmounted by ball finials flanking stylised spearheads. 62cm.: 24ins. high

Left, a detail of a plant stand from Humphry Repton's painting 'Sunshine After Rain' *(see p.225)*

A late Victorian wrought iron plant stand of D-section arranged in three graduated tiers, on plain supports joined by stretchers. 92cm.: 36ins. high

An unusual four-tier graduated wrought iron plant stand with collar tied scrolling backplate on four supports joined by stretchers. Late nineteenth century. 101cm.: 40ins. high. Simpler forms of this design continued to be made into the 1930s

A most attractive cast and wrought iron plant stand of curved form arranged in two tiers. Circa 1840. 420cm.: 165ins. wide

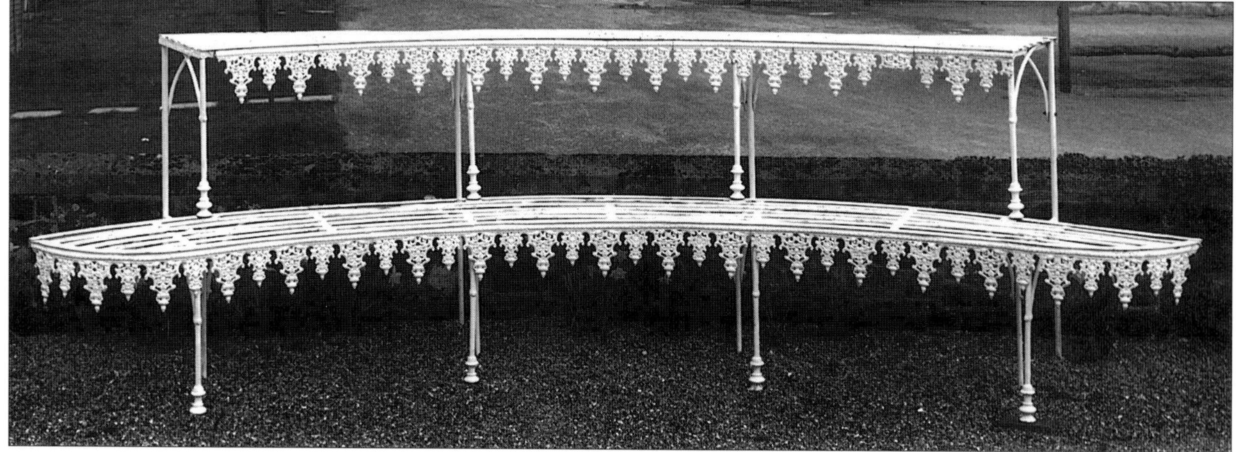

The design of this cast iron plant stand appears in the Coalbrookdale catalogue (see engraving above). It is arranged on four tiers pierced with foliage decoration and stamped 'C B Dale Co.' with diamond registration mark for 1859. Circa 1860. 112cm.: 44ins. high

A Coalbrookdale cast iron plant stand of triangular form, arranged on five tiers with pierced circular trays to support flower pots. Circa 1870. 109cm.: 43ins. high. A similar design was registered in 1875 in the Coalbrookdale catalogue

A very ornate and rare semicircular cast iron plant stand, probably by Crickley Wright & Co., Burton Weir, Sheffield. Intended to be placed against a wall in a conservatory, the stand is arranged on three graduated tiers supported by brackets of scrolling foliage. Circa 1860. 101cm.: 40ins. high

A cast iron semicircular plant stand with three tiers. Circa 1870. 96cm.: 37½ ins. high

A Coalbrookdale cast iron plant stand arranged on three tiers with pierced circular trays on triform base cast with scrolls and foliage. A variation of the top example on p.113. Circa 1870. 110cm.: 43ins. high

Right, note the 'rustic' influence on this cast iron plant stand. Of circular form with pierced gallery and apron and a central column supporting two tiers of three circular apertures for pots beneath a small central dish, on triform truncated branch supports. Probably late nineteenth century/early twentieth century. 168cm.: 66ins. high

Far right, a Victorian cast iron plant stand with five circular dishes arranged on three tiers above central oval tray and supported on four scroll feet. Circa 1860. 112cm.: 44ins. high

A rare cast and wrought iron conservatory plant stand, its end supports pierced with anthemion motifs. Probably English. Circa 1840

A Victorian cast iron plant stand of circular three-tiered form, the two upper circular tiers pierced with foliage, on four outswept scrolling legs supported by the undertier. Circa 1870. 102cm.: 40ins. high

A rare Victorian cast iron plant stand with three rectangular pierced trays arranged on two tiers, the end supports pierced with foliage. Circa 1870. 94cm.: 37ins. wide. Possibly by Yates Haywood & Co., Effingham Works, Rotherham, Yorkshire, who registered a design for a chair-end incorporating similar features

SEED DEPARTMENT—*contd.*

WIREWORK, &c.—*contd.*

Owing to the advance in price of raw material of Iron and Wire Goods, Catalogue prices are subject to alteration without notice.

ELEGANTLY DESIGNED FLOWER STANDS.

Painted in a superior manner, green and white or any colours that may be desired.

No. 30.

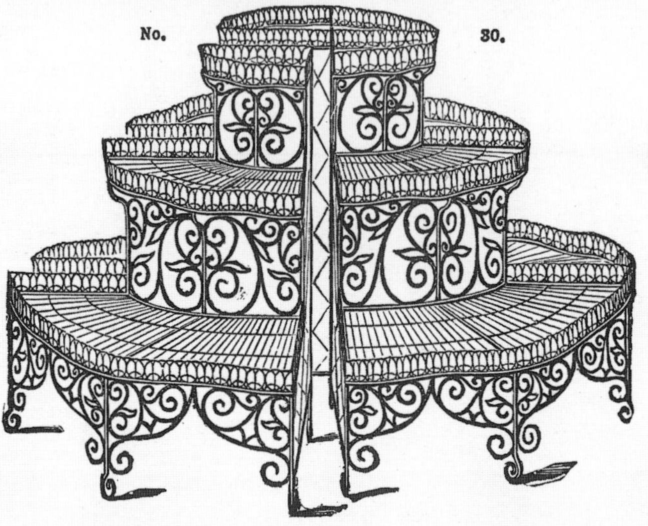

SECTION OF THE ABOVE.

This useful and ornamental Flower Stand is made in *four separate parts*, as shown by the section, fitting closely together, and forming a very unique centre piece; when separated, each part can be used to fit into the corners of the conservatory, or two parts placed together will form a semicircle.

4 ft. 6 in. diameter, 3 ft. 6 in. high	per set of 4,	£5 18 0
Each part separate	,,	£1 10 9
5 ft. diameter, 3 ft. 6 in. high	per set of 4,	£6 11 3
Each part separate	,,	£1 13 9

No. 27.
OVAL STAND.
Painted any colour.

Length.	Width.	Height	Each
2 ft. 6 in.	1 ft.	2 ft. 6 in.	20/9
3 ,, 0 ,,	1 ,, 4 in.	2 ,, 9 ,,	25/0
3 ,, 6 ,,	1 ,, 8 ,,	2 ,, 9 ,,	29/9

No. 25. Painted any colour.

Height.	Width.	Each
4 ft.	3 ft. 6 in.	68/0
4 ft. 6 in.	4 ft.	74/6

No. 24.
CIRCULAR STAND.
Painted any colour.

Diam.	Each
1 ft. 1 in.	10/0
1 ,, 3 ,,	11/3
1 ,, 6 ,,	14/0

Zinc Pans made and fitted to any of the above if required at an additional cost.

NOTE.—Procured to order only, about 10 days required. Sent direct from Works, Carriage paid on orders of 60/0 to the principal Railway Stations in England.

A selection of wirework stands available in 1913. Particularly impressive is No. 30, created in four separate units, though the most ornate and expensive is No. 25. Zinc pans were available at additional cost

94 THE ARMY & NAVY AUXILIARY C. S., L. [April, 1913.

SEED DEPARTMENT—*contd.*

WIREWORK, &c.—*contd.*

Owing to the advance in price of raw material of Iron and Wire Goods, Catalogue prices are subject to alteration without notice

ORNAMENTAL WIRE FLOWER STANDS.

No. 2. STRONG,

Outside measurement.

Length.	Width.	Height.	Painted Green.
2 ft. 6 in.	11 in.	2 ft. 6 in.	5/0
3 ,, 0 ,,	11 ,,	2 ,, 9 ,,	5/8
3 ,, 6 ,,	11 ,,	3 ,, 0 ,,	6/7

No. 13.

Width.	Height.	Painted Green.	Painted Green and White.
3 ft. 0 in.	3 ft. 0 in.	12/0	13/3
3 ,, 6 ,,	3 ,, 6 ,,	13/9	15/9
4 ,, 0 ,,	3 ,, 6 ,,	17/0	19/3

THREE STAGE STAND. No. 15.

Painted any colour.

Width.	Height.	Price.
3 ft. 0 in.	3 ft. 0 in.	17/6
3 ,, 6 ,,	3 ,, 6 ,,	20/3
4 ,, 0 ,,	3 ,, 6 ,,	23/9

No. 16.

Diameter.	Painted Green. Each.	Painted Green and White. Each.
1 ft. 2 in.	6/2	6/7
1 ,, 6 ,,	7/11	8/6
2 ,, 0 ,,	10/6	11/0

No. 29.

Length.	Width.	Height.	Price.
3 ft.	1 ft.	3 ft.	22/0
3 ft. 6 in.	1 ,,	3 ,,	26/3

OVAL STAND No. 28.

Painted any colour.

Length.	Width.	Height.	Price.
1 ft. 6 in.	1 ft. 3 in.	2 ft. 8 in.	13/9
1 ,, 9 ,,	1 ,, 4 ,,	2 ,, 8 ,,	15/6
2 ,, 0 ,,	1 ,, 6 ,,	2 ,, 8 ,,	18/6

No. 8.

Length.	Width.	Height.	Painted Green.
2 ft. 6 in.	7 in.	2 ft. 6 in.	11/0
3 ,, 0 ,,	7 ,,	2 ,, 9 ,,	12/3
3 ,, 6 ,,	8 ,,	3 ,, 0 ,,	13/9
4 ,, 0 ,,	9 ,,	3 ,, 6 ,,	15/9

No. 9.

Length.	Width.	Height.	Painted Green.
2 ft. 6 in.	8 in.	2 ft. 6 in.	13/3
3 ,, 0 ,,	8 ,,	2 ,, 9 ,,	15/9
3 ,, 6 ,,	9 ,,	3 ,, 0 ,,	18/6
4 ,, 0 ,,	9 ,,	3 ,, 6 ,,	21/0

No. 10. Will hold from 9 to 13 Plants.

Outside Measurements.

Width.	Height.	Painted Green.
3 ft. 0 in.	3 ft. 0 in.	17/7
3 ,, 6 ,,	3 ,, 6 ,,	19/6
4 ,, 0 ,,	3 ,, 6 ,,	22/0
4 ,, 6 ,,	3 ,, 6 ,,	26/3

NOTE.—Procured to order only, about 10 days required, Sent direct from Works, Carriage paid on Orders of 60/0 to principal Railway Stations in England,

URNS AND VASES

The Grand Tour traveller of the eighteenth century was in many ways responsible for bringing to England an enormous amount of sculptured ornament and for popularising the 'antique' vase or urn known from Roman times and rediscovered in the Italian Renaissance. English visitors were impressed by the architectural and artistic qualities of the urns they saw and sought old pieces or contemporary reproductions to decorate their homes and gardens. The classical designs are generally those they felt more comfortable with.

Gertrude Jekyll in her book *Garden Ornament* had clear views about the difficulties in choosing a suitable material for such ornament with particular reference to the English climate. 'In Italy', she wrote, 'the marble vase may keep its growing aloe or myrtle, whereas in England for half the year the vase is empty. In fact, white marble is not a stone for English outdoor use, we have more suitable material in home quarries. It is true that the greater number of our native stones encrust too readily from weather and lichen to be quite suitable for delicate sculpture, though in the case of balustrades and urns, seats and bases for sundials this is of less account'. Ignoring terracotta, Miss Jekyll gave her vote: 'There can scarcely be a doubt that the happiest material for our garden sculpture and ornament is lead'.

This section contains examples in stone, terracotta, marble, lead and cast iron. Identical designs may be found in at least three of these materials.

Reproductions continue to be made today, the vast majority imitating earlier styles; these should be clearly offered as modern copies and are perfectly acceptable garden ornaments. For earlier examples it is wise to consult reputable specialist dealers or seek advice from an established auction house.

Stone, Stoneware and Terracotta Urns and Vases

A carved stone urn with lobed body on circular foot, standing on associated square stone plinth. Early eighteenth century. 70cm.: 27½ins high

There is an ecclesiastical influence in this Victorian sandstone urn which looks more like a font; of octagonal form carved with panels, on rising ribbed foot and base. 86cm.: 34ins. high

A Victorian carved stone urn in the 'Jacobean' style, the ovoid body carved in relief with stylised flowerheads surrounded by strapwork beneath egg and dart moulded rim, on rising circular foot, square base and similarly carved and panelled pedestal. An interesting revivalist style incorporating Elizabethan and Jacobean designs. Mid-nineteenth century. 132cm.: 52ins. high

The remarkable Coade factory produced an outstanding range of artificial stone urns, figures and architectural features from the late eighteenth century. The composition of the 'stone' when fired gave it a durable frost-resistant quality. This Coade stone urn in the neo-classical style has fluted ovoid body hung with drapes. Like many Coade pieces it is dated, the square base being stamped 'Coade, London, 1792'. 76cm.: 30ins. high

A rare Austin & Seeley composition stone urn of tall tapering form moulded with stiff leaf decoration and everted rim on associated sandstone base. 129cm.: 51ins. high. The urn is similar to No. 56 in the Austin & Seeley catalogue for 1841, where it is called 'The Oriental Lotus Vase'

An Austin & Seeley composition stone urn, mid-nineteenth century, of tapering octagonal form, moulded with tracery and on raised foot. This urn is a fairly early example of garden ornament in the 'Gothic' taste. It corresponds to a model illustrated in Collection of Ornaments for Gardens, Parks and Pleasure Grounds at Austin's Artificial Stone Works, *of 1835, in which it is simply described as a 'Gothic Vase'. The cost was 2 guineas. Austin & Seeley produced an extensive range of garden ornaments which were well appreciated in their time. An 1841 advertisement talks of extensive stock (comprising about 800 varieties) and the artificial stone 'now so thoroughly established that the most eminent architects and scientific gentlemen have expressed, in the highest terms, their approbation of its durability, and close resemblance to the real stone'*

It is interesting to compare the previous Austin & Seeley urn with this later composition stone urn which also displays a strong ecclesiastical influence. Tapering octagonal form with panels and quatrefoils. 60cm.: 24ins. high

A composition stone urn of shallow lobed form, with everted egg and dart moulded rim on rising circular foot, square base and plinth. A large and impressive example of an otherwise standard pattern. Probably late nineteenth century. 132 cm.: 52ins. high

A similar example to the previous urn, numbered 316, appears in A selection of vases, statues, busts from terra cotta by J M Blashfield, *London, published in 1857 by John Weale of 59 High Holborn, London. Blashfield had works at Poplar, moving to Stamford in 1858. This piece is stamped 'J M Blashfield' and is probably circa 1850*

James Pulham created and developed a composition stone to imitate artificial rockwork and received a number of commissions for 'Pulhamite' rockeries, notably at Battersea Park. This urn is stamped 'Pulhams Terracotta, Broxbourne'. Circa 1870. 90cm.: 35½ins. diameter

A Pulhamite garden urn of shallow semi-lobed form, with everted rim and two scroll handles on rising circular foot and square base stamped 'Pulhams Terracotta, London and Broxbourne'. Mid-nineteenth century. 56cm.: 22ins. high

A similar example of this urn and pedestal is illustrated in the Pulham Garden Ornament catalogue as 'The Brighton Vase', No. 24 priced at £6 5s. (£6.25), the pedestal, No. 267 priced at £6 18s. (£6.90). Circa 1880. 128cm.: 50½ins. high

Above left, a Bath stone urn of plain ovoid form with lug handles. Late seventeenth/early eighteenth century. 70cm.: 27½ins. high

Above, one of a rare set of four Georgian carved stone urns of a style which was popularised later in the nineteenth century in cast iron and composition stone. Late eighteenth/early nineteenth century. 140cm.: 55ins. high

A set of four eighteenth century Cotswold stone jardinières of tall tapering cylindrical form, the sides carved with lobing and flowerheads on ringed circular foot. 61cm.: 24ins. high

The body of this stoneware urn depicts a frieze of figures of various nationalities, each bearing a gift, centred by a seated figure of Queen Victoria, the handles in the form of two seated angels; the square base is stamped 'Garnkirk'. 91cm.: 36ins. high. An example of this urn was shown by Fergusson Miller & Co. at the 1851 Great Exhibition. In 1862 the moulds were obtained by the Garnkirk Fire Clay Company, Glasgow, which appears to date from the 1840s and exhibited at the Great Exhibition of 1851

Nineteenth century Scottish manufacturers were responsible for a large output of stoneware and terracotta garden ornament. This is a good example of an urn by the Garnkirk Fire Clay Company, moulded with masks supporting ribbon-tied flower swags above stylised flowerheads, on circular foot and square base stamped 'Garnkirk'. The square pedestal is moulded with bead and rope twist border and laurel crowns. 88cm.: 35ins. high

Another Scottish company produced this stoneware urn and pedestal in the late nineteenth century. The urn is of squat circular form with egg and dart everted rim and foliate cast lower section beneath a border of trailing fruiting vines, the base stamped 'Lockhead Brick and Tilework, Dunfermline'. 53cm.: 21ins. high, on matching pedestal, similarly stamped. 78cm.: 30½ins. high

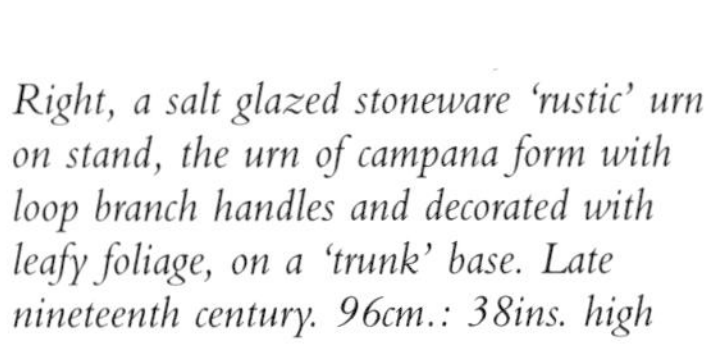

Right, a salt glazed stoneware 'rustic' urn on stand, the urn of campana form with loop branch handles and decorated with leafy foliage, on a 'trunk' base. Late nineteenth century. 96cm.: 38ins. high

Far right, another stoneware 'rustic' urn on stand, this example with tree trunk base and three detachable bowls beneath a trunk moulded urn with applied twigs forming the words 'Royal Oxford' and the date 'MDCCCLXX' (1870)

A most unusual design, a Scottish stoneware urn, its pedestal applied with cows' heads and the bowl with masks and frieze of frolicking putti. Circa 1860. 102cm.: 40ins. high

Following a traditional company form, a Doulton stoneware urn with acanthus leaf moulding and decorated circular foot on square base stamped 'Doulton & Co., Lambeth'. Circa 1860. 76cm.: 30ins. high. The company was started by John Doulton in 1815, becoming Doulton & Watts in 1826. However it was under the direction of Henry Doulton that the company established its pre-eminence with an extensive range of wares including garden ornaments

James Stiff was a former employee of Doulton & Watts and produced a similar range of products. Stiff took his sons into partnership in 1863, and the business was sold to Doulton in 1913. This stoneware urn on stand has acanthus cast bowl with ribbon-tied foliate frieze, on rising socle with stiff leaf decoration and square foot, stamped 'J Stiff & Sons, Lambeth', on square moulded stand applied with lions' masks. Mid-nineteenth century. 104cm.: 41ins. high

Another Stiff stoneware urn with ovoid body cast with a frieze of flowers and stiff leaf decoration, with a square moulded plinth, the urn and base both stamped 'J Stiff & Sons, Lambeth'. Late nineteenth century. 117cm.: 46ins. high

A fine terracotta two handled urn, probably Scottish, the body moulded with swags and with putti carrying grapes, on square pedestal moulded with classical scenes and foliage. Mid-nineteenth century. 137cm.: 54ins. high

A terracotta urn, circa 1880, the square foot stamped 'Royal Pottery Weston Super Mare', on foliage moulded square pedestal bearing similar stamp. The company, perhaps more famed for its flowerpots, started in business in the 1840s, originally produced bricks, tiles and drain pipes, but diversified into a range of garden ornaments including statues, urns and fountains. It went into voluntary liquidation in 1961

A large and impressive composition stone urn, the bowl well modelled with stiff leaf acanthus and a frieze of trailing chestnut leaves, on wrythen circular foot and shown with associated octagonal pedestal. Circa 1870. 152cm.: 60ins. high

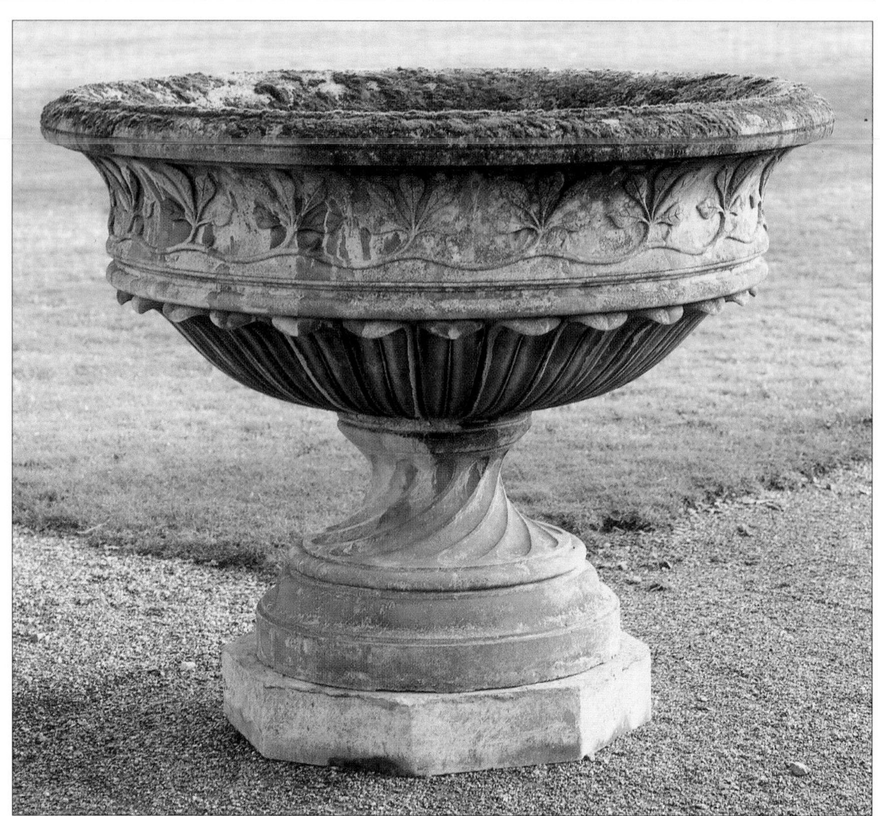

Below, a Scottish glazed terracotta conservatory urn on pedestal, moulded in relief with stylised foliage in brown on a cream ground, with tapering square pedestal. Early twentieth century. 115cm.: 45ins. high

Below right, a substantial stoneware urn, semi-lobed body moulded with geometric decoration and beaded rim, on rising foot with shaped square base. Circa 1860. 97cm.: 38ins. high

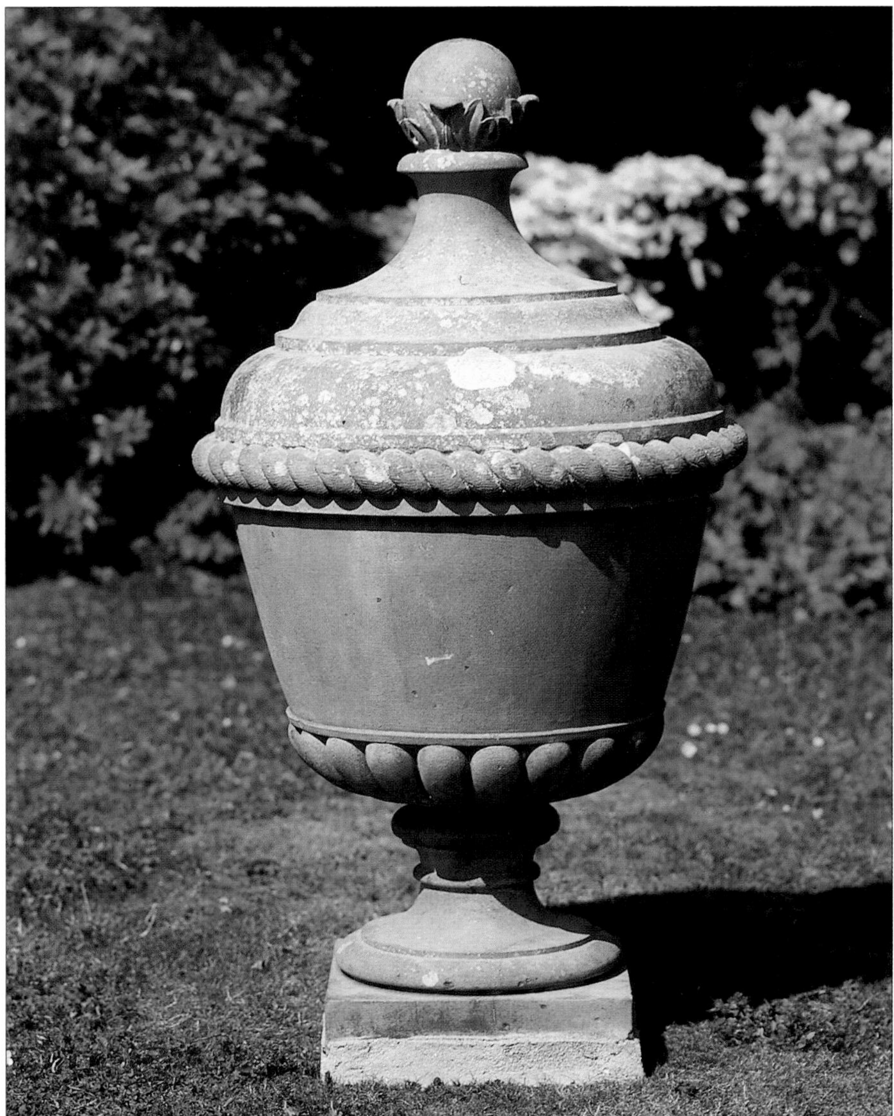

This lidded stoneware urn appears in the Pulham & Son catalogue, circa 1920, as No. 222, 'The Appleton Terminal', priced at £9. 99cm.: 39ins. high

Below left, an identical model of this terracotta urn is illustrated in the 1862 Art Journal *catalogue. This example has Medusa head handles and everted egg-and-dart moulded rim, the foot stamped 'Terra Cotta Mark H Blanchard & Co., Blackfriars Rd., London S. Clay from the estate of Arthur H. . .' Circa 1870. 88cm.: 35ins. high. The clay referred to is from the estate of Sir Arthur Helps, who established the Bishop Waltham Clay Company in 1862. Mark Blanchard served his apprenticeship with Coade & Sealy*

Below, imposing and substantial, this terracotta urn bears no maker's stamp, disappointing since it is of high quality. The body is modelled with swags and ribbon-tied flowerheads beneath a frieze of acanthus and with foliate cast loop handles. Probably English. Circa 1870. 97cm.: 38ins. high

Lead Urns and Vases

An English classical lead garden urn with acanthus handles, tapering gadrooned body and square plinth, probably missing a cover. Late eighteenth/early nineteenth century. 48.5cm.: 19ins. high

Probably of continental manufacture, a large lead urn of campana form, the lower section moulded with acanthus beneath bell flowers, egg-and-dart decorated rim, Greek key pattern handles. Mid-nineteenth century. 87cm.: 34ins. high

A lead Borghese urn. Late nineteenth/early twentieth century. 70cm.: 27½ins. high. A popular design for urns, the famous vase, now in the Louvre, was first recorded in 1594. By 1645 it was in the Villa Borghese, and in 1807 was purchased by Napoleon

Renaissance style urns of this type have been much copied. This example was made in the late nineteenth century. The semi-lobed body is moulded with a frieze of scrolling foliage and masks, the scroll handles terminating in seated classical maidens. 76cm.: 30ins. high

A lead urn, probably by the Bromsgrove Guild, the cylindrical body dated 1900, surrounded by cartouche, the reverse (shown) cast with a verse above lobing on circular foot. 59cm.: 23ins. high

Below left, a similar lead urn, the cylindrical body cast with armorials and dated 1898, the cover with pineapple finial. 96cm.: 38ins. high. Although imitating an earlier style this piece is clearly intended to be seen as late nineteenth century and may well have been a commissioned item

Below, an early twentieth century lead urn in the eighteenth century style, the scale-moulded body with ram-head handles. 73cm.: 29ins. high. A popular style of urn which was reproduced in the 1920s and 1930s by various manufacturers and continues to be reproduced today

Marble Urns and Vases

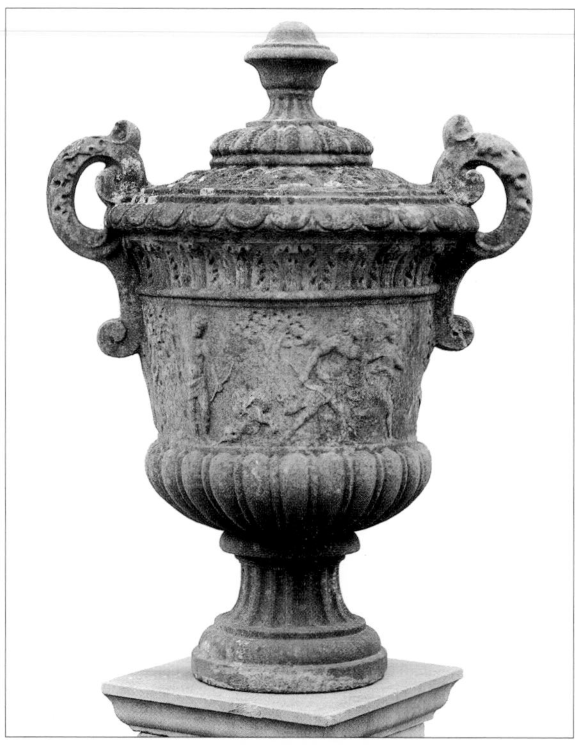

A white marble urn, the semi-lobed body carved with a frieze of Apollo pursuing Daphne, and other classical scenes, scroll and foliate handles, domed cover with ball finial. Mid-nineteenth century. 177cm.: 46ins. high

A pair of fine and large white marble urns, each campana-shaped body carved with a frieze of anthemion and acanthus and with entwined serpent handles. Circa 1840. 169cm.: 63ins. high

A white marble urn, the semi-lobed body carved with acanthus and fluting beneath domed cover with acorn finial. Mid-nineteenth century. 114cm.: 45ins. high

Urns of this more common type were to be found in the gardens of the Crystal Palace in the 1860s. Of shallow form with everted rim, this marble example has a foliate carved lower section, circular foot and square base. 61cm.: 24ins. high, shown on a shaped sandstone base

Cast Iron Urns and Vases

A rare and interesting Handyside cast iron urn, the shallow bowl with everted rim cast with flowerheads above strapwork, the baluster column cast with high relief titled portrait masks including Nelson, Wellington, Watt, Shakespeare, Peel, Scott, Stephenson and Milton, on octagonal shaped foot. Mid-nineteenth century. 126cm.: 49½ins. diameter. A similar urn on stand is illustrated in the catalogue of the Handyside Foundry circa 1855

The manufacturer's plate is just visible at the base of this cast iron campana-shaped two handled garden urn, the body cast with scrolling foliage, looped handles terminating in masks, and stamped 'A Handyside & Co, London and Derby'. Circa 1860. 61cm.: 24ins. high

A substantial cast iron urn of semi-lobed campana form cast with a frieze of scrolling foliage, scroll handles and masks, on fluted circular foot. Second half nineteenth century. 80cm.: 31½ins. high. Urns of a similar design, proportion and size are illustrated in the Handyside catalogue circa 1855

A Handyside cast iron urn, the foliate cast bowl with everted rim on baluster column applied with further foliage, on circular foot with square base, and with square moulded pedestal. Circa 1860. 140cm.: 45ins. high. A similar urn on pedestal is illustrated in the Handyside 1860 catalogue

The antique marble Medici vase provided the inspiration for this cast iron version. Circa 1880. 72cm.: 28ins. high. The Medici vase was first recorded in the Villa Medici in the sixteenth century. It is often paired with the Borghese vase and reproduced in a variety of sizes and mediums

A cast iron copy of the Borghese vase, moulded with a frieze of figures and with loop handles on rising circular foot and square base. Second half nineteenth century. 50cm.: 20½ins. high

A large Warwick urn, the body applied with masks on entwined wrythen handles. Second half nineteenth century. 58cm.: 23ins. diameter. The original Greek vase was found at Hadrian's Villa in 1770 and eventually became the property of the Earl of Warwick. A similar model is illustrated in the 1860 Handyside Foundry catalogue

A pair of Coalbrookdale cast iron urns, each bulbous body moulded with panels of stylised foliage and with lion-mask and ring handles beneath waved rim, stamped with registration mark and 'C B Dale Co.', on rising circular foot and square base. The design was included in the Coalbrookdale catalogue for 1875. 66cm.: 26ins. high

Although this cast iron urn is in the style of Thomas Hope (1769-1831) it was probably produced in France circa 1860. The Handyside Foundry also produced similar urns. The ovoid body is moulded with a frieze of figures in classical dress beneath swan head and anthemion cast handles, a design untraced in Hope's Household Furniture and Inventory *which was published in 1807. 82cm.: 32ins. high*

A large and impressive Coalbrookdale bronzed cast iron urn of truncated ovoid form, the plain semi-fluted body with a beaded rim above a ribbon-tied leaf border, on rising fluted circular base stamped 'Coalbrookdale' and with registration stamp and number. Circa 1880. 82cm.: 32ins. high. A similar vase appears in the 1875 Coalbrookdale catalogue

Right, a rare Coalbrookdale cast iron model of the Milton Vase, circa 1880, the body cast with 'The Expulsion of Adam and Eve' on the obverse and 'The Expulsion of Satan' on the reverse. Flanked by mask and scroll handles on serpent entwined circular foot and square base. 124cm.: 49ins. high. Unlike the majority of Coalbrookdale vases and urns, this example is of multi-piece construction which made for a greater degree of relief in the figures in the frieze as well as a higher quality of casting

Far right, an unusual cast iron urn, the waisted octagonal body cast with fruit and flowers and with registration stamp and number, on rising base. Circa 1870. 74cm.: 29ins. high

A rare Coalbrookdale cast iron urn, identified as 'Ram's Head' in the 1875 catalogue. The body modelled in low relief with a frieze depicting mythological scenes with classical figures and with ram-head handles hung with swags of fruit, fluted circular foot and stepped square base. Circa 1880. 80cm.: 35ins. high. This model was available 'bronzed or painted white, pink inside'

Far left, a Scottish cast iron urn, the cylindrical body cast with ribbon-tied flowerheads and drapes and stamped 'Walter MacFarlane, Saracen Foundry, Glasgow'. Circa 1870. 71cm.: 29ins. high. The Saracen Foundry was begun in 1850 by Walter MacFarlane at Saracen Lane but moved to larger premises at Possilpark in 1871. The company produced a wide range of cast iron products for architectural and domestic use; it was taken over by Allied Ironfounders in 1965

Left, simple but attractive, a cast iron urn, the plain cylindrical body moulded with masks, on rising circular foot. Early nineteenth century. 51cm.: 20ins. high

A Victorian cast iron urn, the ovoid body with lobed and foliate cast lower section, the everted rim with trailing flowers and leaves, on similarly decorated rising circular base with registration stamp and circular foot. Circa 1860. 80cm.: 31½ins. high

A rare cast iron basket urn, the body pierced with roundels beneath a scrolling foliate frieze on fluted circular base and square plinth pierced with stylised flowerheads. Late nineteenth century. 120cm.: 47ins. high

A more traditional form of cast iron urn of semi-lobed and fluted campana form on rising circular foot. Second half nineteenth century. 76cm.: 30ins. high

A Falkirk Iron Company cast iron urn, Scottish, the body moulded with stiff leaf decoration, on rising circular foot and base, stamped 'Falkirk No. 7' and with registration number. Nineteenth century. 63cm.: 25ins. high

A large cast iron urn, the shallow lobed bowl with scrolling handles centred with lions' masks, on scroll and quatrefoil base on circular column pedestal and stone plinth. Circa 1875. 162cm.: 64ins. high. Although not stamped, this design is shown with pedestal in the 1875 Coalbrookdale catalogue as 'Mask Vase'

A cast iron urn, the semi-lobed body with everted upper section cast with laurel wreaths, the baluster lower section cast with acanthus, on stepped rising square base. Nineteenth century. 112cm.: 44ins. high

An interesting cast iron urn and pedestal, the urn with squat campana body, on rising circular foot and on tapering stiff leaf cast column pedestal with stepped square base. Nineteenth century. 150cm.: 51ins. high

A rare cast iron urn of tapering octagonal form, cast in relief with Gothic tracery. Second half nineteenth century. 76cm.: 30ins. high. This design corresponds to a model illustrated in A Collection of Ornaments for Gardens Parks and Pleasure Grounds. *Although extensively reproduced in recent times in composition stone it is rare to find examples in cast iron. Compare with the Austin & Seeley examples on p.119*

An American cast iron urn, of semi-lobed campana form with everted fruit cast rim and mask and loop handles, on rising circular foot stamped 'Spicers Peckham prov. R.I. pat'd, Aug't 13, 1887', on square base and square plinth. Nineteenth century. 82cm.: 32ins. high

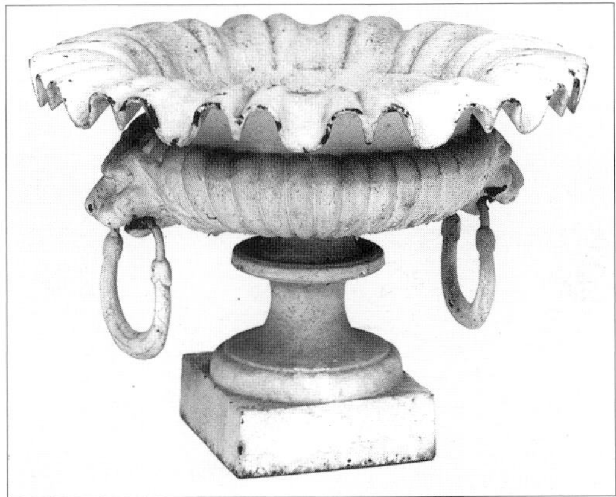

The frilled rim and ringed handles are distinctive features of this cast iron urn with squat ovoid lobed body. Circa 1870. 42cm.: 16½ins. high

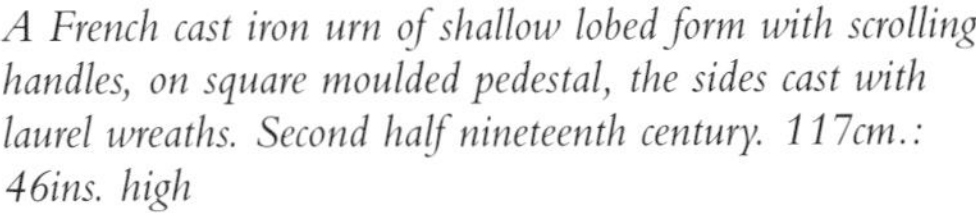

A French cast iron urn of shallow lobed form with scrolling handles, on square moulded pedestal, the sides cast with laurel wreaths. Second half nineteenth century. 117cm.: 46ins. high

A rare bronze vase with applied frieze of scrolling foliage centred with flowerheads, the base inscribed 'Syston Vase, J.H. & M.A. Thorold, July MDCCCXXX'. Mid-nineteenth century. 76cm.: 40ins. high. Sir J.H. Thorold of Syston House, Lincolnshire, married his second wife, Mary Ann, on 12 July, 1830. It is likely the vase was specially commissioned to commemorate that occasion or an anniversary. This model was extensively produced in cast iron by English and French foundries in the second half of the nineteenth century

An impressive French cast iron urn, the bowl cast with festoon-hung masks and with female herm handles, on rising circular foot and square base, and on circular pedestal decorated with a frieze of putti, roundels depicting Pan, and musical trophies. Circa 1870. 290cm.: 114ins. high. An urn of identical design is illustrated in the catalogue of the Société Anonyme des Hautes Fourneaux et Fonderies du Val d'Osne

A French cast iron urn, the lobed body with lion mask and ring handles, on rising circular foot and square base. Second half nineteenth century. 33cm.: 13ins. high. The design for a similar urn is illustrated in the catalogue of the Société Anonyme des Hautes Fourneaux et Fonderies du Val d'Osne, Plate No. 364

It is interesting to see how the winged bird handles accentuate the form of this cast iron French urn with ovoid lobed body on rising fluted circular foot and canted square base. Nineteenth century. 80cm.: 31½ins. high

A fine French cast iron urn, the ovoid body cast with a frieze of sea shells and foliage beneath bead and stiff leaf decoration, with twin headed handles above boar head terminals, the lobed lower section on ribbon-tied rising circular foot and square base, bearing bronze plaque inscribed 'Fonderies du Val d'Osne, 58 Bd. Voltaire, Paris'. Late nineteenth century. 70cm.: 27ins. high. The top portion of the urn after an original in bronze at Versailles, originally designed by Louis XIV's goldsmith Claude Ballin

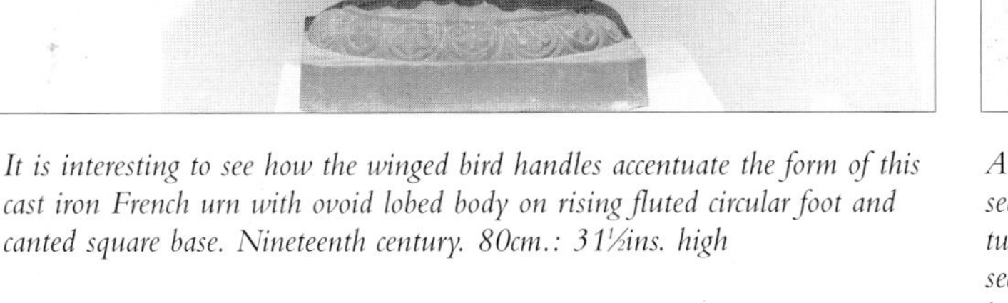

A selection of cast iron vases available in the early 1900s, including examples with lidded covers

ORNAMENTAL VASES AND PEDESTALS

(Cast Iron)

For Walls, Pleasure Grounds, &c.

Fig. 7.

Vase, Fig. 7 .. 8/4

Catalogue of other designs to be had on application.

Painted in colours and well finished.

Fig. 8.
Vase only.. — .. each 77/0
Top for do... — ,, 11/10
Pedestal for do. ,, 45/6

Fig. 9.
Vase only, Fig. 9 .. each 47/6
Top for ditto — — ,, 7/10
Pedestal for ditto — ,, 37/0

Fig. 12.
Vase only, Fig. 12 .. each 56/9
Pedestal for ditto .. ,, 45/6

NOTE.—Procured to order only, about 10 days required. Sent direct from Works, Carriage paid to any Railway Station in Great Britain. Packing extra, if required.

Planting and Protecting

HANDLIGHTS

This section includes a variety of nineteenth to early twentieth century glass or ceramic wares used for protecting and encouraging plant development.

Handlights, or hand glasses as they were called in the early nineteenth century, came in a variety of shapes, the most common being square sectioned with removable pyramidal top. The materials used for the frames also varied. Early nineteenth century types are usually of cast iron, although they were also available with copper bars as well as wrought iron and lead bars. Cast iron framed examples were included in the 1875 Coalbrookdale catalogue.

In the early twentieth century zinc frames were offered, the glass being held in place by zinc clips so that no putty was required.

The most common form of handlight, this nineteenth century cast iron frame example has a pyramidal top with handle. The lower section is made up of four separate sections which would be screwed or bolted together. To accommodate plant growth, two or three lower sections could be used, stacked one on top of each other. 46cm.: 18ins. high

Two scarcer handlights of octagonal form, both with removable tops with handles. Nineteenth century. The tallest 51cm.: 20ins. high

A selection of terracotta garden wares, including a sea-kale forcing pot stamped 'T Parker', circa 1860, 48cm.: 19ins. high; square seed pans by Sankey Bulwell Potteries, Nottingham, early twentieth century; three scarce Sanders' 'Patent Orchid Pans', multi-perforated pots, circa 1920; a range of flowerpots from 1½ to 9ins. diameter, nineteenth and twentieth century, including leaning lower right, a flower pot stamped 'E R' for Elizabeth Regina, circa 1953; two Gothic influenced border markers, circa 1860, one stamped 'Barry & Son, Scarborough'; in the background, resting on a Victorian chimney pot is a cast iron 'Please Keep Off the Grass' sign, circa 1890.

The variety of the common hand-thrown flowerpot makes it an interesting area for the specialist collector. The nineteenth century saw the usual fascinating and curious selection, including Palmers' improved flowerpot which would not blow over in windy weather or allow worms to enter when the pot was standing on the ground, or Browns' flowerpot which had two walls, the space between them filled with water through a small opening

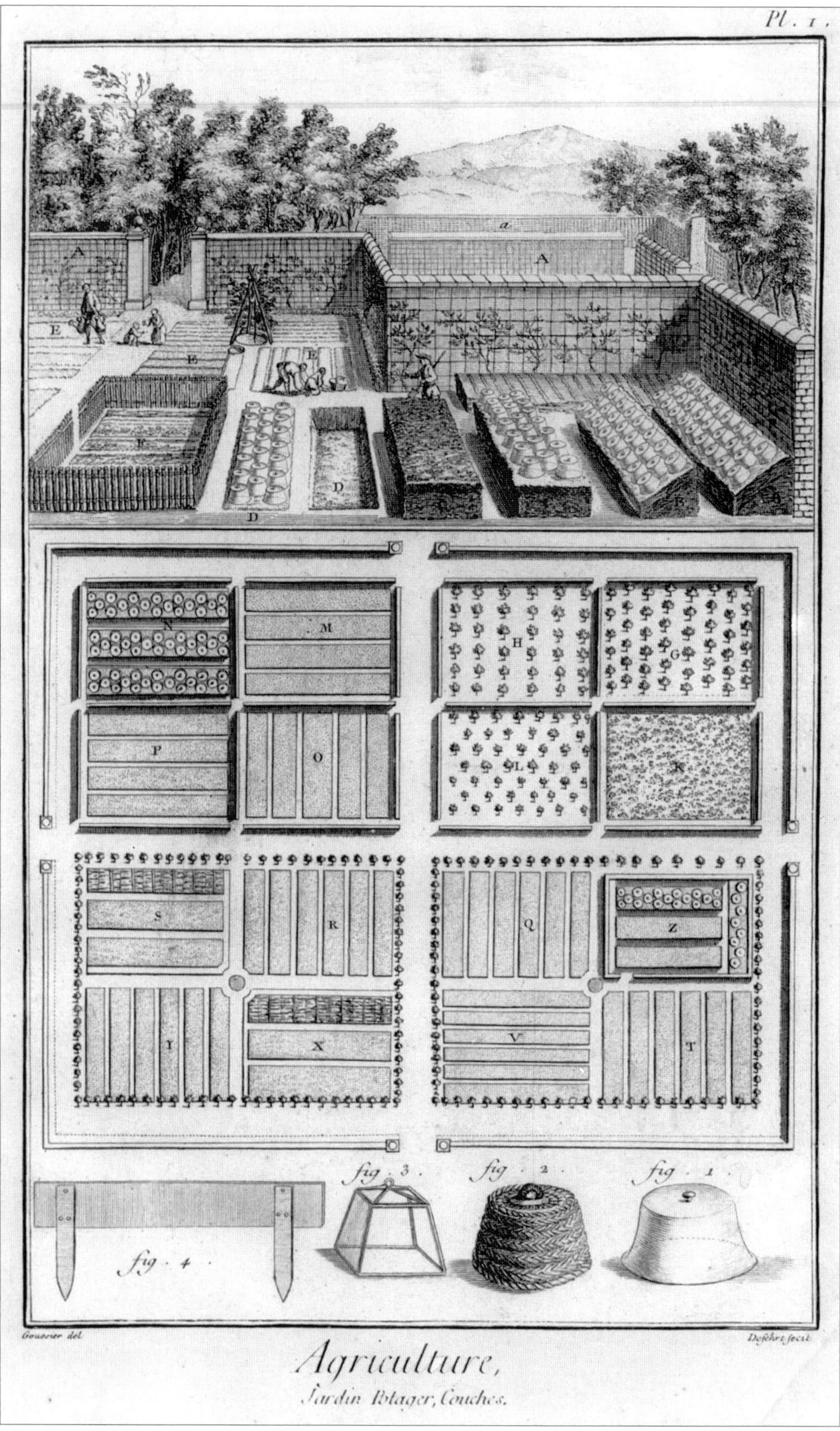

A late eighteenth century French engraving relating to fruit and vegetable cultivation. Note the handlight and cloche at the bottom of the engraving, and the cloches in use in the top section

CLOCHES OR BELL GLASSES

Cloches or bell glasses, very much a French contribution, are formed from one piece of glass, generally bell-shaped, although semi-globular or cylindrical forms are also found. In eighteenth century England broken bottles were used to cover and bring on plants. However in the early nineteenth century Loudon referred to the 'common green glass bell' formed by bottle glass and used for protecting cauliflowers or other culinary plants. Early twentieth century catalogues also refer to the 'correct greenish glass, which does not allow the sun to burn the lettuces or cause them to run quickly to seed.'

About this time advertisers offered English-made cloches without knobs, which they claimed had the advantage of allowing light and heat to be equally diffused through the top. The cost in 1914 for a 16ins. diameter cloche without knob was 1s. 8d. (8p), available with knob at 1d. each extra.

Two large bell glasses. Examples this size could give cover to a number of small plants. Late nineteenth century. 48 cm.: 19ins. high

Two further bell glasses of very distinctive 'bell' shape. Probably nineteenth century

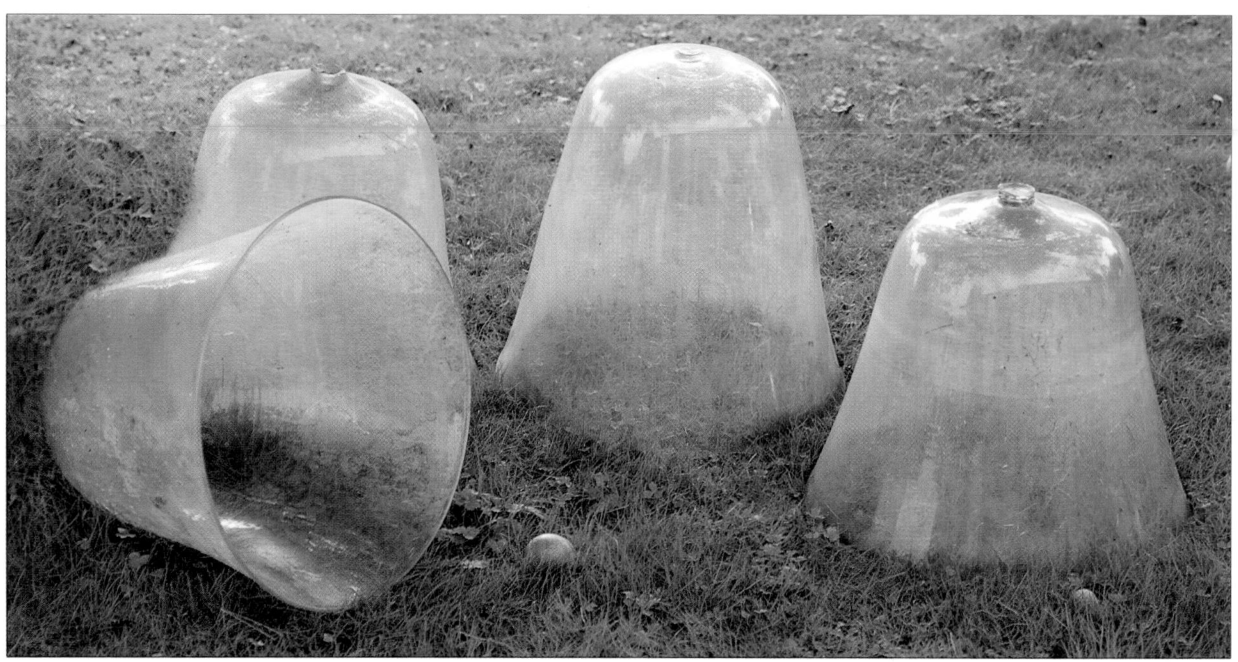

Four glass cloches or bells jars, all early twentieth century

FORCING POTS

Loudon refers to the blanching pot 'which is used to exclude light from sea-kale and rhubarb stalks, and some other culinary vegetables, where the green colour is to be avoided.' Usually the 24ins. size is used for rhubarb and the 16ins. for sea-kale. A lid should be used so that progress can be monitored without completely exposing the plant.

Early examples are scarce and those generally seen date from the early twentieth century. They were certainly commonly available before the Second World War. Terracotta forcing pots are enjoying something of a revival and modern products are available.

Left, a terracotta rhubarb forcing pot, probably late nineteenth or early twentieth century. This 61cm.: 24ins. high conical form, rather like a chimney pot, seems more popular than the more common rounded type shown far right. In the centre are two sea-kale forcing pots. 41 and 46cm.: 16 and 18ins. high

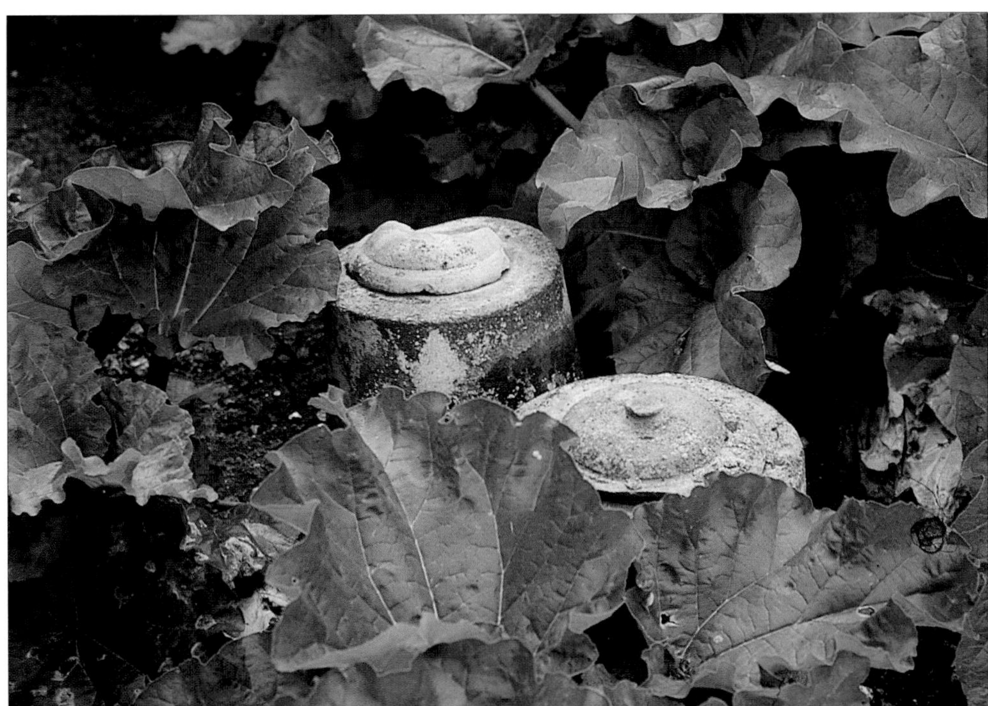

Two early twentieth century forcing pots with lids in a bed of rhubarb

Two late nineteenth/early twentieth century forcing pots with unusual lifting handles

SPECIFIC-PURPOSE PRODUCTS

Some items for growing plants in are not only ingenious and functional, but also, like the cucumber straightener, amusing conversation pieces

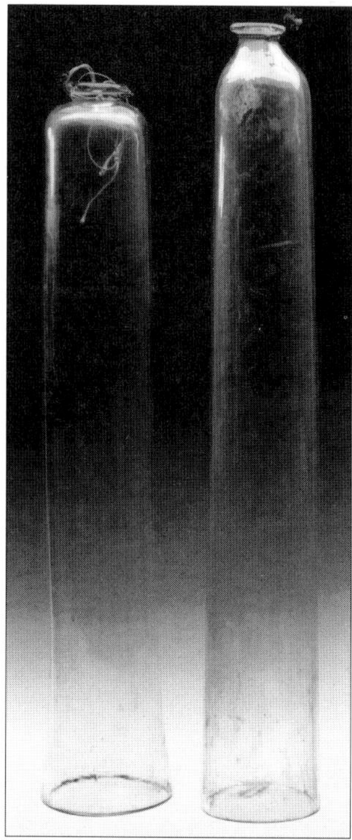

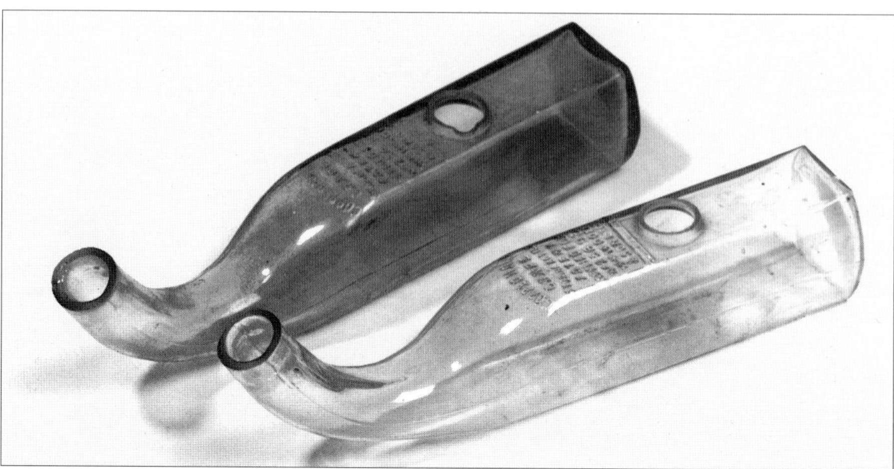

A glass product of some novelty as well as practical use is the grape storage bottle, the most common example of which is the Copped Hall patent made by Wood & Son. A section of vine with a bunch of grapes was placed in the neck of the bottle and the bottle filled with water to which charcoal was added for purification purposes. The two grape bottles shown here date circa 1910 to 1930. 31cm.: 12½ins. long

Cucumber straighteners were very much Victorian gardening accessories. The neck of the straightener was tied by string to a vine support. The young fruit was enclosed in the straightener and was forced to grow straight. Not noted by Loudon, they do not appear to have been advertised after 1914. The most common size is about 56cm.: 22ins. long

Left, the idea of protecting plants in closed containers was popularised by Nathaniel Ward in the late 1820s, and a variety of case incorporating glass was named the Wardian case. These later developed for use as fern cases; some also held water and fish and were known as Warrington cases. The case consisted of a metal frame with glass panels, while some examples were provided with a reservoir and tap to allow a flow of water to the lower section. The example shown is of the more usual form with domed top and etched decoration to glass panels. Circa 1900. 76 cm.: 30ins. wide

Right, the collecting of ferns was highly popular in Victorian times and cases such as this were ideal for their cultivation and protection. Late nineteenth century. 69cm.: 27ins. wide

GREENHOUSES AND GARDEN FRAMES

The vulnerability of glass garden items means that they are rarer than more substantial garden items. Greenhouses are particularly prone to fall into disrepair and because of the cost involved in restoring them, old greenhouses are few and far between.

Orangeries and greenhouses are recorded from the seventeenth century, the 'plant house' reaching its golden age in the nineteenth century.

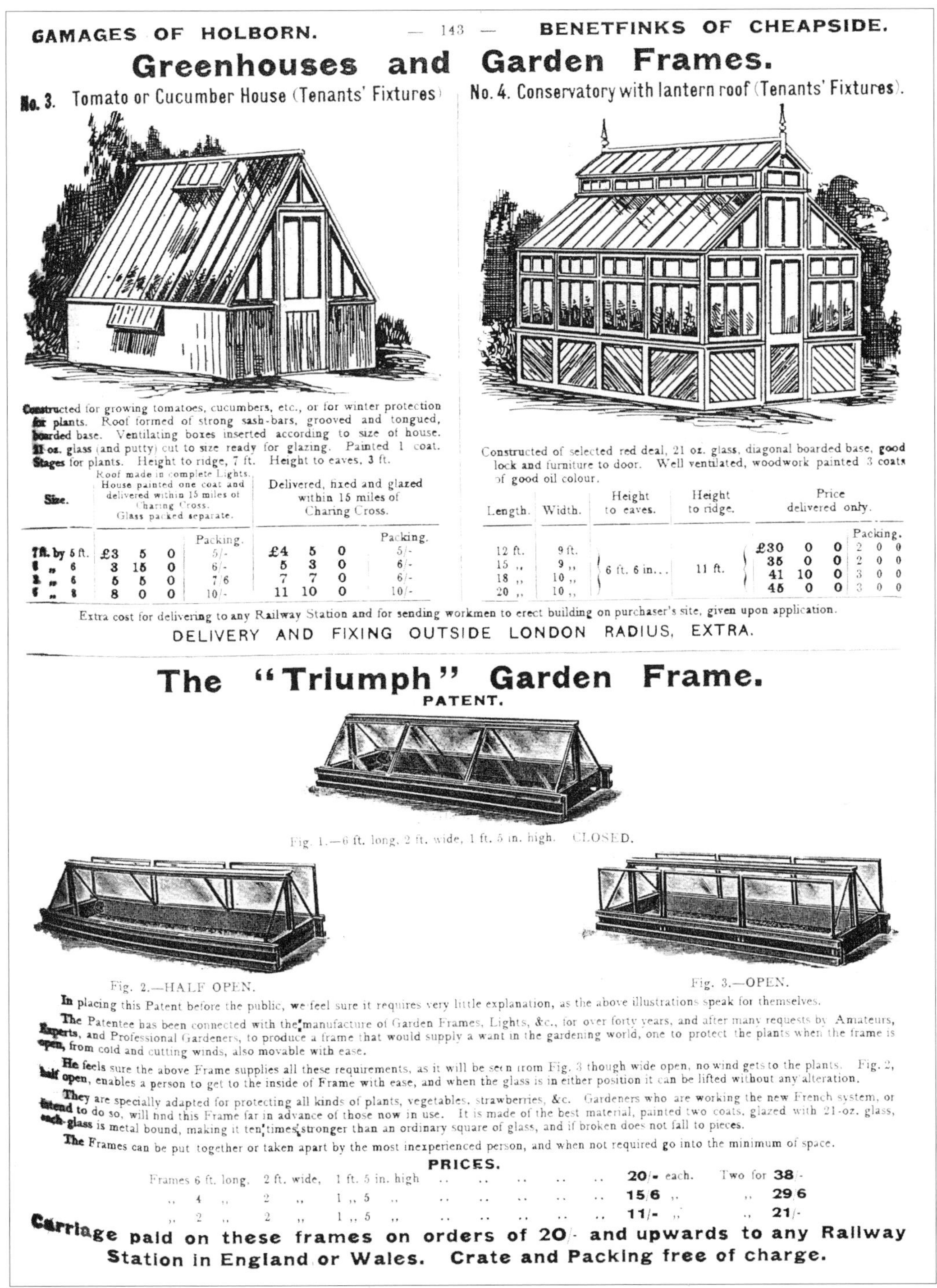

GAMAGES OF HOLBORN. — 143 — BENETFINKS OF CHEAPSIDE.

Greenhouses and Garden Frames.

No. 3. Tomato or Cucumber House (Tenants' Fixtures)

Constructed for growing tomatoes, cucumbers, etc., or for winter protection for plants. Roof formed of strong sash-bars, grooved and tongued, boarded base. Ventilating boxes inserted according to size of house. 21 oz. glass (and putty) cut to size ready for glazing. Painted 1 coat. Stages for plants. Height to ridge, 7 ft. Height to eaves, 3 ft.

Size.	Roof made in complete Lights. House painted one coat and delivered within 15 miles of Charing Cross. Glass packed separate.	Packing.	Delivered, fixed and glazed within 15 miles of Charing Cross.	Packing.
7ft. by 5 ft.	£3 5 0	5/-	£4 5 0	5/-
[illegible] ,, 6	3 15 0	6/-	5 3 0	6/-
[illegible] ,, 6	5 5 0	7/6	7 7 0	6/-
[illegible] ,, 8	8 0 0	10/-	11 10 0	10/-

No. 4. Conservatory with lantern roof (Tenants' Fixtures).

Constructed of selected red deal, 21 oz. glass, diagonal boarded base, good lock and furniture to door. Well ventilated, woodwork painted 3 coats of good oil colour.

Length.	Width.	Height to eaves.	Height to ridge.	Price delivered only.	Packing.
12 ft.	9 ft.	6 ft. 6 in...	11 ft.	£30 0 0	2 0 0
15 ,,	9 ,,			35 0 0	2 0 0
18 ,,	10 ,,			41 10 0	3 0 0
20 ,,	10 ,,			45 0 0	3 0 0

Extra cost for delivering to any Railway Station and for sending workmen to erect building on purchaser's site, given upon application.

DELIVERY AND FIXING OUTSIDE LONDON RADIUS, EXTRA.

The "Triumph" Garden Frame.

PATENT.

Fig. 1.—6 ft. long, 2 ft. wide, 1 ft. 5 in. high. CLOSED.

Fig. 2.—HALF OPEN.

Fig. 3.—OPEN.

In placing this Patent before the public, we feel sure it requires very little explanation, as the above illustrations speak for themselves.

The Patentee has been connected with the manufacture of Garden Frames, Lights, &c., for over forty years, and after many requests by Amateurs, Experts, and Professional Gardeners, to produce a frame that would supply a want in the gardening world, one to protect the plants when the frame is open, from cold and cutting winds, also movable with ease.

He feels sure the above Frame supplies all these requirements, as it will be seen from Fig. 3 though wide open, no wind gets to the plants. Fig. 2, half open, enables a person to get to the inside of Frame with ease, and when the glass is in either position it can be lifted without any alteration.

They are specially adapted for protecting all kinds of plants, vegetables, strawberries, &c. Gardeners who are working the new French system, or intend to do so, will find this Frame far in advance of those now in use. It is made of the best material, painted two coats, glazed with 21-oz. glass, each glass is metal bound, making it ten times stronger than an ordinary square of glass, and if broken does not fall to pieces.

The Frames can be put together or taken apart by the most inexperienced person, and when not required go into the minimum of space.

PRICES.

Frames 6 ft. long,	2 ft. wide,	1 ft. 5 in. high	.. ..	20/- each.	Two for 38/-
,, 4 ,,	2 ,,	1 ,, 5 ,,	.. ..	15/6 ,,	,, 29/6
,, 2 ,,	2 ,,	1 ,, 5 ,,	.. ..	11/- ,,	,, 21/-

Carriage paid on these frames on orders of 20/- and upwards to any Railway Station in England or Wales. Crate and Packing free of charge.

Page from a 1913 catalogue showing two greenhouses, and the wide range of sizes and forms in which they could be ordered, and the 'Triumph' garden frame

Furniture

In furnishing a garden one of the most important decisions will be the choice of seat, which is why this section is the largest in the book and contains the greatest variety of designs and styles. Most examples were made in the last two hundred years. As to material, be it stone, marble, wrought iron, wood, stoneware or cast iron, this must be influenced by the design and size of the garden. Although carved stone or marble examples are likely to be more expensive and need to be permanently established, wooden seats are easily transported but require some weather proofing attention from time to time. Examples in wrought iron may have design aspects that attract rust, while those in cast iron should be reasonably trouble free, apart from occasional repainting.

A final section is devoted to the works of the Coalbrookdale foundry, since it was the most important and prolific manufacturer of garden furniture in the nineteenth century and its products are still seen and sought after today.

In addition to seats a number of garden chair and table designs are also included. Many follow the design of a seat and could be purchased *en suite* or separately.

STONE

Portland stone is a compact limestone from the Isle of Portland. It was extensively used in buildings and for garden ornaments. It is soft when quarried but hardens on exposure to the atmosphere. This late eighteenth century Portland stone seat in attractive weathered condition has a panelled back with scroll decoration, the end supports in the form of seated lions beneath lobed finials. 183cm.: 72ins. wide

A Portland stone seat, similar to the previous example, but in three sections with arched panelled back, lions' heads arms and monopodia supports. 430cm.: 169ins. wide

A curved carved stone bench on three Bath stone supports in the form of seated griffins. Nineteenth century. 260cm.: 102½ins. wide

An impressive nineteenth century carved stone seat that would look at home on a Scottish baronial estate, with plain panelled back, the panelled end supports with carved arms and side panels and surmounted by pointed finials. 374cm.: 174ins. wide

A simple classical carved stone bench with rectangular moulded top, on three fluted and volute stepped rectangular supports. Early nineteenth century. 259cm.: 102ins. wide

This Portland stone seat, also displaying a classical influence, is of curved form, the plain back with a fluted panel and with downswept fluted arms; the rope twist and beaded seat on shaped supports. Nineteenth century. 153cm.: 60ins. wide

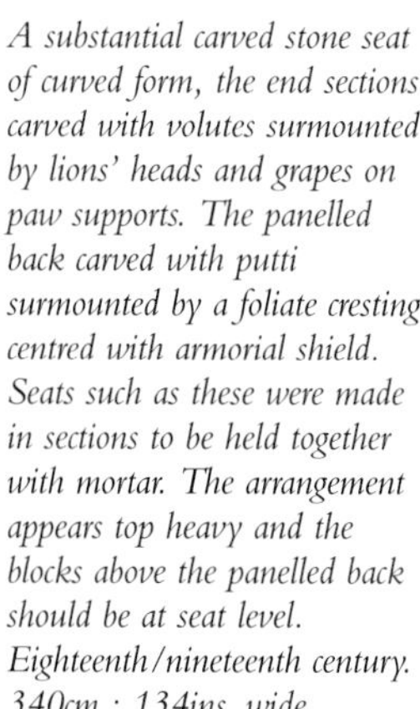

A substantial carved stone seat of curved form, the end sections carved with volutes surmounted by lions' heads and grapes on paw supports. The panelled back carved with putti surmounted by a foliate cresting centred with armorial shield. Seats such as these were made in sections to be held together with mortar. The arrangement appears top heavy and the blocks above the panelled back should be at seat level. Eighteenth/nineteenth century. 340cm.: 134ins. wide

MARBLE

Very much influenced by examples from ancient Rome, an Italian Rosso Verona marble chair, the arms in the form of winged lions, the front carved with anthemion and scrolls. A pinkish colour usually, this type of marble turns a wonderful reddish hue when wet. Late nineteenth century

The 'Ravenna' marble seat from J.P. White's catalogue Garden Furniture and Ornament, *circa 1910. 198cm.: 78ins. wide. The seat cost £37 10s. (£37.50) 'in best hard Carrara marble'.* *See also p.150*

An Italian white marble seat, the plain back with Vitruvian scroll frieze, end supports in the form of eagles' heads, and on claw feet. Late nineteenth century. 170cm.: 67ins. wide

A highly decorated marble seat, with arched back centred by shield and flowerheads, the arms in the form of grotesque winged lions. This is very similar to the 'Ravenna' seat on p.149. Early twentieth century. 180cm.: 71ins. wide

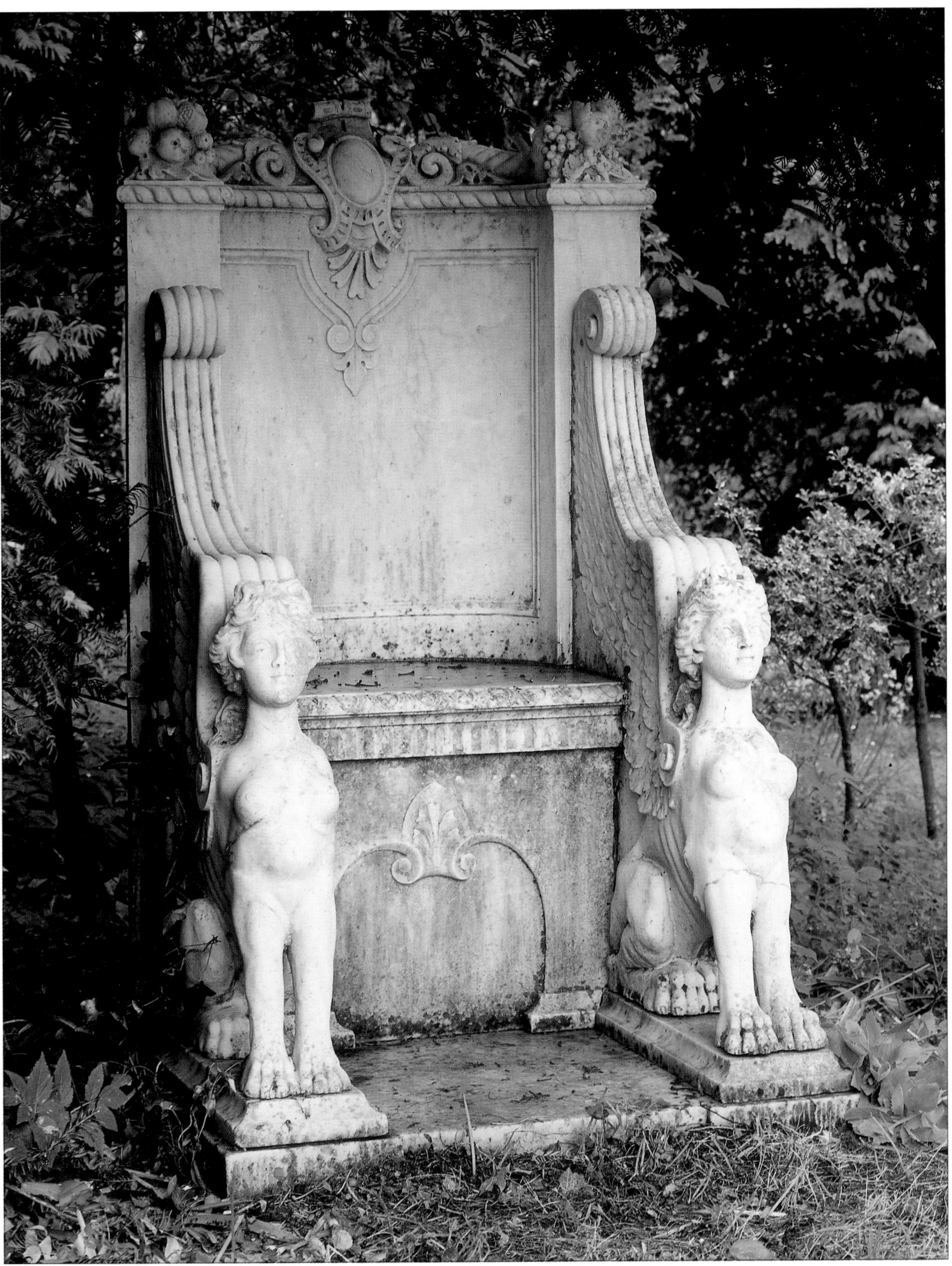

A fine late nineteenth century Italian marble garden chair, in the form of a throne, the curved back with a cartouche flanked by cornucopia, the scrolling console arms supported by winged sphinxes. The quality and style of this piece combine to make it an attractive and valuable item. Circa 1870. 150cm.: 59ins. high

WROUGHT IRON

A wrought iron games seat with plain slatted back and seat, the end supports joined by arched stretchers, with hinged footrest and a pair of wheels to one end. These practical seats could be wheeled to a suitable spot, while the folding footrest gave protection from damp grass to the sitters' feet and long dresses of the period. Nineteenth century. 244cm.: 96ins. wide

A wrought iron games seat with plain slatted seat and segmented back, the legs with wheels at one end, joined by stretchers. Hinged footrest on paw supports. The mobility and practicality of these seats has secured them a timeless popularity. Early nineteenth century. 155cm.: 61ins. wide

A rare Regency wrought iron garden seat, the back with unusual latticework decoration, with plain slatted seat and curved arm supports. Early nineteenth century. 110cm.: 43½ins. wide

Right, an early nineteenth century reeded wrought iron garden seat, with slatted seat and back, the supports joined by bowed stretcher. A good example of a small sized seat of pleasing proportions and in attractive condition. 122cm.: 48ins. wide

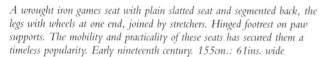

Far right, a wrought iron garden armchair, early nineteenth century

A reeded wrought iron garden seat with plain slatted seat and arched segmented back. Note the simple paw feet to front supports. Early nineteenth century. 159cm.: 62½ins. wide

Another variation of design, this reeded wrought iron seat has segmented back, plain slatted seat and curved protruding arms. A small seat which works well to the design. Early nineteenth century. 115cm.: 45ins. wide

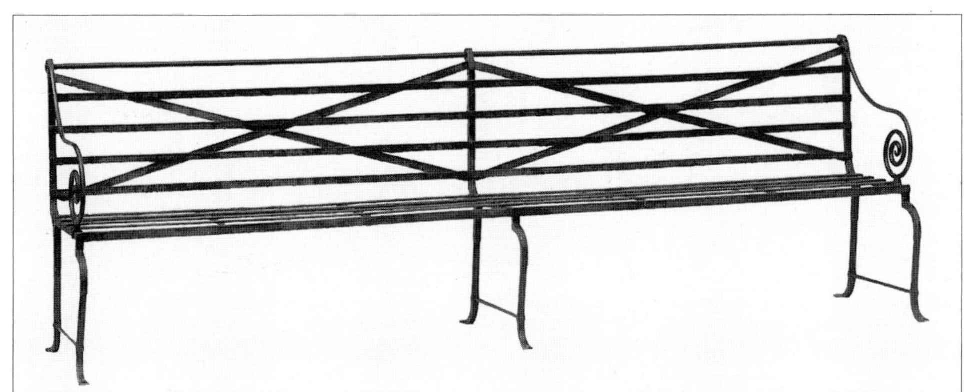

A Scottish mid-nineteenth century wrought iron garden seat with slatted back and seat, the overscroll arms on outswept supports joined by stretchers. Here the width of the seat suggests it was intended for public rather than private use. 304cm.: 120ins. wide

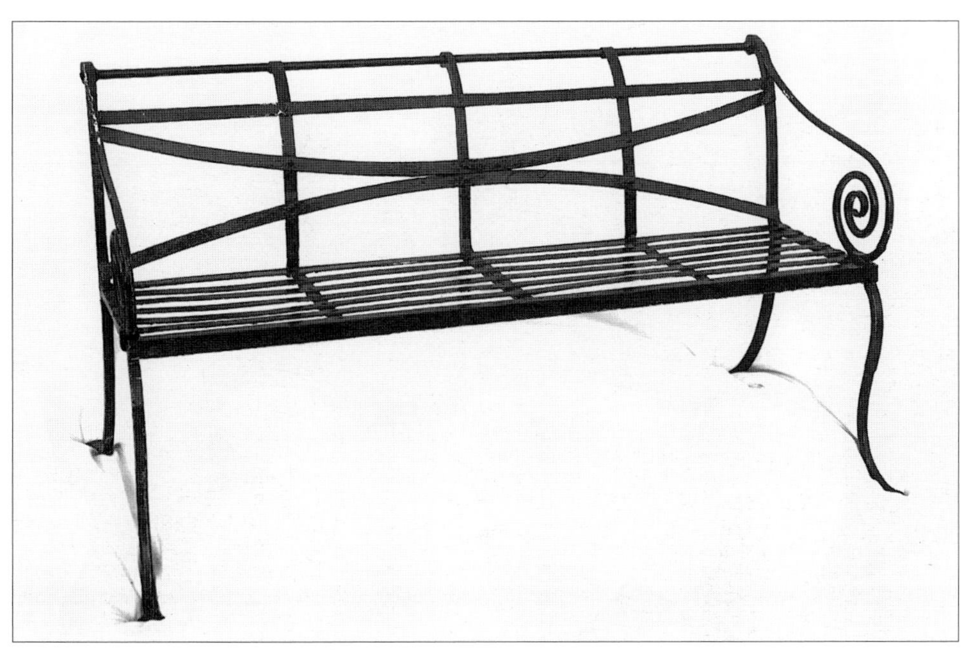

A more compact solid looking mid-nineteenth century wrought iron seat, the back with bowed stretchers and with scrolled arms similar to the previous example. 154cm.: 60½ins. wide

Right, an early nineteenth century reeded wrought iron seat with segmented back, the legs with paw feet joined by stretchers. 104cm.: 40ins. wide

Far right, note the Sheraton influence to the back of this early nineteenth century wrought iron garden chair. A practical attempt to translate a contemporary dining chair design into a garden seat. 122cm.: 48ins. wide

Right, an early nineteenth century reeded wrought iron garden chair with segmented back, the supports with paw feet joined by stretchers. Here the segmented back works very well with a single chair. Compare the stretchers with those on the garden armchair on p.152

Far right, wrought iron garden seat, with plain slatted seat and segmented reeded back, the supports with paw feet joined by stretchers. Early nineteenth century. 160cm.: 63ins. wide

A similar but wider seat than the previous example, and therefore requiring additional support. Early nineteenth century. 183cm.: 72ins. wide

A reeded wrought iron seat, the back decorated with scrolls. A pleasing design and a welcome change from the usual segmented back design. Nineteenth century. 154cm.: 60½ins. wide

A similar seat to the previous example, but with an arched back and on paw feet. Circa 1830. 180cm.: 71ins. wide

A reeded wrought iron seat with wonderful overscroll arms, the back with segments and roundels. Early nineteenth century. 200cm.: 79ins. wide

It is rare to find a maker's stamp on seats of this type. This bears the stamp of Brown & Freer, Stourbridge, a company recorded in Slater's 1850 Worcestershire Directory as 'Iron Bar, Hoop and C. Manufacturers'. Note scrolling supports with inverted hearts. Mid-nineteenth century. 122cm.: 48ins. wide

A late nineteenth century wrought iron seat similar to a design offered by Barnard Bishop & Barnards, Norwich Iron Works, with slatted seat, trellis back and overscroll arms and supports. 124cm.: 48ins. wide

A French wrought iron seat with overscroll back and seat, with tubular slats on five outswept supports. Late nineteenth century. 196cm.: 77ins. wide. Shown with a garden chair of similar form, the back with brass plate inscribed 'St Saveur'

Known variously as tête-à-tête, double garden chair, or conversation seat, this nineteenth century wrought iron example has arcaded back, the supports formed by stretchers with scroll feet. 135cm.: 53ins. wide

For those who prefer the shade, what could be more practical than a tree seat, curved to follow the contours of the trunk? This is a quarter curved section with the more usual segmented back. Early nineteenth century. 147cm.: 58ins. wide

A wrought iron tree seat without arms so that it could be joined to a similar semicircular section. Early nineteenth century. 140cm.: 55ins. wide

A mid-nineteenth century wrought iron tree seat of curved form, with slatted seat and back, the legs with scroll terminals. 188cm.: 74ins. wide

For a large tree, a wrought iron tree seat comprising two halves, each with four sections, plain slatted seat and segmented back, on paw supports joined by stretchers. Early nineteenth century. 236cm.: 93ins. diameter

A wrought iron tree seat comprising two halves, with plain slatted seat and back. A contemporary advertisement for a similar tree seat (circa 1880) suggests 'A seat 4½ft in diameter, to fit round a tree 18ins. in diameter'. Probably late nineteenth century. 175cm.: 69ins. wide

A smaller version of the centre tree seat on the opposite page. This reeded wrought iron example shows how the two halves would be joined. Early nineteenth century. 145cm.: 57ins. diameter

Far left, a French wrought iron garden chair, with sprung hoop shaped back, on circular seat stamped 'Carre, Paris'. Seats of this type became popular in England with manufacturers such as Barnard Bishop & Barnards who offered 'Improved Steel Chairs' of similar design. 'The seats and backs of these chairs are formed of flat steel springs which render them very elastic and easy'. Seats of this type were still being advertised in early twentieth century catalogues. Circa 1880

Left, another popular design of wrought iron sprung chair, with circular seat and back. French. Circa 1880

WOOD

Gertrude Jekyll in her book *Garden Ornament* (1918) suggested that 'For Gardens of lesser pretension we may have wooden seats, either of hard wood or painted. The common habit of painting garden seats a dead white is certainly open to criticism.' Miss Jekyll preferred a grey or 'some very quiet tone of green'.

Probably influenced by a revival of enthusiasm for 'Chinese Chippendale' in the 1860s, a wooden garden seat with plain slatted seat, the back and arm supports with 'Chinese' latticework decoration. 208cm.: 82ins. wide

A French pine conservatory bench, with slatted seat, the downswept arms and back with X-shaped stretchers. Simulated wood grain painted finish. Late nineteenth century. 159cm.: 63ins. wide

A Chinese style garden seat with arched and slatted back with overscroll arms centred with roundels on plain supports joined by stretchers. We have come to associate this form of wooden garden seat with Lutyens and the style he popularised in the early twentieth century. In fact, this design has its origin in the seventeenth century. Twentieth century. 238cm.: 94ins. wide

Included in the J.P. White catalogue of 1910 was this painted wooden garden seat known as their 'Carlton' design. It was available in painted deal at 7 guineas (£7.35), dark oak varnished at 10 guineas (£10.50), or oiled teak at 11 guineas (£11.55). The back is pierced with 'Chinese Chippendale' latticework and with a central panel dated 1901 and inscribed with the quotation:

> *'Here, with a loaf of bread beneath the bough/A flask of wine, a book of verse and thou/Beside me in the wilderness/And wilderness were Paradise enow'*

A choice of some ten such verses could be ordered. 289cm.:114ins. wide

Another J.P. White offering, the 'Pyghtle' painted wooden garden seat. This model with slatted seat and arched slatted back was available in deal, oak and teak. The name was taken from the White works address in Bedford. Circa 1910. 214cm.:84ins. wide

More conventional seat designs from a 1913 catalogue. Known as 'Man-O'-War' garden seats, they were made from teak wood of old navy ships, which 'being thoroughly seasoned, is impervious to the effects of sun or rain, and requires neither paint nor varnish'. From left to right the 'Alexandra' seat, the 'Duke' chair and the 'Hannibal' seat

STONEWARE AND EARTHENWARE

An amusing Minton 'Majolica' ware conservatory or garden seat in the form of a crouching monkey holding fruit and supporting a tassel-trimmed cushion. Circa 1860

A rare J. & R. Howie Scottish glazed stoneware 'rustic' garden chair in the form of a tree stump sprouting oak leaves, with green and brown glazed seat and amorphous branch arms and back. Stamped at base 'Hurlford Fire Clay Works, Kilmarnock'. Circa 1870. 100cm.: 39½ins. high

Enthusiastically embracing the 'rustic' influence of the late nineteenth century, a pair of Scottish glazed earthenware garden seats, each formed with truncated branches and stamped 'Moss End' (Moss End is some ten miles from Glasgow), on rectangular bases. 111cm.: 43½ins. wide. Shown with a 'rustic' table, the circular top on truncated stump support. 91cm.: 36ins. diameter

A George Jones majolica garden seat moulded in relief with waterlilies, bulrushes, sparrows and dragonflies. Circa 1875. 45cm.: 17¾ins. high

Right, a glazed stoneware 'rustic' style garden chair in the form of a tree stump with branch pierced back and arms. Seats such as these need to be permanently located since they are extremely heavy and awkward to manoeuvre. Circa 1870. 112cm.: 44ins. high

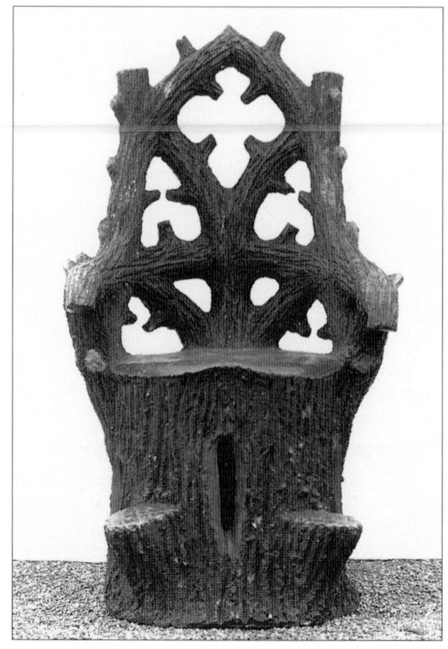

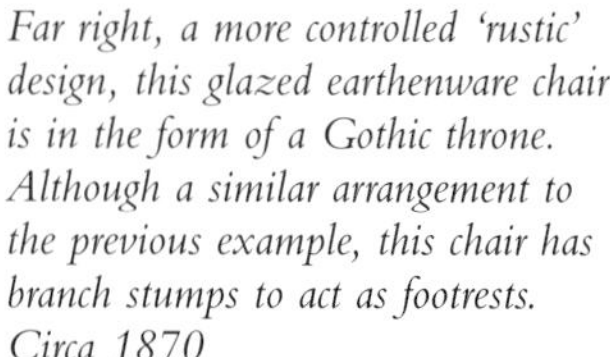

Far right, a more controlled 'rustic' design, this glazed earthenware chair is in the form of a Gothic throne. Although a similar arrangement to the previous example, this chair has branch stumps to act as footrests. Circa 1870

Most 'rustic' seats appear to be Scottish in origin, so it is interesting to identify an English manufacturer. The one on the left stamped 'Chadwick Barker & Co., Totley, Sheffield', the one on the right stamped 'Lindsay & And..., Lillie Hill, Terracotta Works, Dunfermline'. Both late nineteenth century. Both 107cm.: 42ins. high

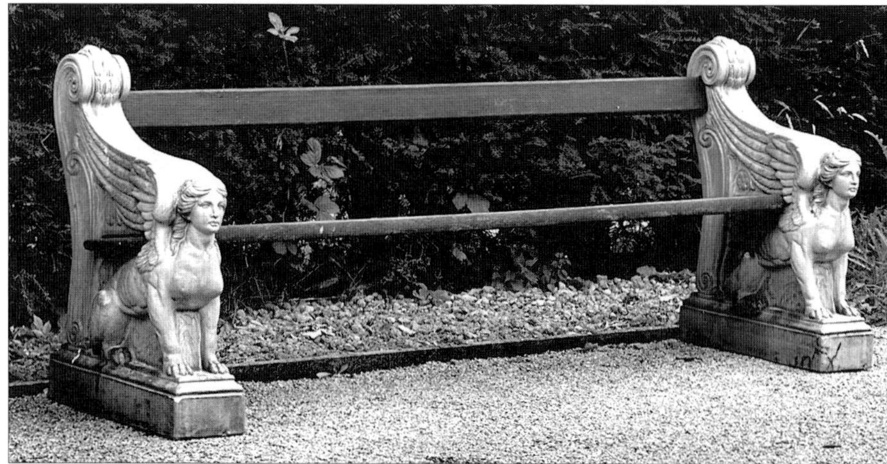

A Doulton glazed stoneware garden seat with plain slatted back and seat, each end support in the form of a sphinx with accentuated scrolling wings, on rectangular base, stamped 'Doulton, Lambeth, London'. The arrangement of the simple planked back and seat would suggest a variable length seat could be easily achieved. Circa 1900. 234cm.: 92ins. wide

CAST IRON

Buyers should be aware that the popularity of cast iron examples and the relative ease with which moulds can be taken from originals has led to a number of designs being reproduced. Whilst most copies can be identified from the poor finish to the seams, artificial ageing and overpainting may prove a hazard to the inexperienced. Casts taken from nineteenth century examples will still incorporate registration masks and foundry stamps. It is therefore important to buy from reputable sources who can confirm the genuineness of the item.

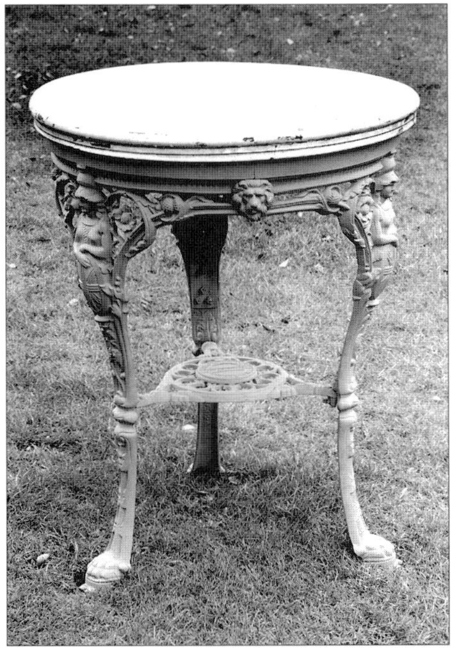

Far left, originally intended for use in public houses and thus known as a pub table, the 'Britannia' model is the most common pub table design. Cast iron with circular wooden top, on three sabre supports cast with a figure of Britannia holding a Union flag shield. This example has a foliate pierced undershelf cast with maker's name 'Gaskell and Chambers Ltd., Bar fitters, Manchester'. Circa 1890. 70cm.: 28ins. high

Left a cast iron pub table with circular wooden top, the triform base cast with heads of the bearded W.G. Grace wearing cricket cap, beneath the initials 'W G' flanked by swags. On sabre supports centred by an undertier. 66cm.: 28ins. high

Two views of one of the most attractive garden chairs manufactured in the nineteenth century, produced by the Lion Foundry, Northampton, probably from a set of four representing the Four Seasons. Circular back pierced with thistles and flowers, and a central roundel decorated with putti and a chariot, surmounted by a cartouche inscribed 'Autumn', with rams' heads arms, serpentine leaf-pierced seat, shaped apron and foliate cabriole legs joined by stretchers. Circa 1860. See also p.166

The Lion Foundry at Northampton produced this rare two-seater cast iron garden chair with serpentine foliate pierced seats in the mid-nineteenth century. The end supports and central arm are cast with scrolls, leaves and fruit. The shaped circular backs representing Spring and Summer are each centred with a roundel cast with putti inside borders of spring and summer flowers and flanked by sheeps' heads, the back stamped 'Lion Foundry Northampton, registered by W. Roberts' on each roundel. 105cm.: 41½ins. wide. *See also p.165.*

In 1830 a John Brettell set up the Beehive Foundry which became the Lion Foundry and was operated by Brettell and William Roberts from 1849 to 1851. Roberts then operated on his own from 1851 to 1868. The firm ceased trading in 1929

An American cast iron tree seat, the seat pierced with scrolls and the back cast with trailing vines and grapes. Late nineteenth century. 110cm.: 43ins. diameter

The 'Hissing Serpent' cast iron garden seat with wooden slatted seat and back, the end supports in the form of serpents. Late nineteenth century. 165cm.:65ins. wide

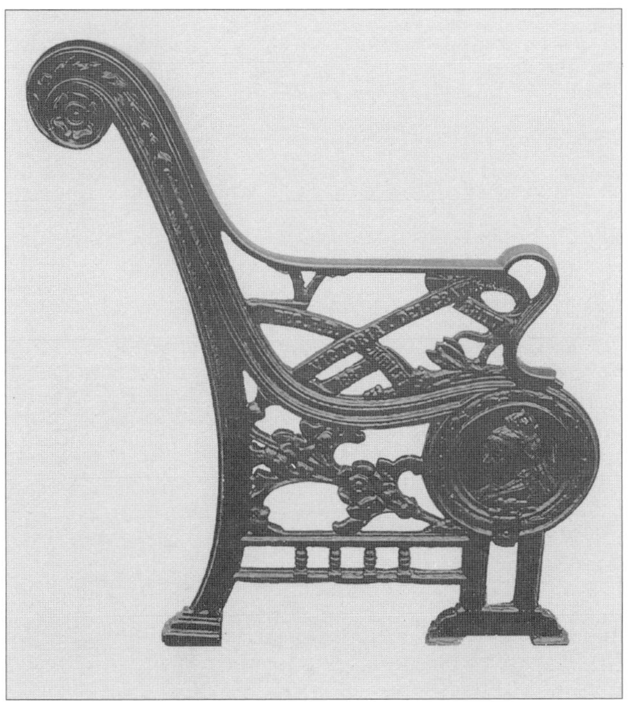

A rare end section cast iron 'Jubilee' seat, produced to celebrate the Golden Jubilee of Queen Victoria, 1887. The supports cast with scrolls and foliage, a portrait medallion of the queen, and a Latin legend 'Victoria Dei Gratia Britt Reg. FD Jubilee 1887' to the arm supports

A nineteenth century 'Rustic' style cast iron garden chair, the back and seat pierced with branches and foliage, the end supports entwined with serpents. *See also p.170*

Above, displaying a strong Gothic influence, this French Val d'Osne foundry cast iron chair has rectangular seat pierced with hexagons, the back and arms pierced with quatrefoils and tracery. Circa 1860

Above right, French cast iron seat similar in design to the previous example, circa 1860. Also shown (right) an engraving of the seat from a contemporary pattern book

Right, the design of the back of this American cast iron chair may well have been influenced by the shield and eagle emblem as depicted on the reverse of some United States coins in the late nineteenth century. The style of seat is similar to those by Robert Wood. Circa 1900

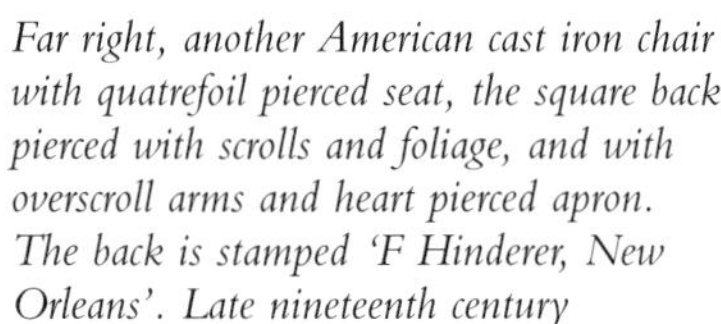

Far right, another American cast iron chair with quatrefoil pierced seat, the square back pierced with scrolls and foliage, and with overscroll arms and heart pierced apron. The back is stamped 'F Hinderer, New Orleans'. Late nineteenth century

A 'modern' cast iron garden chair designed by Edward Bawden, with wooden slatted seat, the back, sides and apron pierced with geometric patterns. Second quarter twentieth century. Edward Bawden, RA, was born at Braintree, Essex in 1903. He is better known as a book illustrator and mural painter

A matching cast iron seat designed by Edward Bawden, with wooden slatted seat, segmented back pierced with geometric patterns and with similarly pierced end supports and apron. Second quarter twentieth century. 121cm.: 47½ins. wide.

A set of Victorian style cast iron chairs, early twentieth century, each arched back cast with a portrait medallion flanked by foliage. Possibly originally intended as hall or conservatory chairs. Also shown a cast iron pub table with foliate pierced top on three supports cast with masks supporting an undertier. 60cm.: 23½ ins. diameter

A rare cast iron seat by James Haywood, the back and arms pierced with truncated branches and maker's stamp 'J Haywood, Phoenix Foundry, Derby', and diamond registration mark for 20 June, 1853. Mid-nineteenth century. 130cm.: 51ins. wide

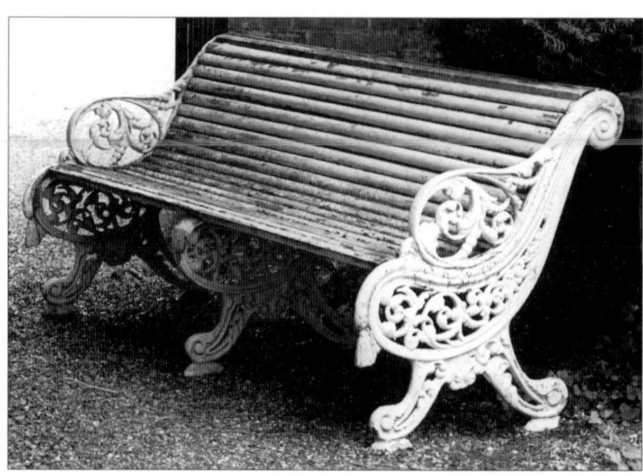

A cast iron seat, probably from the Falkirk Iron Works, as a very similar example is shown in their catalogue of circa 1875-80 under the heading 'Seats, Royal Park Pattern'. Slatted back and seat, the end terminals and central section with overscroll ends and supports and pierced with scrolling foliage, hung with tassels. 188cm.: 74ins. wide

The irregular form of this seat suggests that it might be rather uncomfortable! The seat and back pierced with truncated branches and oak leaves, the sides entwined with serpents. Circa 1870. 132cm.: 52ins. wide. See also p.167

A cast iron seat with slatted back and seat from the firm of Illingworth Ingham, and with some design similarities to the example above

An interesting cast iron example with wooden slatted seat and arcaded foliate cast back, the end supports cast with serpents, grapes and with dogs' heads terminals. This appears to be a variation on the Coalbrookdale 'Serpent and Grape' pattern seat, see p.175, although the arcaded iron back does not appear in any known foundry catalogue of the time. Circa 1870. 151cm.: 59ins. wide

The functional design suggests this seat may have been intended for public use. It has a plain wooden back, foliage pierced end supports and a geometrically pierced seat stamped 'Geo. Smith & Co., Sun Foundry, Glasgow'. Circa 1860. 155cm.: 61ins. wide. The company was operating in Glasgow in 1858, and moved to Chippers, Renfrewshire in 1894. It became a limited company in 1895 and went into voluntary liquidation in 1899

The Lion Foundry, Kirkintilloch, Glasgow, produced this cast iron seat, probably circa 1890. With wooden slatted back and seat, the end supports are cast with foliage and scrolls and with eagle head terminals. It is stamped 'Lion Foundry, Kirkintilloch'. 152cm.: 60ins. wide. The company, as the Lion Foundry Co. Ltd., was listed in local directories for 1918

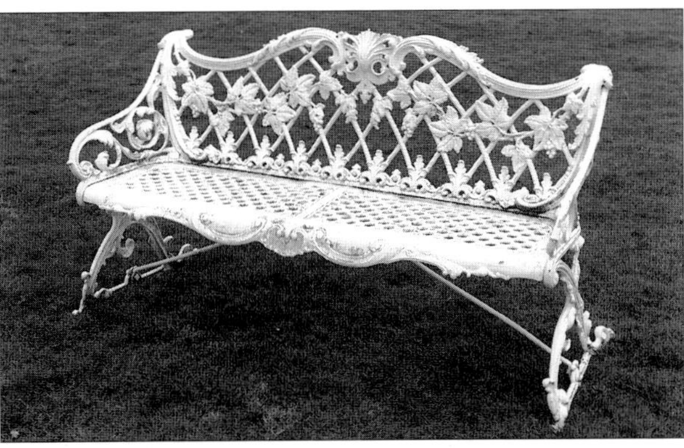

A very attractive cast iron garden seat with elegant arched and scrolled back pierced with trelliswork and fruiting vines, the seat pierced with geometric patterns, on X-scroll supports joined by stretcher. Strong rococo influence with barely the hint of a straight line. Circa 1870. 147cm.: 58ins. wide

A cast iron garden seat with plain solid seat, the back and sides with trailing twigs, foliage, birds and snails and with pierced apron. Note how the wooden seat is fitted to the frame. 148cm.: 58½ins. wide

A nineteenth century cast iron garden seat, possibly American, the back cast with a profusion of scrolls centred by a bunch of grapes, the seat pierced with geometric patterns, on four scrolled legs joined by stretchers and a scroll pierced apron. 106cm.: 42ins. wide

One of a rare pair of cast iron benches from the Yates Haywood Foundry, with unusual and attractive pierced foliate end supports, the seat pierced with circle and lattice decoration. Circa 1860. 91cm.:36ins. high.

The foundry was formed from the merger of J. Yates and J. Haywood & Co. which exhibited work at the Great Exhibition of 1851

Probably by Coalbrookdale, one of a pair of double-sided bench ends, centred by anthemion and with overscroll arms. Circa 1870

A rare Carron Foundry cast iron seat, the seat pierced with arabesques and foliage. The serpentine shaped back cast with hoops beneath foliate cresting, on cabriole supports with foliate cast apron and ring turned back legs. Stamped 'Carron' and with diamond registration mark for 16 March, 1846. Mid-nineteenth century. 113cm.: 44½ins. wide

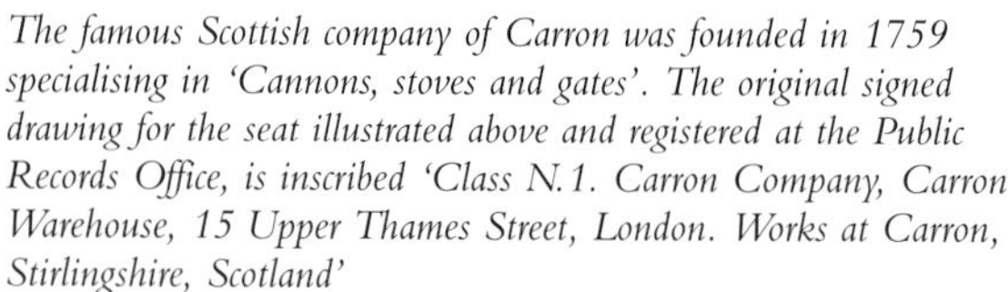

The famous Scottish company of Carron was founded in 1759 specialising in 'Cannons, stoves and gates'. The original signed drawing for the seat illustrated above and registered at the Public Records Office, is inscribed 'Class N.1. Carron Company, Carron Warehouse, 15 Upper Thames Street, London. Works at Carron, Stirlingshire, Scotland'

The design of this seat, although in the Louis XV style, is confidently and powerfully eclectic, the pierced serpentine back with central flower motif, flanked by latticework and panels of fruiting plants, the angled arms ribbon tied with scroll ends. On cabriole legs. Diamond registration stamp for 8 March, 1865. 190cm.: 75ins. wide

Catalogue engraving for the seat. The design is registered for the Dalkeith Ironworks, Dalkeith, Scotland. The company was certainly operating from circa 1810 until the end of the nineteenth century, and may well have been founded by David Mushet the famous metallurgist, born in Dalkeith in 1772 and brought up as an ironfounder. An advertisement in an 1860 directory presents the company as 'W R Mushet, Dalkeith Iron Works'. Apart from stoves and garden seats the company also offered fountains, Villa metallic greenhouses and arbours

A Scottish cast iron seat, with wooden slatted seat, arched back pierced with wheatsheaves and cockleshells, the back stamped 'Falkirk' and with registration number. The design was first registered by the Falkirk Iron Company (instituted in 1819) as number 198596 in 1866. Circa 1870. 165cm.: 65ins. wide. In 1929 the Falkirk Iron Company became part of Allied Ironfounders Ltd.

A cast iron seat (left) and catalogue engraving (above) from a design registered by Andrew McLaren & Co. Seat with diamond registration stamp for 8 January, 1869, and numbered 15. Circa 1870. 163cm.: 64ins. wide.

Research has so far failed to identify the McLaren foundry. An Alexander McLaren is listed in a 1918 Glasgow directory as an ironfounder's agent and gave a London address of 174 Upper Thames Street, probably warehousing and retailing premises, close to those used by the Carron and Falkirk foundries

A rare cast iron seat by John Finch, the back and end supports pierced with foliage and strapwork and with diamond registration stamp for 10 August, 1866, No.44. Circa 1870. 153cm.: 64ins. wide. The company was established in 1830 and manufactured fenders, hat, coat and umbrella stands, tables, school desks and garden seats

The original engraving for the seat above is registered in the Public Records Office, number 199811, with John Finch of Priory Street, Dudley, Worcestershire, as the manufacturer

A Gothic influence can be seen in this French cast iron seat with scroll pierced seat, the back with ogee panels and quatrefoils, the end supports with rayed decoration and plain legs joined by stretchers. Circa 1860. 126cm.: 49½ins. wide

A cast iron seat with quatrefoil and tracery pierced back, stamped 'Crawfords, Glasgow'. Circa 1860. 107cm.: 73½ins. wide. This is probably a product of J. & E. Crawfords (see p.168). Eagle Foundry, Port Dundas, Glasgow. The company operated circa 1838 to 1878

The design of the seat above is registered in the catalogue of the Société Anonyme des Hautes Fourneaux et Fonderies du Val d'Osne who manufactured identical seats at the same time as Crawfords (see p.168). It is rare for this design to be produced by a British foundry. The Val d'Osne seat was available in various sizes from 101cm. to 190cm.: 40ins. to 75ins. wide

COALBROOKDALE

This was the most important English foundry of the nineteenth century for manufacturing an extensive range of garden related products from gates to boot scrapers, fountains to garden rollers. Benjamin Pitts Capper in his *Topographical Dictionary of the United Kingdom,* published 1813, recorded that 'Colebrook Dale [sic] lies in a winding vale between two vast hills, which break into various forms, with beautiful hanging woods. Here are erected the most considerable iron works in England, the first iron bridge in England being set up here over the river Severn. From the manufactory were supplied most cast iron bridges since erected in different parts of the Kingdom'.

The cast iron garden seats shown here and on the following pages are from the Coalbrookdale Company range circa 1850 to 1900. The 1875 company catalogue noted: 'The increasing use of iron garden seats has led to the introduction of a number of new designs. For this country wooden seats are generally preferred to iron, and are more suitable, and in most of the newer patterns the staves are fitted in an iron frame, thus forming the seat entire; and while stronger and more convenient for packing the trouble of fixing each stave separately is avoided. For hot climates, however, metal staves have to take the place of the wooden ones, and these are secured in a similar manner for the bottom or seat. Designs can be submitted and special estimates furnished for any large number of chairs for public parks or grounds, and coats of arms etc. may be introduced as required.'

The fact that this company produced such an extensive range of attractive garden seats which are also reasonably well recorded has no doubt contributed to their present popularity and desirability.

Far left, a late nineteenth century Coalbrookdale cast iron table, the shaped rectangular top pierced with arabesques and stylised foliage, the similarly cast end supports joined by an arched stretcher. 110cm.: 43ins. wide

Left, both this and the previous example were intended for a hall or conservatory rather than for specific garden use. Circa 1875

The 'Serpent and Grape' is one of the earliest popular Coalbrookdale patterns. This example has wooden slatted back and seat, the end supports entwined with serpents and dogs' heads terminals. Circa 1870. 158cm.: 62ins. wide

The 'Serpent and Grape' design was registered at the Public Record Office and dated from 1844. The 1875 catalogue offered the seat 3ft. to 10ft. long and in permutations of painted or bronzed finish, oak or iron seat and back. The original painted colours were green or chocolate

The earliest recorded pattern registered by Coalbrookdale at the Public Record Office, numbered 2286. A drawing of a panel of 'Convolvulus' (above) registered by the company at the Public Record Office, and also numbered 2286, was adapted shortly afterwards by the foundry into a garden seat. On the right, a Coalbrookdale 'Convolvulus' pattern cast iron seat with diamond registration stamp for 12 November, 1842. Circa 1860. 188cm.: 74ins. wide

A Coalbrookdale cast iron seat circa 1860. The design appears to have a strong Indian influence. Registration stamp date for 28 April, 1853. The seat was available with three or two arches, as well as a single arched version (see below), the sizes ranging from 122cm. to 183cm.: 48ins. to 72ins. wide

The single arched version of the seat was registered at the Public Record Office under number 90929. It was also registered as pattern number 20 in the 1860

A 'Rustic' pattern cast iron seat, with diamond registration stamp for 7 April, 1851, and numbered 78766. Iron slatted seat, the back and end supports pierced with twigs and foliage. Circa 1860. 127cm.: 50ins. wide. The 1875 Coalbrookdale catalogue offers the seat also as a 'single' chair

A Coalbrookdale garden chair in the 'Oak and Ivy' pattern. Wooden slatted seat, arched back, rounded arms, and with pierced apron on cabriole supports with paw feet. Note the overscroll arms with dogs' heads terminals. The 'Oak and Ivy' pattern was designed by the sculptor John Bell and was registered in the 1875 Coalbrookdale catalogue, Section III, page 256

A Coalbrookdale 'Gothic' pattern cast iron seat, stamped 'C B Dale Co. No. 99277', with diamond registration stamp for 5 February, 1854, and numbered 22. Circa 1860. 153cm.: 60ins. wide. The design is included in the 1875 Coalbrookdale catalogue, Section III, page 253, number 22 and was available painted green or chocolate or with bronzed finish. A matching chair was also available. The design is a triumph of Gothic revivalism

An example of what is probably the most common survivor of the Coalbrookdale seat range, the popular 'Fern and Blackberry' pattern with wooden slatted seat, the back and end supports pierced with foliage. Registration stamp for 30 April, 1858. Circa 1875. 145cm: 57ins. wide. See also pp.180 and 183

The 'Fern and Blackberry' design is identified in the 1875 Coalbrookdale catalogue, Section III, page 254, number 29. A similar version was numbered 29A

A rare Coalbrookdale 'Medallion' pattern cast iron seat with wooden slatted seat, the arched back centred with an oval medallion cast with classical maiden and monogrammed 'JK' (see detail) and stamped 'C B Dale Co. with diamond registration stamp for 13 March, 1862. It is extremely unusual to find artists' monograms on Coalbrookdale seats, and it has been suggested that this is the work of J. Kershaw who was working as a designer at the Coalbrookdale Foundry in the 1860s. Circa 1870. 188cm.: 74ins. wide

The original signed engraving for this seat was registered in the Public Record Office and numbered 149933 in 1862. The design also appears in the 1875 Coalbrookdale catalogue

Not dissimilar to the 'Horse Chestnut' pattern (see p.181), an example of the 'Passion Flower' pattern seat, painted in naturalistic colours and stamped 'Coalbrookdale, No 74, Registered No.3511'. Back altered. Circa 1870. 142cm.: 56ins. wide

One of the rarer Coalbrookdale designs, an 'Osmunda Regalis' pattern garden seat, circa 1875, with plain slatted seat stamped 'Coalbrookdale', the back and end supports pierced with a profusion of leaves and flowers, the end supports with registration stamp and number and pattern number 57a. This seat, included in the 1875 catalogue, was available with or without bracket shelves to attach to end sections. Could be had bronzed or painted, in sizes 'about 4ft.10ins. and 6ft.4ins'. This example 142cm.: 56ins. wide

A Coalbrookdale 'Fern and Blackberry' pattern chair, with wooden slatted seat and diamond registration stamp, numbered 113617. Identified as 529 in the 1875 catalogue and available bronzed or painted with pine wood or iron seat, a 'real oak seat extra'. Circa 1875. *See also pp.177 and 183*

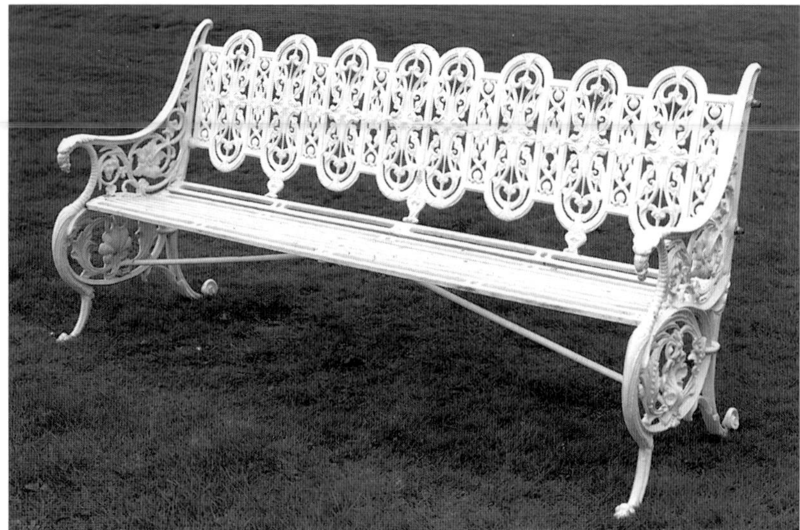

A single-sided version of a double-sided seat offered in the 1875 Coalbrookdale catalogue. Iron slatted seat, panelled back pierced with stylised foliage, the end supports decorated with flowerheads and scallop shells, stamped 'C B Dale Co.', with diamond registration stamp for 18 May, 1866, design number 104791 and numbered 26, on paw feet with stretchers. 185cm.: 73ins. wide.

Below, the double-sided version of the seat shown above was also offered in the 1875 Coalbrookdale catalogue

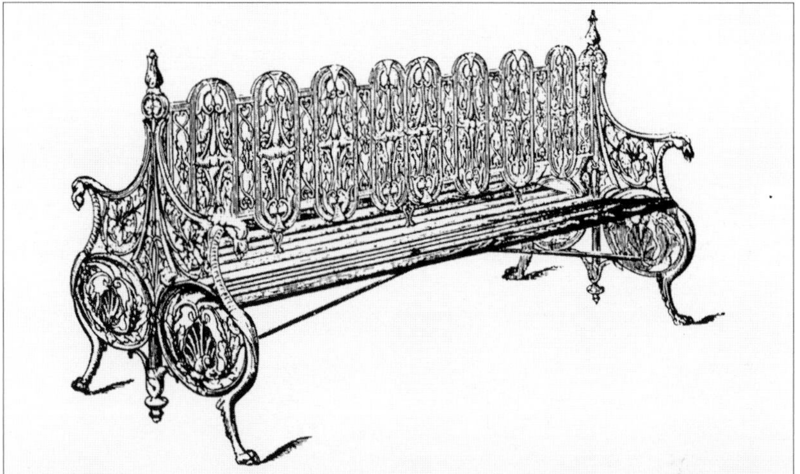

Designed by Christopher Dresser, a Coalbrookdale 'Water Plant' pattern cast iron chair, circa 1870, with wooden slatted seat, the back stamped 'Coalbrookdale' and with diamond registration stamp for 18 January, 1867. The side supports joined by stretchers

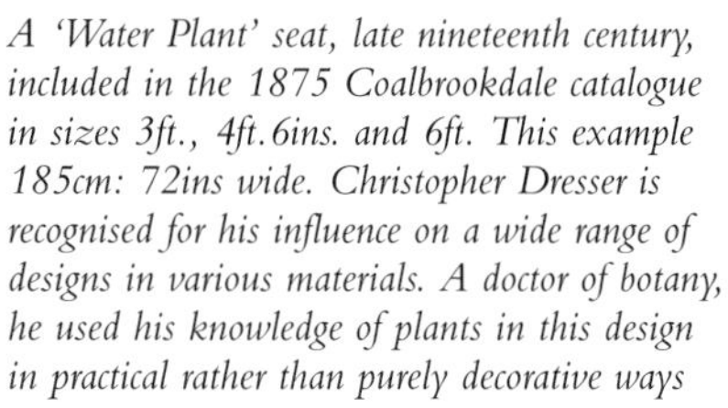

A 'Water Plant' seat, late nineteenth century, included in the 1875 Coalbrookdale catalogue in sizes 3ft., 4ft.6ins. and 6ft. This example 185cm: 72ins wide. Christopher Dresser is recognised for his influence on a wide range of designs in various materials. A doctor of botany, he used his knowledge of plants in this design in practical rather than purely decorative ways

A Coalbrookdale 'Horse Chestnut' pattern cast iron seat painted in naturalistic colours, stamped 'Coalbrookdale Co.'. Circa 1870. 186cm.: 72ins. wide. It is shown below as a single seater

An example of the rare 'Osmunda Fern' pattern, a version of 'Osmunda Regalis', see p.179, with wooden slatted seat, the back stamped 'Coalbrookdale' with registration stamp and number 275254. Circa 1875. 147cm.: 58ins. wide

The 'Horse Chestnut' design was included in the 1875 Coalbrookdale catalogue

The more usual version of the 'Passion Flower' pattern seat, in scroll curved form with foliate pierced seat, the arched back pierced with a profusion of passion flowers and scrolling foliage, on cabriole supports joined by stretchers. The design is included in the 1875 Coalbrookdale catalogue. Circa 1875. 94cm.: 37ins. wide See also p.179

The 'Osmunda Fern' design is shown as number 57 in the 1875 Coalbrookdale catalogue, and was available in four sizes, including a garden chair

A fine example of a Coalbrookdale 'Lily of the Valley' pattern cast iron seat, with wooden slatted seat, the front rail stamped 'C B Dale Co.'. In original burnished condition. Circa 1870. 155cm.: 61ins. wide

A 'Lily of the Valley' pattern cast iron garden armchair, circa 1870, the seat pierced with interlacing scrolls. Identified as number 536 in the 1875 Coalbrookdale catalogue

Coalbrookdale 'Fern and Blackberry' seat, circa 1870. *See also pp.177 and 180*

Detail from a Coalbrookdale chair showing the registration marks and 'C.B.Dale Co. No.195629'

A good example of a 'Nasturtium' pattern seat, the back stamped 'C B Dale' and with registration stamp for 1872 and stamped 'Coalbrookdale No 44'. Circa 1880. 183cm.: 72ins. wide.

The design was included in the 1875 company catalogue as number 44 (below), and came in four sizes, including an armchair

A 'Nasturtium' pattern garden armchair with wooden slatted seat, the back and end supports pierced with trailing nasturtiums, stamped 'C B Dale' and with registration stamps. This example has been successfully restored by shot blasting which has revealed detail lost through repainting and general deterioration. Circa 1880

The more simple design of the 'Laurel' pattern seat with rayed wooden slatted seat, the back cast with panels of laurel wreaths, the arm terminals with grotesque heads above winged cabriole supports with paw feet. Circa 1865. 119cm.: 47ins. wide. The design is included in the 1875 Coalbrookdale catalogue

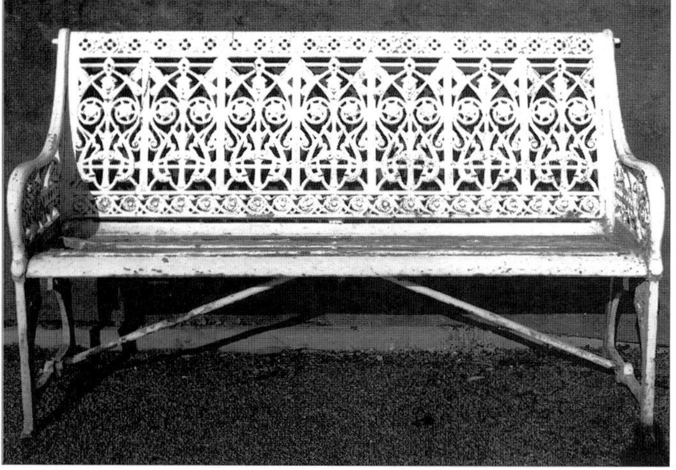

A rare Coalbrookdale 'Medieval' pattern cast iron garden seat with wooden slatted seat, the back pierced with roundels and stylised foliate motifs, with similarly decorated end supports joined by stretchers. Circa 1875. 148cm.: 58ins. wide. Included as number 52 in the 1875 Coalbrookdale catalogue

A late nineteenth century Coalbrookdale design, the back with oval panels of flowering plants flanked by paterae, the end supports with overscroll arms on oval feet, cast with 'Pattern No.75' and diamond registration stamp for February 1883. 191cm.: 75ins. wide

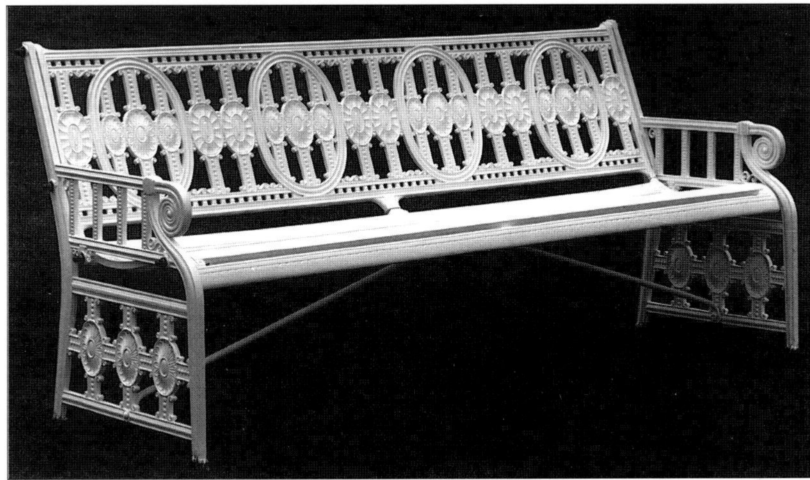

Similar to the previous example, a Coalbrookdale cast iron seat with wooden slatted seat, the back pierced with oval paterae and with diamond registration number 397749 and numbered 71-2. Circa 1890. 104cm.: 72ins. wide

The original signed engraving for this seat (below left) was registered in the Public Record Office and correspondingly numbered 397749 in 1883 under the Coalbrookdale Company Limited, Shropshire. It subsequently appeared in the Coalbrookdale catalogue Garden and Park Furniture, *1907*

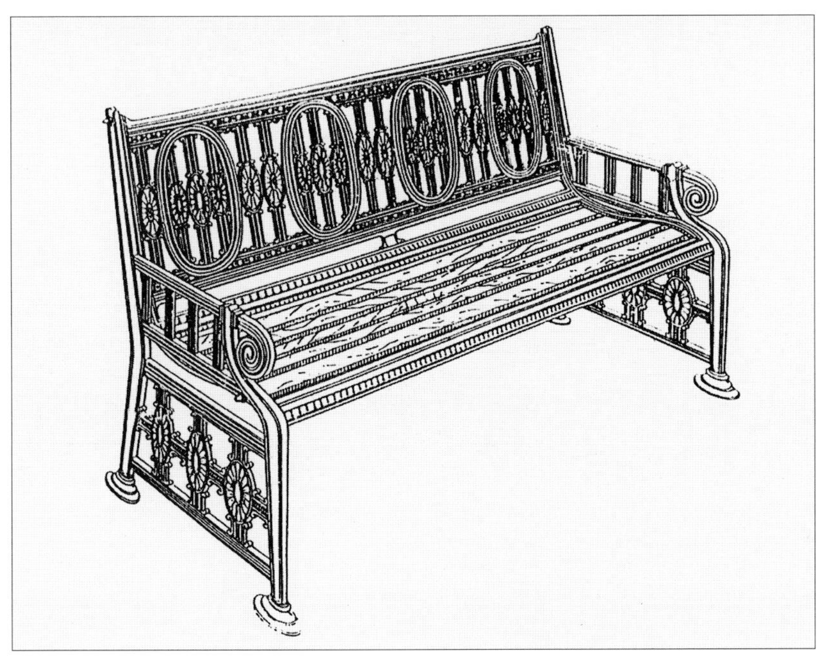

A matching Coalbrookdale cast iron garden armchair. Circa 1890

Garden lines can be of the most simple form, but the variety of spool shapes in wrought, or later cast, iron make this a natural collecting area; larger lines may well be intended for agricultural use. Interestingly copies of some Victorian designs are now being reproduced.

A selection of lines. 1 – eighteenth century, 56cm.: 22ins. long; 2 and 4 – late nineteenth century; 3 and 7 – late nineteenth/early twentieth century; 5, 11 and 12 – early nineteenth century; 6 – cast iron, late nineteenth century; 8 – mid-nineteenth century; 9 – cast iron with patent stamp and star and tapering triangular spike, late nineteenth century; 10 – early twentieth century

Implements and Tools

Until the sixteenth century, tools employed by gardeners were simple, basic, and usually heavy. They had evolved from agricultural implements that had been in use for hundreds, if not thousands, of years. In themselves these tools – an iron shod spade, a sickle, hoes of various forms, mattocks and rakes, together with knives and saws – might seem sufficient enough, but the increased interest in gardens, and the need for gardeners to be well equipped led to a number of innovations and modifications, so that by the middle of the seventeenth century we can see from contemporary illustrations an extensive range of purpose-made tools and accessories. These included refined tools for pruning and grafting as well as hedging shears, digging forks and trowels, in fact, practically all the non-mechanical tools generally known today.

Of course these tools were not mass-produced, and it was not until the nineteenth century that such items could be purchased easily in common weight, design and finish. Naturally the variety and range expanded, particularly for spades, forks and hoes. Most tools became lighter and in some cases more elegant, for use not only by the labourer but also by the master or lady of the house.

After the Second World War, tools generally returned to a more limited standard range. The age of electrical power driven tools was about to dawn.

Exact dating of tools is not an easy exercise, since in some cases designs remained popular for half a century or more; even the more sophisticated implements, such as the Dubois flower gatherer (illustrated below), had a production life of over twenty-five years.

DIGGING, GATHERING AND WEEDING

The range of everyday tools produced circa 1860 to 1930, is amazing in terms of variety and speciality. As late as 1927 C.T. Skelton of Sheffield made thirty-five different types of spade, most of which could be had in different finishes and sizes and with either 'T'- or 'D'-shaped handles. Skelton also offered thirty-five different forks, including asparagus, beetroot and potato, and regional styles such as 'Cheshire', 'Guernsey', 'Irish', 'Kent', 'Lancashire' and 'Scotch'.

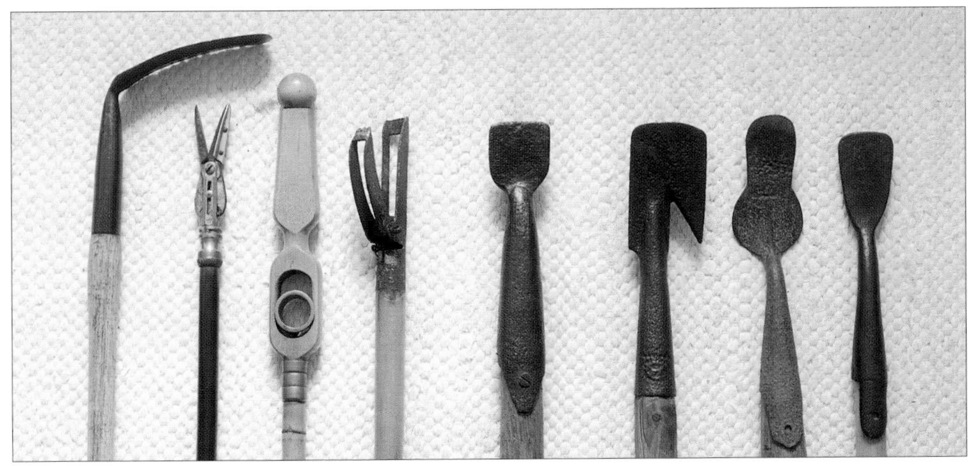

A selection of traditional and novelty implements. Left to right, a scarce garden/golf practice implement which encouraged the user to practise their swing at the same time as decapitating daisies and weeds, and which, with protective head cover, could also be used as a walking stick (an example of an item which today would be far more valuable to a collector of golfing items than a gardener – the Army & Navy Stores marketed this, or a very similar product, as the 'Niblick', 25s. (£1.25), in 1935); a Dubois patent flower gatherer, marketed in 1913 as 'an exceedingly light and useful article, expressly adapted for ladies' use', was operated by a pull 'trigger' incorporated in the handle (shown beside the gatherer), French circa 1910-35; a Little Gripper flower/fruit picker, English, circa 1935; a spud or weeder, known from the days of Samuel Pepys who records using one, this chisel-like implement dates from the seventeenth century or earlier, the example shown probably dating to mid-nineteenth century; a steel weed hook, the notch to hook and pull weeds, late nineteenth century or later; a light steel thistle-head shaped spud, late nineteenth century; a well made nineteenth century spud, head 20cm.: 8ins. long

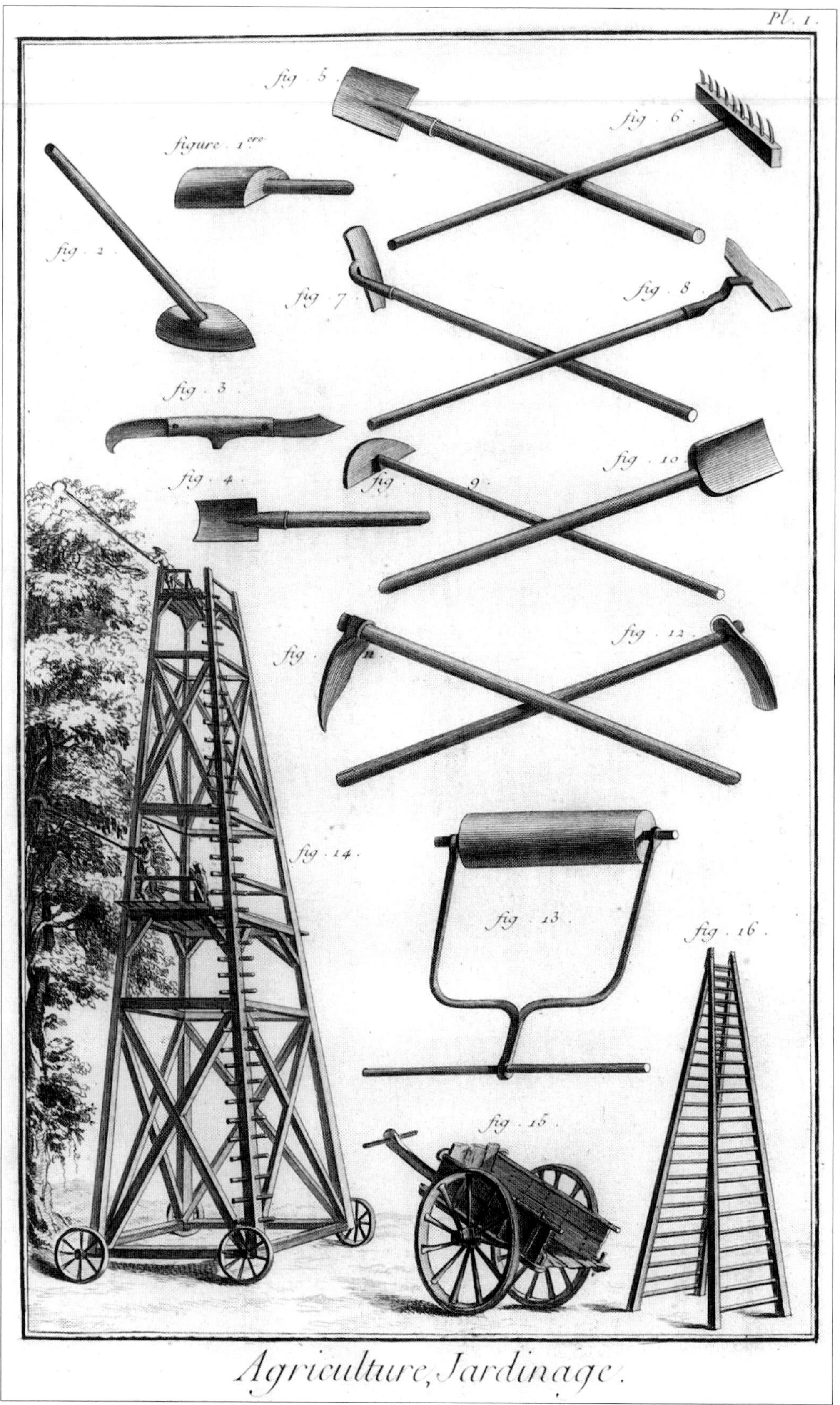

A selection of tools, including hoes, spades, and a rake, from a series of late eighteenth century French engravings

Prize Medals awarded at the Great Exhibition of 1851, and the Exposition Universelle, 1855.

WALTER THORNHILL,

MANUFACTURER OF CUTLERY IN ALL ITS BRANCHES,

By Appointment to Her Majesty, H.R.H. the Prince Albert, and the Royal Family,

No. 144, NEW BOND STREET, & 42, CORNHILL, LONDON.

ESTABLISHED A.D. 1734.

Walter Thornhill begs to submit to the Nobility and Gentry the following list of Pruning and Horticultural Instruments, manufactured by him, of which drawings will be found on the other side corresponding with the numbers attached.

Every article is of the best quality, and as he is a Manufacturer, he is enabled to undertake the making of any Gardening Implement, or to carry out any improvement or alteration that may be suggested in the form of the article now in use.

He would particularly call attention to the Averuncator (No 24), a Pruning Instrument for cutting off branches of Trees at any height with perfect ease, also to the Pruning Shears (Nos. 1 and 28), the form and sliding cut of which greatly increases their power; they are made of all the intermediate sizes.

The New Gardening Chatelaine (No. 18), will be found a most useful appendage by the Ladies; also the Cases of Pruning Instruments (No. 34), which can be fitted with any Instrument selected.

Gardening Spuds made in all forms. Tool Chests from 15s. to 20 guineas.

1. Slide Pruning Shears.
2. Slide Pruning Shears, with bows.
3. Pruning Scissors.
4. Grape Thinning Scissors.
5. Flower Gatherer to cut and hold at the same time.
6. Grass and Box Clippers.
7. Pruning Hatchet with Saw and Hammer.
8. Pruning Hatchet and Hammer.
9. Pruning Knives in every variety of size and form.
10. Budding Knives, of improved shape.
11. Garden Trowel.
12. Pruning Saw.
13. Bill Hook, with cutting edge at back.
14. Large Slide Pruning Shears of all sizes.
15. Walking Stick Spud, double edged.
16. Walking Stick Spud, single.
17. Scotch Thistle Spud.
18. Ladies' Garden Chatelaines fitted to order.
19. Long Handled Grass Clipper with wheel.
20. Long Handled Pruning Saw.
21. Flower Gatherer with long handles. 12/6
22. Spring Grape Gatherer for Hot-houses. 20/.
23. Pruning Switch with long handle.
24. Averuncator for pruning trees at any height.
25. Horticultural Hammer.
26. Lever Pruning Shears with long handles.
27. Long Handled Spring Grape and Flower Gatherer. 20/.
28. Pruning Shears for large branches.
29. Rose Tree Pruning Knife.
30. Hedge and Box Cutting Shears.
31. Flower Gatherer suitable for Conservatories. 35/.
32. Gentlemen's Portable Cases of Gardening Instruments fitted to order.
33. Tool Chests fitted in every variety.
34. Ladies' Portable Case of Gardening Implements.

***Ladies' Spades, Rakes, Hoes, Trowels, &c., made of Steel, in a very light and superior manner.** Also, small sets, suitable as presents for Children.*

The front cover of Walter Thornhill's catalogue of cutlery and bladed garden implements, circa 1860 (see also p.204). Thornhill had offices in New Bond street and was primarily a manufacturer and retailer of cutlery and good quality garden tools and implements and the advertisement states 'Ladies' Spades, Rakes, Hoes, Trowels, &c., made of Steel, in a very light and superior manner'. Their tools would have been relatively more expensive than other mass-produced products

A selection of gardening implements. 1 – weeding fork with twisted prongs, circa 1920-40; 2 – billhook with maker's mark 'I.L' within a heart, probably late eighteenth century; 3 – trowel, late nineteenth century; 4 – child's rake, early twentieth century; 5 – planting spade, early twentieth century; 6 – weeding fork, circa 1900; 7 – small rake, probably for a child or lady, circa 1900; 8 – weeding fork mid- to late nineteenth century; 9 – weeding fork with short 'squared' handle, mid-nineteenth century; 10 – trowel, circa 1900-30; 11 – fern trowel, circa 1900; 12 – weeding fork, circa 1900-30; 13 – asparagus knife, mid-nineteenth century

A selection of daisy grubbers for extracting daisies and levering out small weeds. From left to right, long handled with three prongs, circa 1910, 61cm.: 24ins. long; traditional form, circa 1920; shaped form, circa 1900; simple flat form, circa 1910; cast iron headed grubber with 'bowl' fulcrum, circa 1900; Brades forged steel head with long handle, circa 1900. At the top, a simple two-prong example, mid-twentieth century, 26.5cm.: 20½ins. long

GARDEN CHESTS.

No. 10.—Contains A set of Garden Tools as under:—A rake, a saw, a bill-hook, a paddle, a hoe, and a fruit-knife with hook; these six articles are made to screw into a ferrule, to fix upon a staff. Also, a hammer, a fork, a pair of scissors, and a partition with some nails and list . . .	1	10	0	1	15	0
No. 11.—Contains A set of Garden Tools as under:—A rake, a saw, a bill-hook, a paddle, a hoe, and a fruit-knife with hook; these articles are made to screw into a ferrule, to fix upon a staff. Also, a hammer, a fork, a pruning-knife, a pair of scissors, a pair of shears, a line and reel, a small hand-saw, and a hatchet, three gimlets, and a partition with some nails and list.	2	4	0	2	16	0

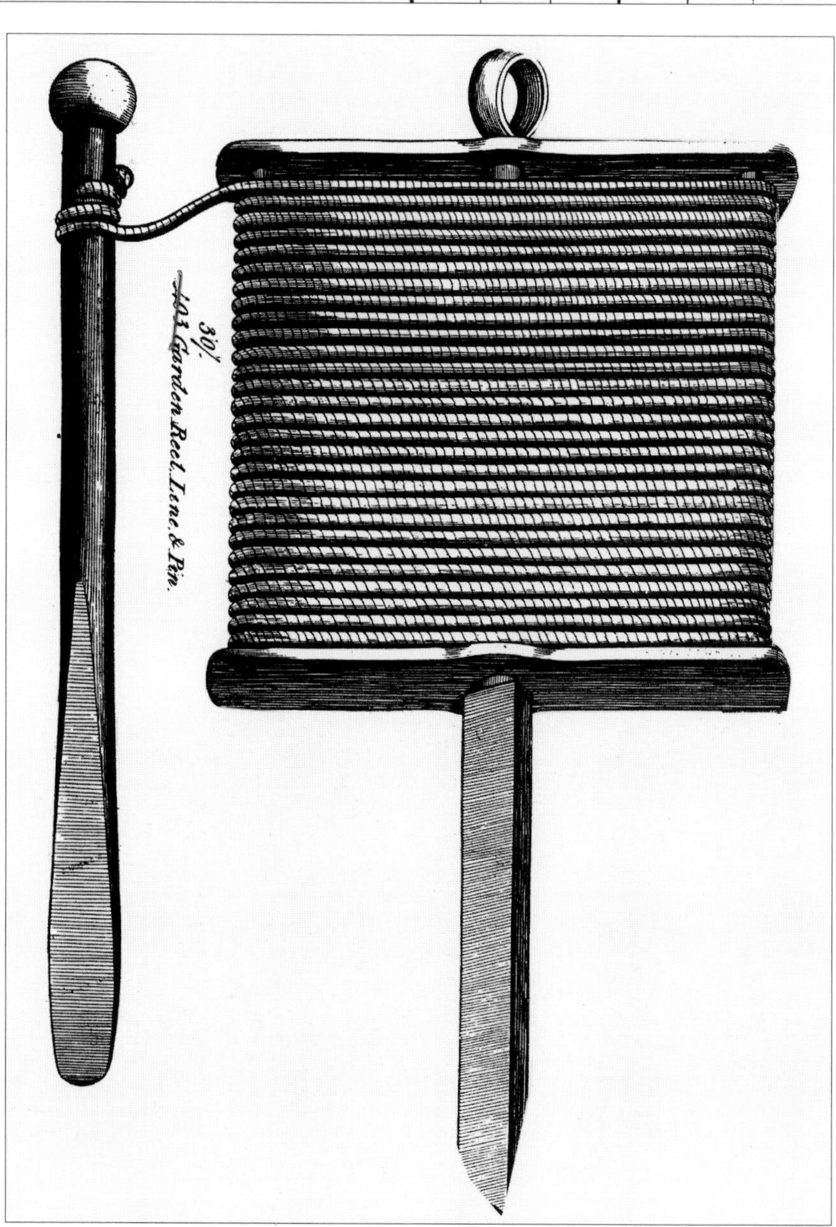

Richard Timmins & Sons of Birmingham published their pattern book which included gardening and agricultural tools, c.1845. Above, the details in the pattern book of garden tool chests. No. 10 (some of the contents illustrated opposite top) cost £1 10s. (£1.50p) in oak, £1 15s. (£1.75p) in mahogany, while No. 11 included some further items. Right, '403 Garden Reel Line & Pin' from the pattern book, circa 1830-40. Opposite top, the idea of interchangeable tool heads has been proposed many times over the last one hundred and fifty years. It is unlikely many sets, as illustrated in the Timmins pattern book, were produced, and it would be rare to find a similar set. Opposite bottom, Timmins' pattern book engraving for 'Ladies Garden Tools also Weeding Forks and Common Garden Trowels', c.1840. All from Tools for the Trades and Crafts, *Kenneth D. Roberts, 1976*

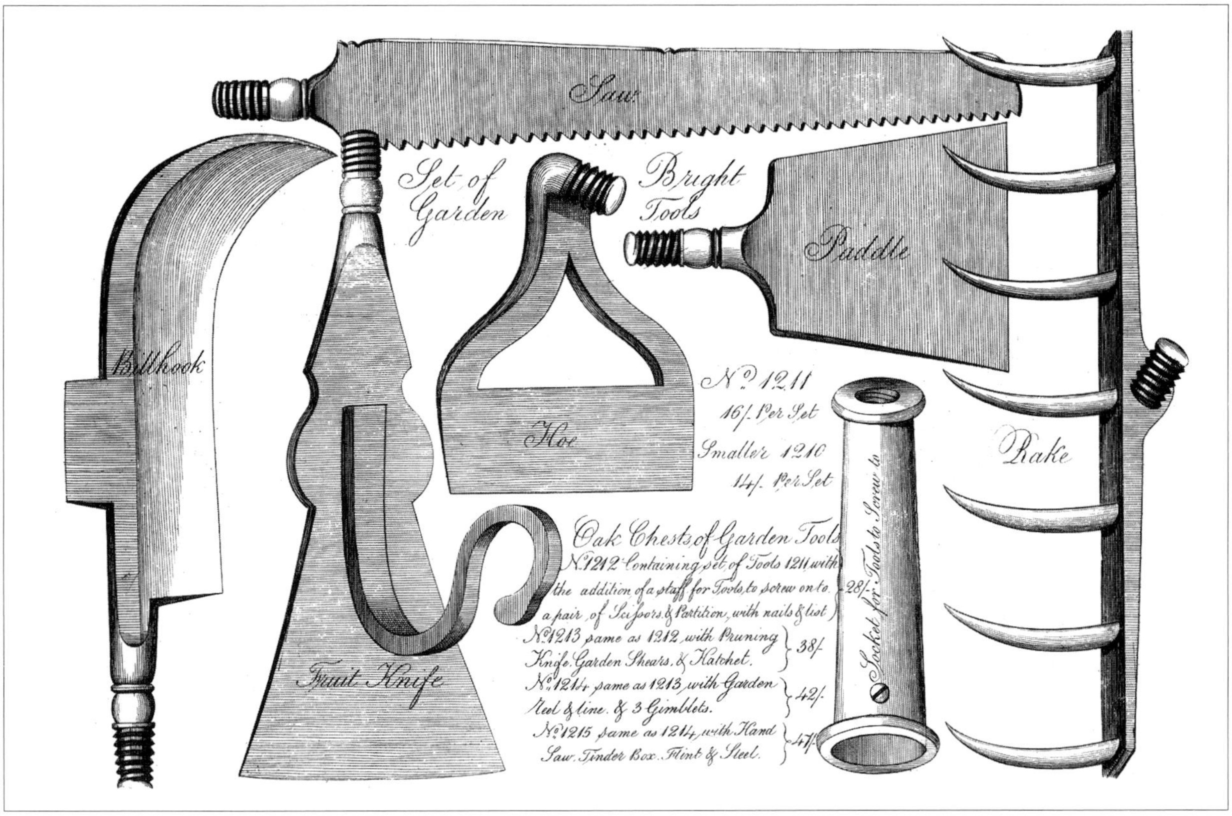

Saw
Set of Garden
Bright Tools
Paddle
Billhook
Hoe
Rake
Fruit Knife
Socket for Tools to Screw to
No. 1211
16/- Per Set
Smaller 1210
14/- Per Set
Oak Chests of Garden Tools
No. 1212 Containing set of Tools 1211 with the addition of a staff for Tools to screw on to. a pair of Scissors & Partition, with nails & list } 28/-
No. 1213 same as 1212, with Pruning Knife. Garden Shears. & Hatchet. } 38/-
No. 1214 same as 1213, with Garden Reel & line. & 3 Gimblets. } 42/-
No. 1215 same as 1214, with Hand Saw. Tinder Box. Flint & Steel. } 47/-

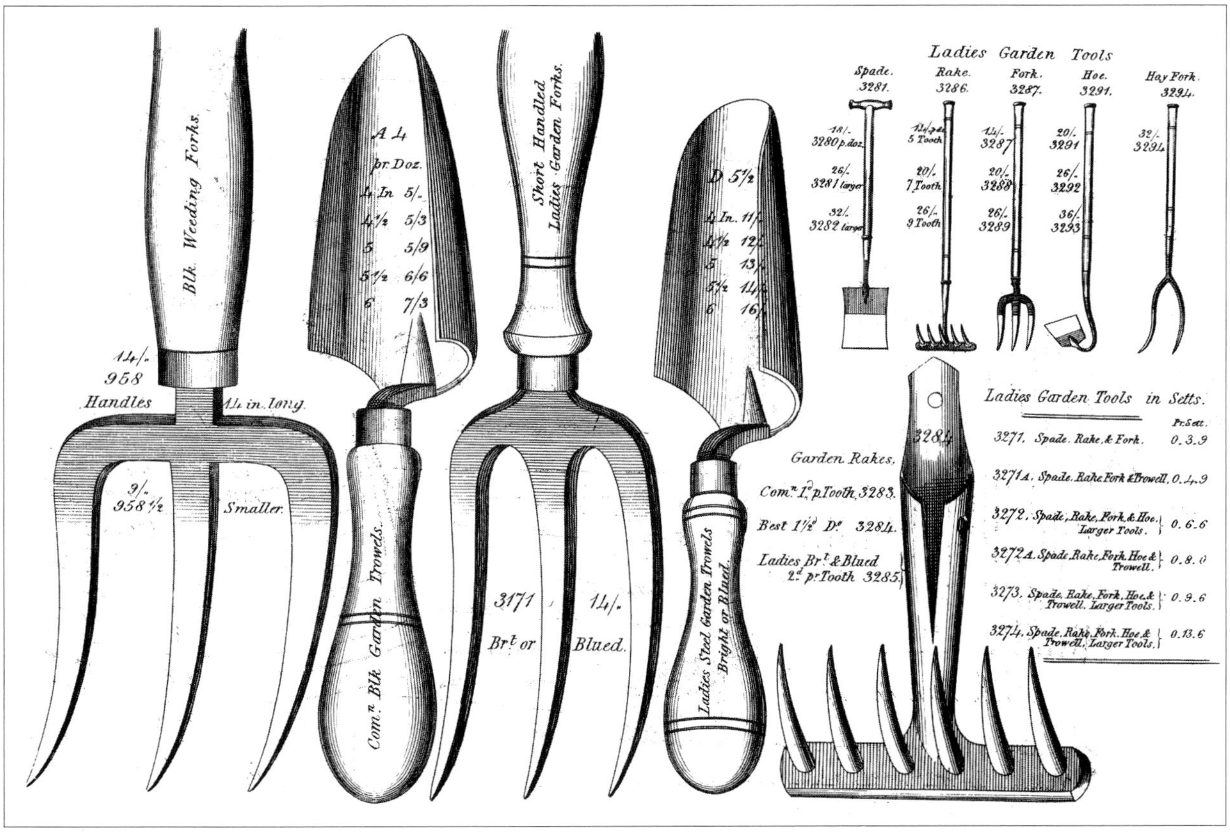

Blk. Weeding Forks.
14/-
958
Handles 14 in. long.
9/-
958 1/2
Smaller.
A 4
pr. Doz.
4 In. 5/-
4 1/2 5/3
5 5/9
5 1/2 6/6
6 7/3
Comn. Blk Garden Trowels.
Short Handled Ladies Garden Forks.
3171 14/-
Brt or Blued.
D 5 1/2
4 In. 11/-
4 1/2 12/-
5 13/-
5 1/2 14/-
6 16/-
Ladies Steel Garden Trowels Bright or Blued.
Ladies Garden Tools
Spade. 3281.
Rake. 3286.
Fork. 3287.
Hoe. 3291.
Hay Fork. 3294.
18/- 3280 p. doz.
26/- 3281 larger
32/- 3282 larger
14/- p. doz. 5 Tooth
20/- 7 Tooth
26/- 9 Tooth
14/- 3287
20/- 3288
26/- 3289
20/- 3291
26/- 3292
36/- 3293
32/- 3294
3284
Garden Rakes.
Comn. 1d. p. Tooth 3283.
Best 1 1/2d. Do. 3284.
Ladies Brt. & Blued 2d. pr. Tooth 3285.
Ladies Garden Tools in Setts.
Pr. Sett.
3271. Spade. Rake. & Fork. 0.3.9
3271A. Spade. Rake Fork & Trowell. 0.4.9
3272. Spade, Rake, Fork & Hoe. Larger Tools. 0.6.6
3272A. Spade Rake, Fork Hoe & Trowell. 0.8.0
3273. Spade. Rake, Fork, Hoe & Trowell. Larger Tools. 0.9.6
3274. Spade. Rake. Fork. Hoe & Trowell. Larger Tools. 0.13.6

1 – hodding spade by Skelton, early twentieth century; 2 – three-tined fork, early to mid-nineteenth century; 3 – grafting spade, late nineteenth century; 4 – parsnip fork, mid-nineteenth century; 5 – bulb planter by Skelton, early twentieth century; 6 – roguing fork, to remove rogue plants from a crop, early twentieth century; 7 – mule open-faced spade, early nineteenth century; 8 – unusual two-tined fork, possibly for taking up roots, early nineteenth century; 9 – unusual turfing iron with semicircular head, late nineteenth century; 10 – turfing iron with 'Ace of Spades' head, late nineteenth/early twentieth century; 11 – continental (French or Low Countries) fork, early nineteenth century; 12 – dock grubber, a larger version of a daisy grubber, early twentieth century

A selection of forks and spades. 1 – double-strapped garden spade with treaded blade, D-shaped handle, circa 1915, 69cm.: 27ins.; 2 – Brades Co. 'Spring Temper' No.748 potato fork, circa 1930; 3 – unusual spade with riveted central strap, blade stamped 'cast steel' and 'Birmingham', circa 1900; 4 – Victorian garden fork with flattened prongs, circa 1875; 5 – Brades Co. No. 987 'Youth's' spade, double strapped, ash handle with D-grip, 64cm.: 25ins., circa 1900; 6 – Brades Co. edging knife for trimming grass borders, circa 1915; 7 – 'Dreadnought' three-prong garden fork, the trade name 'Dreadnought' adopted by many manufacturers around the early years of the twentieth century, circa 1900; 8 – Wm. Park & Co. Wigan No.3 ground breaking spade, a more unusual and attractive variation to the normal design, circa 1910; 9 – Brades 'Criterion' boys' or ladies' border fork with square prongs and T-handle, circa 1920; 10 – short lawn piercing fork with four rounded prongs (not shown), used for aerating, circa 1915; 11 – digging fork with four prongs and D-handle, circa 1915; 12 – Brades No. 2 'Youth's or Lady's' spade, a lightweight version of the more general garden spade, circa 1910; 13 – five-prong digging fork, double strapped, ash handle with D-shaped grip, circa 1920

'Spring work in a Dutch garden in the sixteenth century'. From The Popular Encyclopedia of Gardening, *circa 1920*

William Small (1843-1929), 'The Kitchen Garden', 1871, watercolour and bodycolour. (Courtesy Christopher Wood Gallery)

Garden Tool Kit Holders.

Made entirely of unbreakable metal.

Preserve your Garden Tools.

The "Gardeners' Complete" Tool Kit Holder.

Floor space occupied, only 18 inches square.

Weight only 16 lbs.

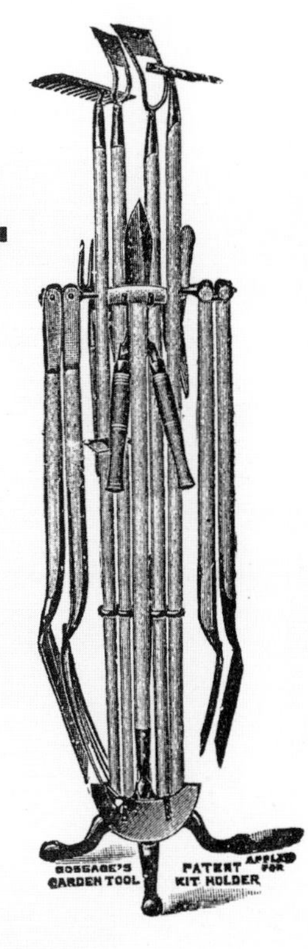

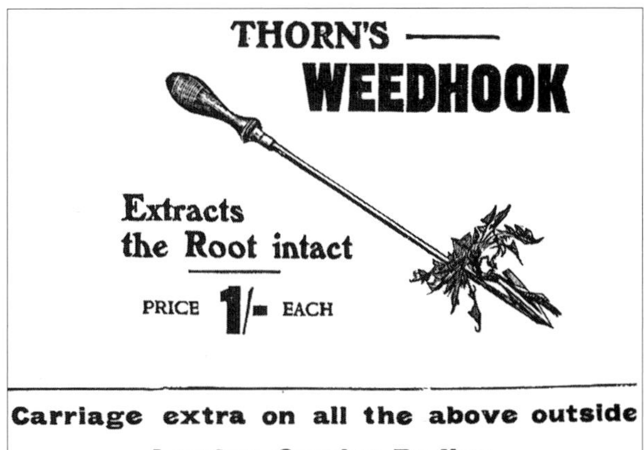

THORN'S ——
WEEDHOOK
Extracts the Root intact
PRICE 1/- EACH
Carriage extra on all the above outside London Carrier Radius.

Gamages of Holborn offered this weedhook in their catalogue, claiming that it 'Extracts the Root intact'. Early twentieth century

Designed to hold eighteen different garden tools, this holder could also be converted into a lawn sprinkler by attaching the sprinkler to the top and a hose to the bottom of the foot. Circa 1911

Complete Garden Tool Baskets.

Buff Gardening Baskets, fitted with Weed Fork, Trowel, Budding Knife, Pruning Scissors, Vine Scissors, Secateurs, Garden Hammer and Reel of Bouquet Wire.

Large size .. **17/9**
Medium size .. **15/6**

A useful selection of gardening tools, well presented for the lady gardener. Circa 1911

An early twentieth century fruit picking ladder

Two open-faced spades. Left, a modified form of mule spade, an early twentieth century Phillip's patent 'Acme Diagonal' digger, the promotion for which reads: 'This tool transforms labour into a pleasant exercise. It enters the earth as easily as a fork. It sub soils the earth and perfectly aerates it. Lightness and strength are its special recommendation.' Although fairly scarce, it must have sold reasonably well since it was in production for at least twenty-five years. Right, a mule spade (sometimes called a fork) for digging heavy soil or clay, the open head attached to the handle by long straps with D-shaped grip, late nineteenth century

A scarce conservatory flower gatherer by Underwood, Haymarket, London, circa 1860, shown against an extract from Thornhill's catalogue of about the same date illustrating their version of a similar product

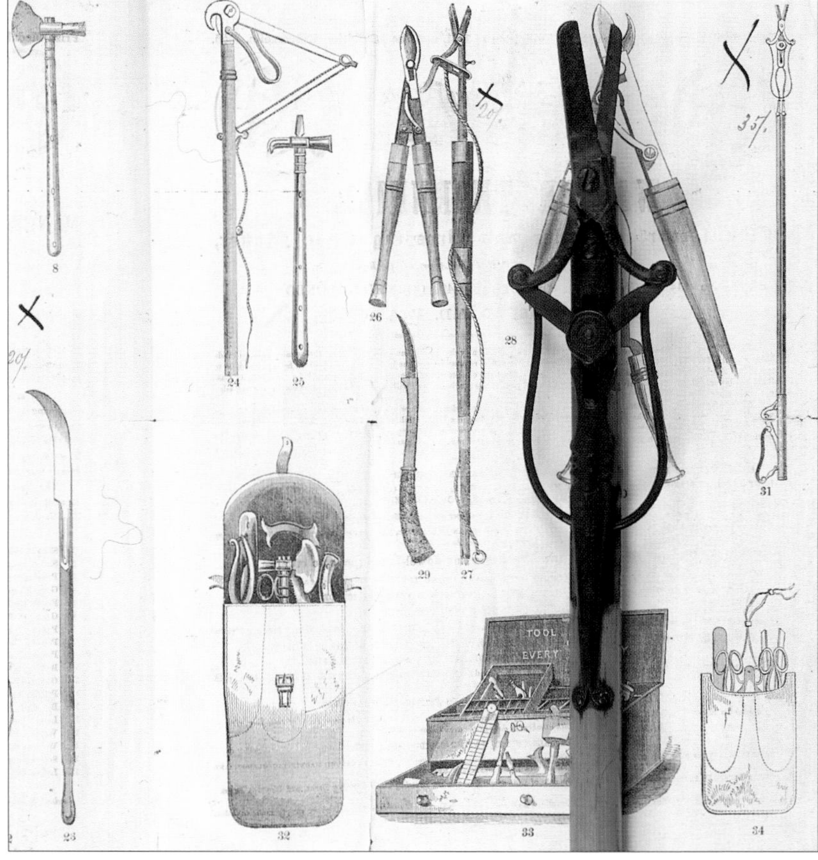

Humphry Repton, from 'Designs for the Pavilion at Brighton' (detail)

Edward George Handel Lucas (1861-1936), 'When the Cat's Away, the Mice Will Play', 1881, oil on panel. (Courtesy Christopher Wood Gallery)

'Garden Shears and Grass or Border Shears', as illustrated in Richard Timmins & Sons, Birmingham, pattern book, c.1845

Thomas James Lloyd (1849-1910), 'Scything the Lawn', 1903, watercolour. (Courtesy Sotheby's)

CUTTING AND TRIMMING

The knife has always been one of the gardener's most useful implements, and the requirement for specialist knives developed strongly in the nineteenth century. Particularly appreciated were folding knives. These came in a wide variety of shapes and sizes and were made by leading Sheffield manufacturers such as William Rodgers and Thomas Turner.

After the knife, shears are another important bladed implement. Examples encountered can date from the eighteenth century and these may carry a maker's stamp; later nineteenth century shears are not usually stamped with makers' marks. Although a specialised field of manufacture, the Sheffield District Trades Directory of 1876 listed no less than fifteen manufacturers.

In the same way scissors for pruning, propagating, etc. were widely available. The secateur was introduced from France in the early nineteenth century, and superseded pruning shears.

Also included in this section are small saws including folding varieties, and another nineteenth century favourite, the asparagus knife; this has a long blade, blunt on both edges except for a short serrated edge on one side.

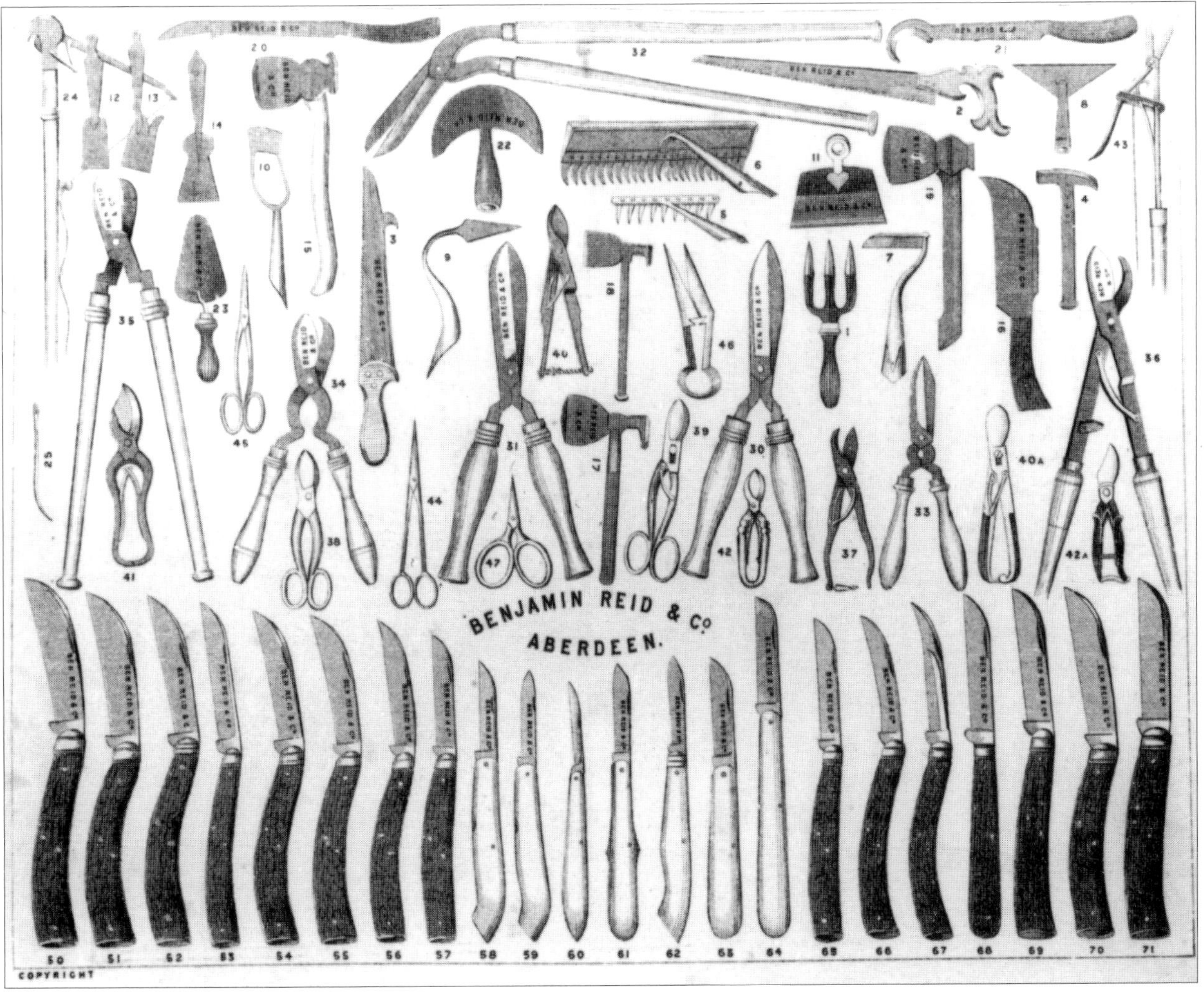

A selection of secateurs, shears, pruning scissors, staghorn pruning knives and ivory handled budding knives, as advertised in the Benjamin Reid & Co. catalogue of circa 1875

A selection of garden hand shears. From top to bottom, small hand shears, early nineteenth century; heavy hand shears with butterfly blade-tightening nut, stamped with initials 'P D' (probably the maker's mark), 60cm.: 25ins. long, probably late eighteenth century; hand shears with large tightening nut to blades, stamped with maker's mark 'V' in oval, early nineteenth century; hand shears with turned handles, early nineteenth century

A selection of shears and secateurs. 1 – extra long shears, 72.5cm.: 28½ins. long, late nineteenth century; 2 – lady's or child's shears, early twentieth century; 3 – Barrow's patent pruning secateurs by Burman & Sons, Birmingham, early twentieth century; 4 – hand shears, early to mid-nineteenth century; 5 – Aubert's patent secateurs by Robt. Sorby, Sheffield, circa 1910; 6 – Levin patent secateurs, circa 1900; 7 – pruning/gathering secateurs with patent date 'Mar.16.97', circa 1900; 8 – lady's or child's shears, circa 1910; 9, 10 and 12 – secateurs, circa 1910-30; 11 – large hand shears, probably eighteenth century, but similar to seventeenth century design, 63cm.: 25ins. long

A selection of multi-cut hedge trimmers. From top to bottom, Code 'Halftime' slide action clipper, centre handle with side acting push/pull ball handle, circa 1930, 53cm.: 21ins. wide; Spong's Garden Hedge Trimmer, with nine teeth arranged in semicircular pattern, 38cm.: 15ins. long, circa 1910 (the company was well known for a range of kitchen equipment, including knife sharpeners); two 'Astor' garden shears, manufactured by the Flexa Lawnmower Co. Ltd., Woking, England, circa 1935, original price 13s. 9d. (68p); the All British 'Little Wonder' hedge clipper, a one-man machine for side cuts up to 4ft. high in one operation, and a one- or two-man machine for top cuts. The promotional material stated: 'Two men with a "Little Wonder" can do in one hour the work that two men with shears would do in an ordinary working day'. Cost in 1938 was £6 18s. 6d. (£6.92 ½p) – quite an intimidating machine; the 'Remex' hedge trimmer, spring operated multi-cut with seventeen teeth, English, mid-twentieth century; 'Astor' type shears, circa 1920

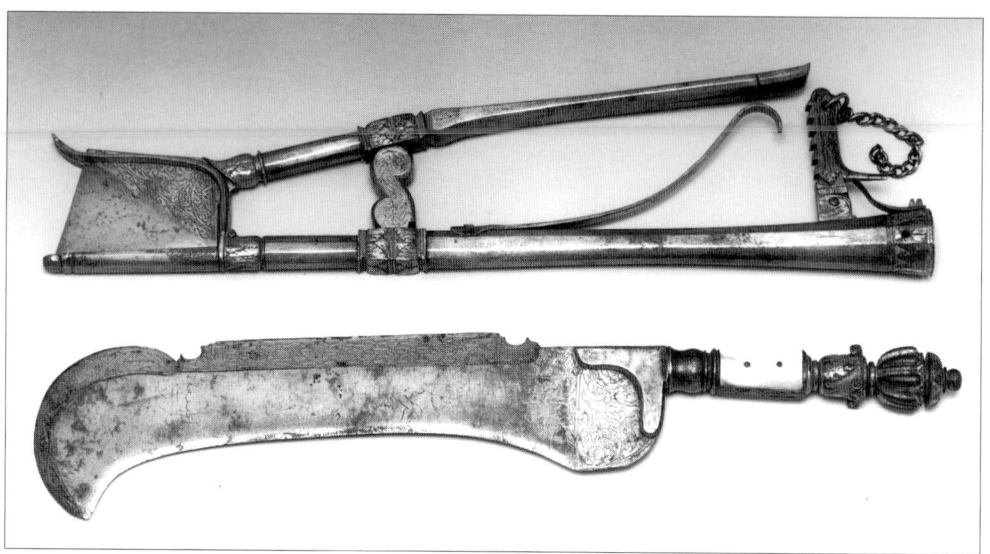

Two fine sixteenth century Italian steel pruning implements, both with engraved decoration. A snickersnee with spring loaded rachet mechanism, 34 cm.: 13½ins. long, and a pruning knife 35 cm.: 13¾ins. long. Whilst most early gardening implements are crudely made these are attractive and desirable collector's pieces

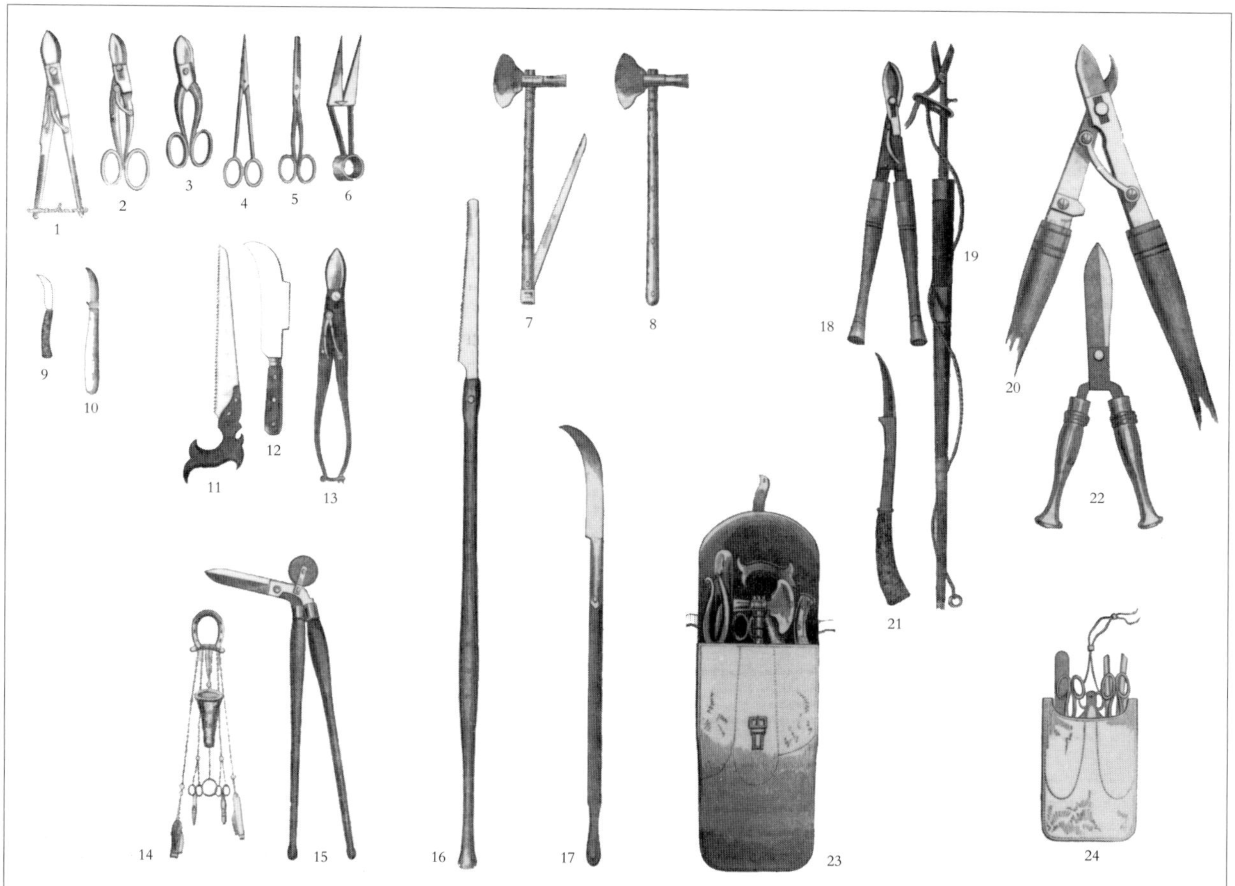

A selection of bladed garden implements from Walter Thornhill's catalogue circa 1860 (see p.189), including 1 – slide pruning shears; 2 – slide pruning shears with bows; 3 – pruning scissors; 4 – grape thinning scissors; 5 – flower gatherer; 6 – grass and box clippers; 7 – pruning hatchet with saw and hammer; 8 – pruning hatchet and hammer; 9 – pruning knife; 10 – budding knife; 11 – pruning saw; 12 – bill hook; 13 – large slide pruning shears; 14 – lady's garden chatelaine; 15 – long handled grass clipper with wheel; 16 – long handled pruning saw; 17 – pruning switch with long handle; 18 – lever pruning shears with long handles; 19 – long handled spring grape and flower gatherer; 20 – pruning shears for large branches; 21 – rose tree pruning knife; 22 – hedge and box cutting shears; 23 – gentleman's portable case of gardening instruments, fitted to order; 24 – lady's portable case of gardening implements

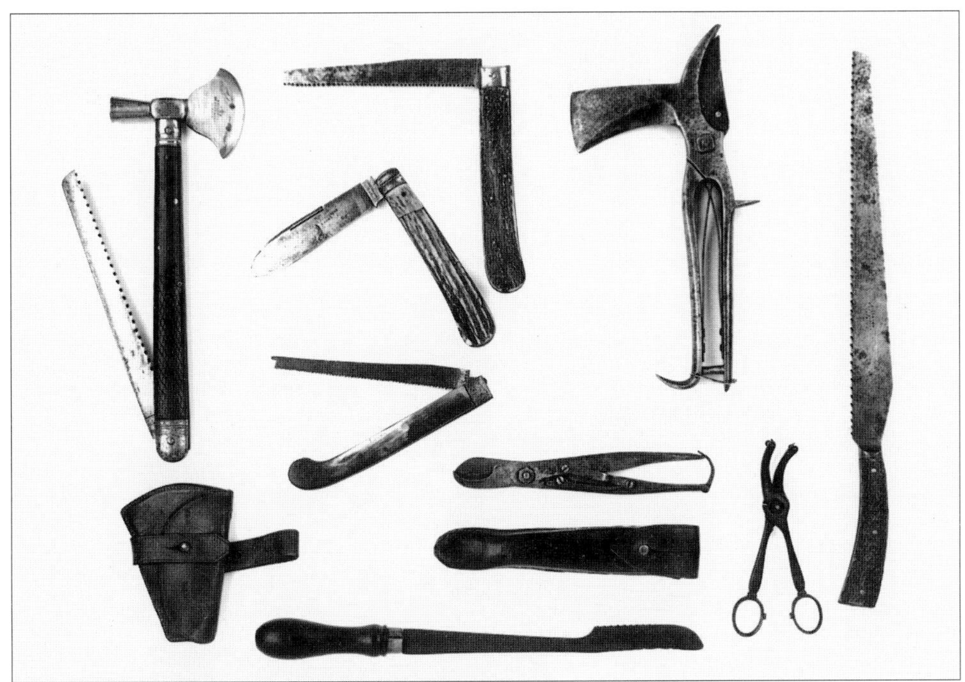

A selection of cutting tools. Top row from left to right, a gardener's axe/hammer/saw by Underwood, stamped with crown and 'VR', mahogany handle with chequered grip incorporating pruning saw, leather cover and belt loop, circa 1860; to the right of the axe, a folding pocket pruning saw and a folding knife, both mid-nineteenth century, and a folding pruning saw, early nineteenth century; a pair of French vine secateurs, mid-nineteenth century; a pruning saw by Hill & Son, early nineteenth century. Bottom row from left to right, a pair of pruners by Skelton, with case, late nineteenth century; a pair of flower gatherers, circa 1912. At the bottom of the picture an asparagus knife, circa 1900

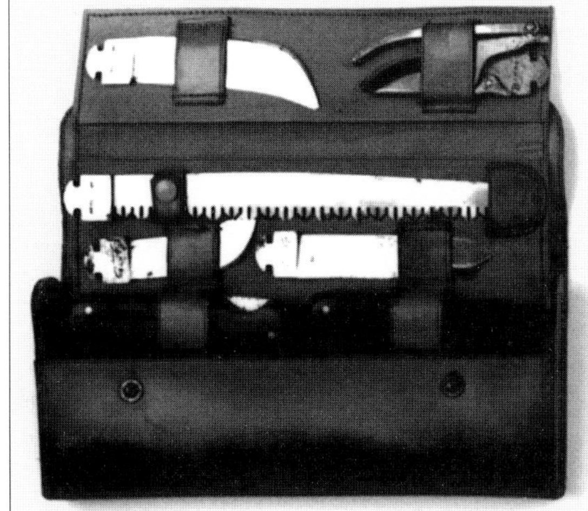

An ingenious and well made Bonsa multi-use garden knife/saw tool set, with interchangeable blades and folding knives in fitted case. German. Circa 1920

The 'Little Wonder' mechanical hedge trimmer. Circa 1930. This 'All British' machine was advertised by Marshalls of New York in their 1927 catalogue in three sizes, a 30ins. one-man machine, 40ins. one- or two-man machine, and 60ins. two-man machine. The largest size cost $35. Also advertised was the electric 'Little Wonder' operated with a one tenth HP General Electric Motor, price $90

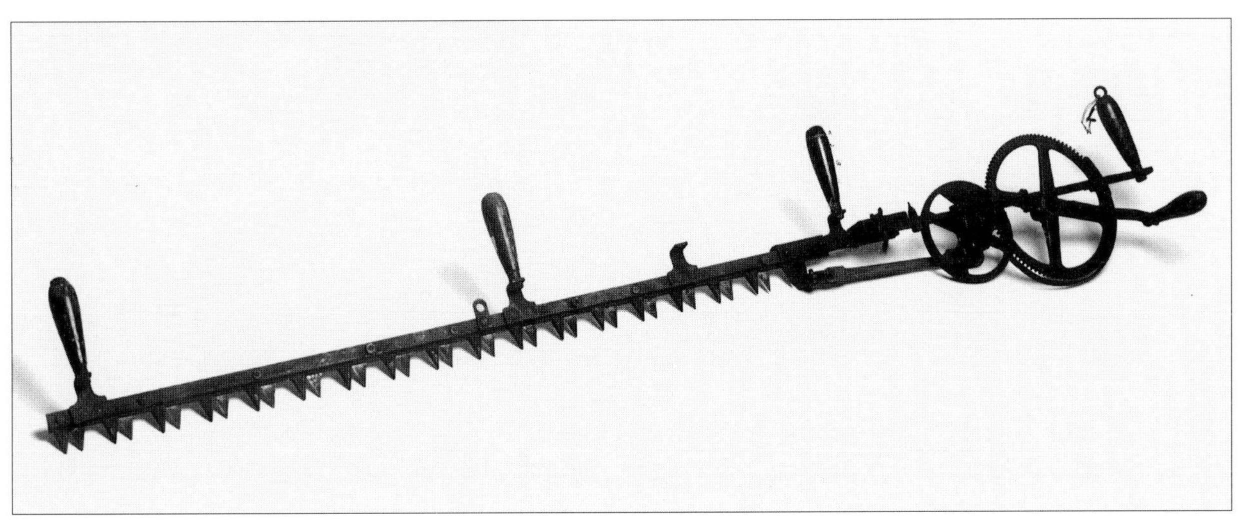

Lawns and Borders

MOWING

Although it may be a tiresome chore, nevertheless great satisfaction can be derived from a well cut lawn. Until the middle of the nineteenth century most lawns had to be cut with a scythe.

In 1830 an engineer, Edwin Budding, invented the lawnmower (see p.208), and this must rank as one of the greatest inventions, if one takes into account of its benefit to gardeners, garden design and maintenance, and recreation. Although an immediate success in terms of efficiency over the scythe, Budding's machine had design faults and other designers and manufacturers, such as Shanks of Arbroath, Ransomes of Ipswich and Green of Leeds, introduced improvements so that the original simple gear-driven machines were overtaken by chain-driven models.

Towards the end of the nineteenth century, competition ensured prices were competitive and almost anyone who wanted a lawn could afford to maintain it. Almost inevitably the Victorians looked to steam to power their mowers, but these were soon superseded by petrol-powered models. Interest in lawnmowers and their development is already strong and a number of museum collections have been formed.

Thomas Green of Leeds began producing lawnmowers in the 1850s, the early machines being gear driven. This is a charming 6ins. cut 'Multum in Parvo' (much in little) model. It was a well recommended machine, and Sydney Beeton thought it 'one of the best of its kind that has yet been produced'. Cost circa 1880 would have been about one guinea (£1.5p). In 6, 7 and 8ins. cut sizes, it would generally have been used for cutting borders. Circa 1880. 15cm.: 6ins. size

A selection of lawnmowers. From back to front, on the seat a simple Ransomes 6ins. cut side-wheel border mower (smaller machines of this type are generally scarcer and more appealing), circa 1910; a Shanks 10ins. cut side-wheel mower, the smallest size from the range which went up to a 16ins. cut, known as 'The Britisher' and bearing the company's cast badge with thistle motif and 'Arbroath', circa 1910; a Ransomes 'Ajax' lawnmower produced only as a 12ins. model for £4 4s. (£4.20), the promotional material stating 'This machine is fitted with ball bearings to the cutting spindle, and patent "Oilite" self aligning bearings to the land roll spindle, this is a new feature', circa 1935.; a 7ins. cut version of the Green 'Multum in Parvo' gear-driven mower with old (apparently original) grass box (grass boxes were often sold separately and therefore are scarce with earlier models), circa 1880; at the front, a Green 'Silens Messor' (silent mower) chain-driven model introduced in the 1880s and evidently a great success, since it remained in production for decades (its grass box is on the seat), circa 1900

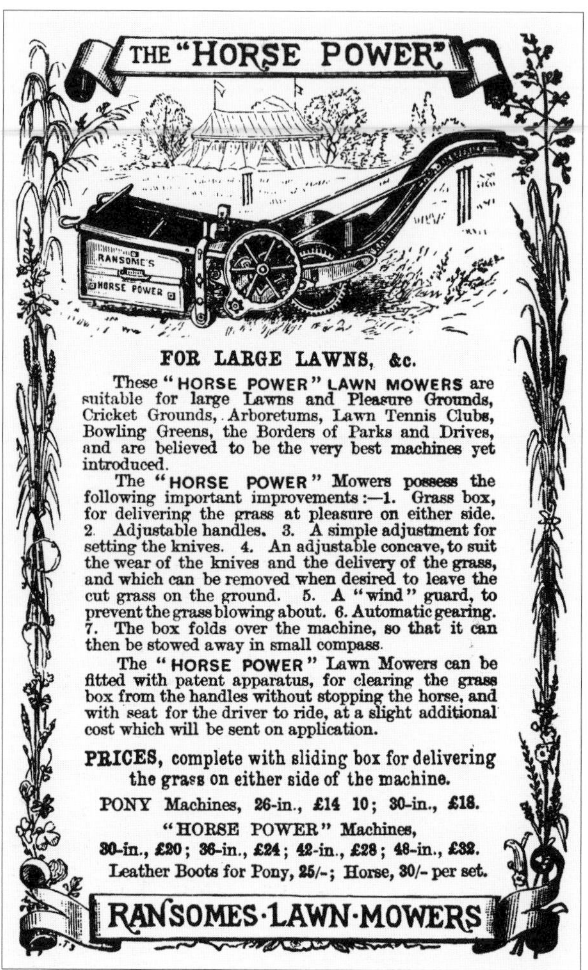

THE "HORSE POWER"
RANSOMES
HORSE POWER
FOR LARGE LAWNS, &c.
These "HORSE POWER" LAWN MOWERS are suitable for large Lawns and Pleasure Grounds, Cricket Grounds, Arboretums, Lawn Tennis Clubs, Bowling Greens, the Borders of Parks and Drives, and are believed to be the very best machines yet introduced.
The "HORSE POWER" Mowers possess the following important improvements:—1. Grass box, for delivering the grass at pleasure on either side. 2. Adjustable handles. 3. A simple adjustment for setting the knives. 4. An adjustable concave, to suit the wear of the knives and the delivery of the grass, and which can be removed when desired to leave the cut grass on the ground. 5. A "wind" guard, to prevent the grass blowing about. 6. Automatic gearing. 7. The box folds over the machine, so that it can then be stowed away in small compass.
The "HORSE POWER" Lawn Mowers can be fitted with patent apparatus, for clearing the grass box from the handles without stopping the horse, and with seat for the driver to ride, at a slight additional cost which will be sent on application.
PRICES, complete with sliding box for delivering the grass on either side of the machine.
PONY Machines, 26-in., £14 10; 30-in., £18.
"HORSE POWER" Machines,
30-in., £20; 36-in., £24; 42-in., £28; 48-in., £32.
Leather Boots for Pony, 25/-; Horse, 30/- per set.
RANSOMES·LAWN·MOWERS

Advertisement for the Ransomes 'Horse Power' lawnmower, also available as a Pony Machine. The harness would be attached to the hooks at the front of the grass box. Circa 1880

SUMNER'S PATENT STEAM
LAWN MOWER.
VERY STRONG
Well Made
AND
Durable.
NO DANGER.
Compact
AND
Neat.
EASY TO WORK.
Steam can be raised in ten minutes from Cold Water.
EASY TO START.
The above represents one of Sumner's patent Steam lawn mowers and roller. As will be seen the engine and boiler is fitted over the machine, and can when desired be fitted to existing Machines.

Advertisement for Sumner's Patent Steam Lawn Mower. Circa 1893

Budding's Patent No.3157 lawnmower. Circa 1832

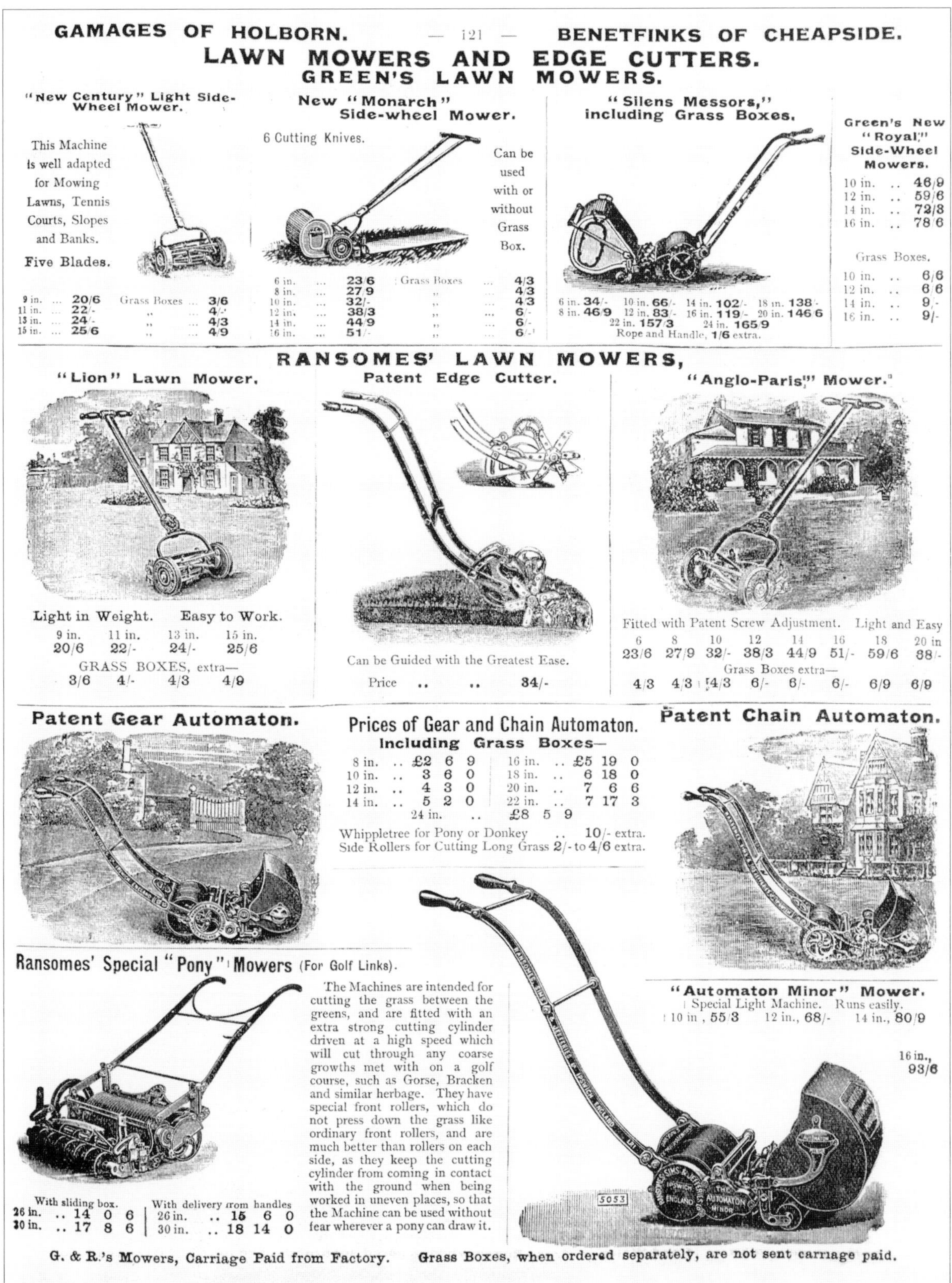

GAMAGES OF HOLBORN. — 121 — BENETFINKS OF CHEAPSIDE.

LAWN MOWERS AND EDGE CUTTERS.

GREEN'S LAWN MOWERS.

"New Century" Light Side-Wheel Mower.

This Machine is well adapted for Mowing Lawns, Tennis Courts, Slopes and Banks.

Five Blades.

		Grass Boxes	
9 in.	20/6	Grass Boxes	3/6
11 in.	22/-	,,	4/-
13 in.	24/-	,,	4/3
15 in.	25/6	,,	4/9

New "Monarch" Side-wheel Mower.

6 Cutting Knives.

Can be used with or without Grass Box.

		Grass Boxes	
6 in.	23/6	Grass Boxes	4/3
8 in.	27/9	,,	4/3
10 in.	32/-	,,	4/3
12 in.	38/3	,,	6/-
14 in.	44/9	,,	6/-
16 in.	51/-	,,	6/-

"Silens Messors," including Grass Boxes.

6 in. 34/- 10 in. 66/- 14 in. 102/- 18 in. 138/-
8 in. 46/9 12 in. 83/- 16 in. 119/- 20 in. 146/6
22 in. 157/3 24 in. 165/9
Rope and Handle, 1/6 extra.

Green's New "Royal" Side-Wheel Mowers.

10 in.	46/9
12 in.	59/6
14 in.	72/3
16 in.	78/6

Grass Boxes.

10 in.	6/6
12 in.	6/6
14 in.	9/-
16 in.	9/-

RANSOMES' LAWN MOWERS,

"Lion" Lawn Mower.

Light in Weight. Easy to Work.

9 in.	11 in.	13 in.	15 in.
20/6	22/-	24/-	25/6

GRASS BOXES, extra—

3/6	4/-	4/3	4/9

Patent Edge Cutter.

Can be Guided with the Greatest Ease.

Price 34/-

"Anglo-Paris" Mower.

Fitted with Patent Screw Adjustment. Light and Easy

6	8	10	12	14	16	18	20 in
23/6	27/9	32/-	38/3	44/9	51/-	59/6	88/-

Grass Boxes extra—

4/3	4/3	4/3	6/-	6/-	6/-	6/9	6/9

Patent Gear Automaton.

Prices of Gear and Chain Automaton. Including Grass Boxes—

8 in.	£2	6	9		16 in.	£5	19	0
10 in.	3	6	0		18 in.	6	18	0
12 in.	4	3	0		20 in.	7	6	6
14 in.	5	2	0		22 in.	7	17	3
					24 in.	£8	5	9

Whippletree for Pony or Donkey .. 10/- extra.
Side Rollers for Cutting Long Grass 2/- to 4/6 extra.

Patent Chain Automaton.

Ransomes' Special "Pony" Mowers (For Golf Links).

The Machines are intended for cutting the grass between the greens, and are fitted with an extra strong cutting cylinder driven at a high speed which will cut through any coarse growths met with on a golf course, such as Gorse, Bracken and similar herbage. They have special front rollers, which do not press down the grass like ordinary front rollers, and are much better than rollers on each side, as they keep the cutting cylinder from coming in contact with the ground when being worked in uneven places, so that the Machine can be used without fear wherever a pony can draw it.

With sliding box.				With delivery from handles			
26 in.	14	0	6	26 in.	15	6	0
30 in.	17	8	6	30 in.	18	14	0

"Automaton Minor" Mower.

Special Light Machine. Runs easily.

10 in., 55/3 12 in., 68/- 14 in., 80/9 16 in., 93/6

G. & R.'s Mowers, Carriage Paid from Factory. Grass Boxes, when ordered separately, are not sent carriage paid.

Gamages' catalogue selection of early twentieth century side-wheel gear- and chain-driven lawnmowers. Note the 'Patent Edge Cutter'. The 'Pony Mower' (also suitable to be pulled by a donkey) was for use on golf courses and larger areas of lawn. Circa 1914

Eyre Crowe (1824-1910), 'A Quiet Read', oil on canvas, 1878. (Courtesy Christopher Wood Gallery)

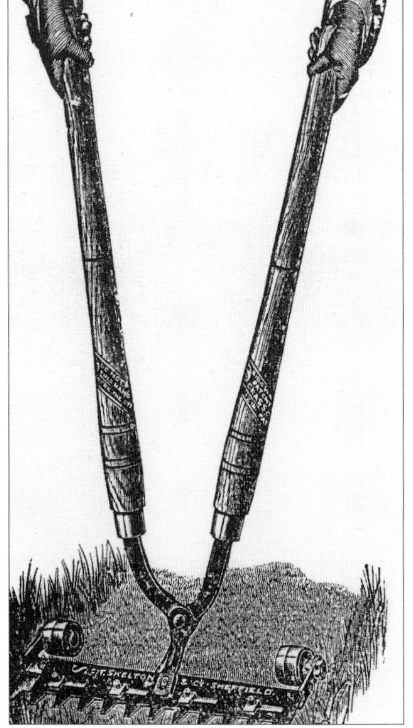

Ridgway's 'Best Black Clippers, a patent grass-cutting machine first introduced circa 1885. The advertisement illustration, showing cutters manufactured by Skelton of Sheffield circa 1911, was accompanied by the directions: 'Always give the full throw of the top knife over the bottom by moving the "right" handle only as far as it will go to and fro'. *See also p.215*

Humphry Repton (1752-1818), from 'Designs for the Pavilion at Brighton'

Lawnmowing with horses, circa 1900

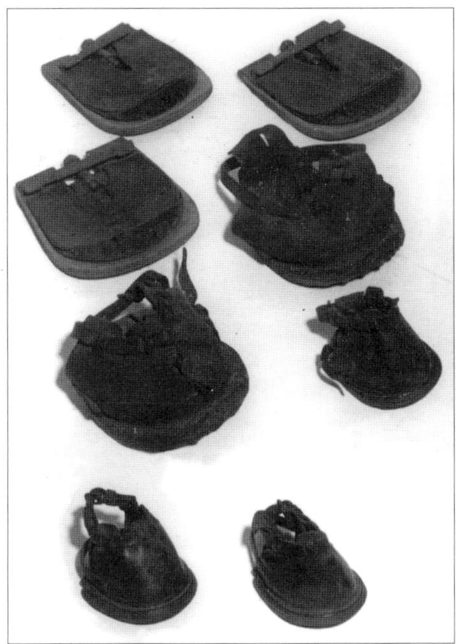

A set of four mint condition block sole leather horse lawnmowing boots for use by a cob. Early twentieth century

As horses, ponies or donkeys were used to pull lawnmowers, their hooves might leave depressions on the grass. To eliminate this problem to some degree leather boots were produced. The illustration shows three bore gauges, two leather horse boots and three leather pony boots. Late nineteenth/early twentieth century

ROLLING

It is generally accepted that rolling is good for an established lawn, and that it is also a requirement for preparation of a lawn or path.

The earliest rollers were of stone or wood, and a number of stone rollers survive from the eighteenth century, usually with wrought iron handles. The stone to the roller is not always perfectly formed and consequently such rollers can be difficult to move and do not necessarily give perfect results. Similarly early wooden rollers would have been made from tree trunks which also tend to give imperfect service. Cast iron was taken up as an obvious improvement and these rollers were in use in the late eighteenth century. Parson Woodforde, who recorded so many interesting snippets of information in his diaries, wrote on Wednesday 11 June, 1794: 'Sent Ben early this morning to Norwich with my great Cart after my new Garden Roller of Cast Iron . . . It is a very clever roller and is called a ballance roller, as the handle never goes to the ground. It is certainly very expensive but certainly also very handy. The roller amounts in the whole to £4.0.0. viz: cast iron 2cwt, 2grs. 26lb, at 2½d per lb, £2.17.6. Hammer'd iron 40lb at 6¾d. £1.2.6.' Woodforde has given us some useful insights to cost – £4 would have represented a costly purchase two hundred years ago; note also the relative costs of cast iron to wrought iron. Wrought iron would have been used for the handle.

Parson Woodforde's ballance [sic] roller must have been the latest thing, and although it is almost certainly a nineteenth century example, the large cast iron balance roller seen on p.215 is probably similar. These rollers would have been single cylinder form. Whilst satisfactory to a certain degree, the sharp edges of the roller might cut into the grass when the roller was being manoeuvred. Improvements in design in the nineteenth century lead to the introduction of the double cylinder roller with rounded edges which could be turned more easily, and to rollers ballasted with water or sand, which greatly increased their weight.

Three stone rollers of eighteenth century type with wrought iron handles, sizes vary from the very small 32cm.: 12½ins. wide (centre) to 76cm.: 30ins. wide (left). Stone rollers would have been heavy to draw and would probably be used for gravel walks. In the early nineteenth century stone rollers were largely superseded by cast iron rollers

Wooden rollers continued to be used for a considerable period, and solid elm rollers were certainly still being produced until the outbreak of the Second World War. Illustrated with the late nineteenth century roller is a turf barrow of about the same period. Roller 49cm.: 19ins. wide

Three stone rollers, late eighteenth/early nineteenth century. Note the varieties of wrought and cast iron handle and frame shape. The largest 112cm.: 44ins. wide

A nineteenth century stone roller with wrought iron frame

English Provincial School, 'On the Terrace, Holmwood, Tunbridge Wells', watercolour, circa 1850

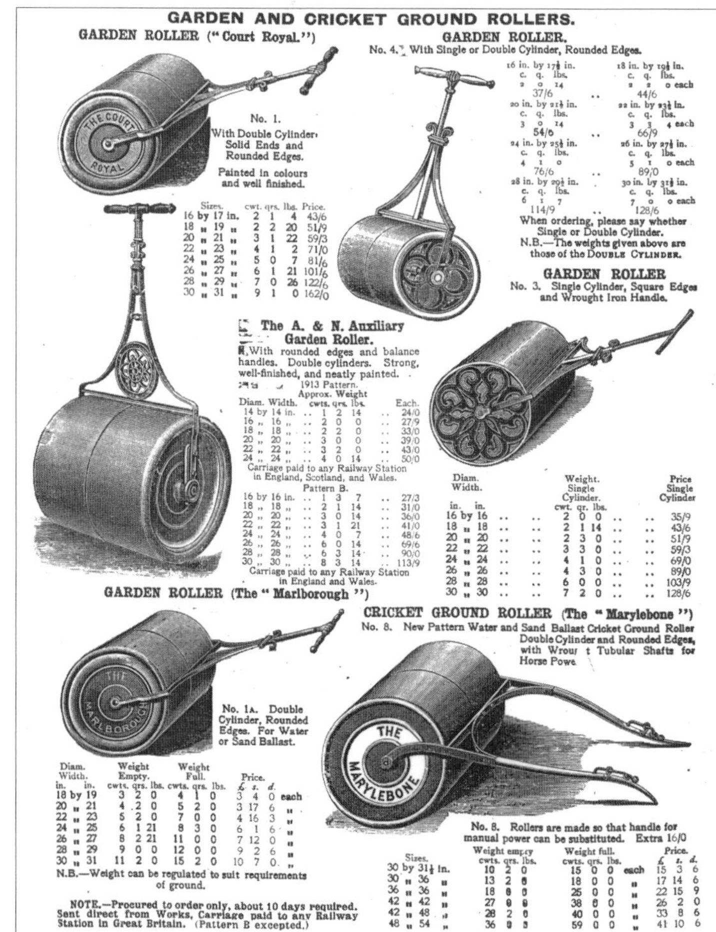

GARDEN AND CRICKET GROUND ROLLERS.

GARDEN ROLLER ("Court Royal.")

No. 1.
With Double Cylinder, Solid Ends and Rounded Edges.
Painted in colours and well finished.

Sizes.	cwt.	qrs.	lbs.	Price.
16 by 17 in.	2	1	4	43/6
18 " 19 "	2	2	20	51/9
20 " 21 "	3	1	22	59/3
22 " 23 "	4	1	2	71/0
24 " 25 "	5	0	7	81/6
26 " 27 "	6	1	21	101/6
28 " 29 "	7	0	26	122/6
30 " 31 "	9	1	0	162/0

GARDEN ROLLER.
No. 4. With Single or Double Cylinder, Rounded Edges.

Size	c. q. lbs.	Price	Size	c. q. lbs.	Price
16 in. by 17½ in.	2 0 14	37/6	18 in. by 19½ in.	2 2 0 each	44/6
20 in. by 21½ in.	3 0 14	54/6	22 in. by 23½ in.	3 3 4 each	66/9
24 in. by 25½ in.	4 1 0	76/6	26 in. by 27½ in.	5 1 0 each	89/0
28 in. by 29½ in.	6 1 7	114/9	30 in. by 31½ in.	7 0 0 each	128/6

When ordering, please say whether Single or Double Cylinder.
N.B.—The weights given above are those of the DOUBLE CYLINDER.

GARDEN ROLLER
No. 3. Single Cylinder, Square Edges and Wrought Iron Handle.

Diam. Width. in. in.	Weight. Single Cylinder. cwt. qr. lbs.	Price Single Cylinder
16 by 16	2 0 0	35/9
18 " 18	2 1 14	43/6
20 " 20	2 3 0	51/9
22 " 22	3 3 0	59/3
24 " 24	4 1 0	69/0
26 " 26	4 3 0	89/0
28 " 28	6 0 0	103/9
30 " 30	7 2 0	128/6

The A. & N. Auxiliary Garden Roller.
With rounded edges and balance handles. Double cylinders. Strong, well-finished, and neatly painted.

1913 Pattern.

Diam. Width.	Approx. Weight cwts. qrs. lbs.	Each.
14 by 14 in.	1 2 14	24/0
16 " 16 "	2 0 0	27/9
18 " 18 "	2 2 0	33/0
20 " 20 "	3 0 0	39/0
22 " 22 "	3 2 0	43/0
24 " 24 "	4 0 14	50/0

Carriage paid to any Railway Station in England, Scotland, and Wales.

Pattern B.

Diam. Width.	cwts. qrs. lbs.	Each.
16 by 16 in.	1 3 7	27/3
18 " 18 "	2 1 14	31/0
20 " 20 "	3 0 14	36/0
22 " 22 "	3 1 21	41/0
24 " 24 "	4 0 7	48/6
26 " 26 "	6 0 14	69/6
28 " 28 "	6 3 14	90/0
30 " 30 "	8 3 14	113/9

Carriage paid to any Railway Station in England and Wales.

GARDEN ROLLER (The "Marlborough")

No. 1A. Double Cylinder, Rounded Edges. For Water or Sand Ballast.

Diam. Width. in. in.	Weight Empty. cwts. qrs. lbs.	Weight Full. cwts. qrs. lbs.	Price. £ s. d.	
18 by 19	3 2 0	4 1 0	3 4 0	each
20 " 21	4 2 0	5 2 0	3 17 6	"
22 " 23	5 2 0	7 0 0	4 16 3	"
24 " 25	6 1 21	8 3 0	6 1 6	"
26 " 27	8 2 21	11 0 0	7 12 0	"
28 " 29	9 0 0	12 0 0	9 2 6	"
30 " 31	11 2 0	15 2 0	10 7 0	"

N.B.—Weight can be regulated to suit requirements of ground.

NOTE.—Procured to order only, about 10 days required. Sent direct from Works, Carriage paid to any Railway Station in Great Britain. (Pattern B excepted.)

CRICKET GROUND ROLLER (The "Marylebone")
No. 8. New Pattern Water and Sand Ballast Cricket Ground Roller Double Cylinder and Rounded Edges, with Wrou t Tubular Shafts for Horse Powe

No. 8. Rollers are made so that handle for manual power can be substituted. Extra 16/0

Sizes.	Weight empty cwts. qrs. lbs.	Weight full. cwts. qrs. lbs.		Price. £ s. d.
30 by 31½ in.	10 2 0	15 0 0	each	15 3 6
30 " 36 "	13 2 0	18 0 0	"	17 14 6
36 " 36 "	18 0 0	25 0 0	"	22 15 9
42 " 42 "	27 0 0	38 0 0	"	26 2 0
42 " 48 "	28 2 0	40 0 0	"	33 8 6
48 " 54 "	36 0 0	59 0 0	"	41 10 6

A catalogue selection of garden rollers, and one cricket ground roller which could be ordered at up to 4½ ft. wide. 1913

A selection of rollers and other garden accessories. At the back in the wooden wheelbarrow a handlight top; just visible leaning against the door Ridgway's 'Best Black Clippers' (see also p.210); outside the shed, at the back on the left, an S.I.F. 'Suffolk' Auto lawn tennis court marker, early twentieth century; at the back on the right, a large cast iron balance roller, probably early nineteenth century, 168cm.: 66ins. high; front left, a stone roller, early nineteenth century, 69cm.: 27ins. wide; front right, a 'Kenbar' double cylinder cast iron garden roller, late nineteenth century, 41cm.: 16ins. wide; hanging on the wall, three garden lines and a Wm. Paul of Paisley lawn aerator with hollow tines, circa 1930; leaning against the wall a simple rotating aerator, circa 1910

FETCHING AND CARRYING

It is not known exactly when the wheelbarrow was invented. Certainly they were in use in the Middle Ages and John Evelyn shows us examples we would instantly recognise in perhaps the most famous illustration of mid-seventeenth century tools and accessories intended for inclusion in his *Elysium Britannicum*. Barrows generally have a frame made of elm or ash, while the sides and bottom may be of softer wood and the wheel iron or wood with iron tyre. They came in various forms depending on the task. Apart from the usual garden barrow, Loudon noted the separating barrow, the ground work barrow, the haulm barrow, the Normandy barrow, the flower pot barrow and the hand barrow. In fact three of these (the hand barrow, the flower pot barrow and the haulm barrow) have no wheel and are merely means of lifting and carrying.

Although metal barrows had been noted in the late eighteenth century, it was not until the late nineteenth century that wrought iron frame barrows with galvanised bodies became popular. Wooden barrows continued in production until the middle of the present century, although they were fitted with pneumatic tyres. The metal wheelbarrow, now finds itself challenged by the plastic ballbarrow.

A late Victorian garden barrow, probably ash frame with elm body, scratch decoration, iron supports, iron tyred wooden spoked wheel. 114cm.: 45ins. long

A Victorian style wooden wheelbarrow, bolted hardwood construction, four spoked wheel with iron tyre. 150cm.: 59ins. long

Clémence van den Broeck (b.1843), 'The Gardener's Barrow'

A child's wooden wheelbarrow with solid wooden wheel. Early twentieth century. 78cm.: 31ins. long

A garden hand barrow with slatted wooden top, the side guards stencilled 'GARDEN', iron supports to frame. Circa 1920. 200cm.: 78ins. long overall. Examples with tray tops are more common and are used for carrying a number of pots and plants

A simple hand barrow, probably late nineteenth century, for carrying large plants in tubs or pots. Beeton noted that 'if a number of plants or pots have to be carried at one time, it is better to add legs to the frame, and place a low railing round the platform'

SEED DEPARTMENT—*contd.*

WHEELBARROWS.

ROUND FRONT BARROW. No. 14 (G). Mounted on strong angle iron frame, fitted with unbreakable steel wheel, extra strong body with band round top; suitable for garden or farm use.

No.	Long.	Wide.	Painted all over.	Galvanized Body.	Galvanized all over.
1	36 in.	26 in.	27/9	33/6	37/9
2	38 "	28 "	32/3	37/9	41/6

COAL BARROW, No. 15 (G). Angle iron frame and unbreakable steel wheel; specially made for carrying coal or coke.

No.	Length. Top.	Width. Top.	Painted all over.	Galvanized Body.	Galvanized all over.
1	32 in.	24 in.	23/9	26/6	31/3
2	35 "	26 "	26/6	29/9	33/9

GARDEN BARROW

No. 16 (G).

On strong frame. Suitable for all general garden purposes.

No.	Size of Bodies.	Galvanized all over.	Galvanized Body.	Painted all over.
0	23 by 21 in.	15/3	18/6	14/6
1	28 " 23 "	17/6	21/2	16/9
2	31 " 26 "	20/9	25/4	19/6
3	36 " 30 "	24/6	29/3	22/9
4	38 " 32 "	27/9	33/9	26/6

ANGLE IRON BARROW, No. 18 (G). Made on strong angle iron frames, unbreakable steel wheels, and strong welded band round the top; galvanized body.

No. 1.	No. 2.	No. 3.
28 by 25 in., 20/10	33 by 27 in., 23/9	35 by 29 in., 26/6

NOTE.—The above procured to order only, about 5 days required. Sent direct from Works, carriage paid on all orders of 35/- within Carter, Paterson & Co.'s London Suburban radius; and of 53/- to nearest Railway Station in England.

This Note applies only to goods marked (G).

STRONG WROUGHT-IRON WHEEL-BARROW

With Steel Body.

Special value.

No. 10. (R)

No. 10 pattern.	Length at top.	Width at top.	Depth at front.	Depth at back.	Painted body.	Galvzd body.
Size 1	2 ft. 6 in.	2 ft. 1 in.	13 in.	5 in.	26/0	28/3
Size 2	2 ft. 9 in.	2 ft. 3 in.	15 in.	6 in.	28/0	30/3

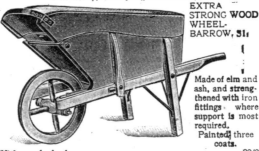

WOOD WHEEL-BARROWS (R).

Made of hard-wood and fitted with strong wrought-iron stays.

No. 71. Size of body inside, 32 by 22½ in. Painted 3 coats.

With wrought-iron wheel 35/8
With wood wheel 35/8

Shifting top boards for the above, 8/8 extra.

No. 71S. A smaller size, with cast wheel; size of body, 25½ by 18½ in. 27/0

No. 72. BOX GARDEN BARROW, unpainted, with wood wheel 22/3

If fitted with top boards 30/9

If painted 3 coats, 4/6 extra.

No. 898. With hardwood frame and 1-in. elm sides, fitted with wood wheel, and removable back board; unpainted.

Length at top.	Width at top.	Length at bottom.	Width at bottom.	Depth at front.	Price.
36 in.	24 in.	22 in.	19 in.	20 in.	25/0

NOTE.—The above procured to order only, about 10 days required. Carriage paid on orders of 49/- to nearest Railway Station in England and Wales; also to Edinburgh, Dublin, and Belfast.

This note applies only to goods marked (R).

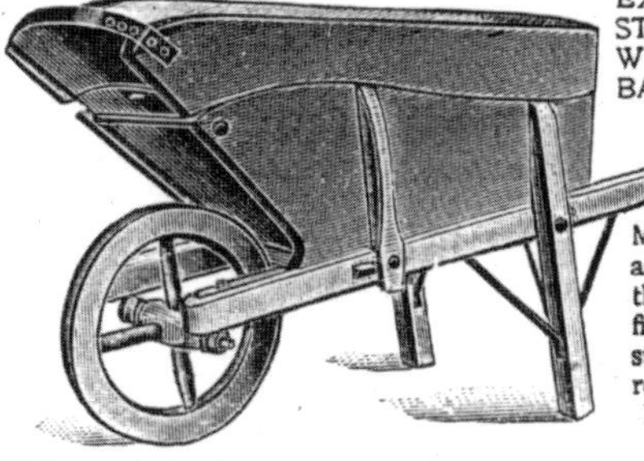

EXTRA STRONG **WOOD** WHEEL-BARROW, **31.**

Made of **elm** and ash, and **strengthened with** iron **fittings** where **support is** most **required.**

Painted three **coats.**

With wood wheel 29/0
Fitted with shifting top boards 36/0

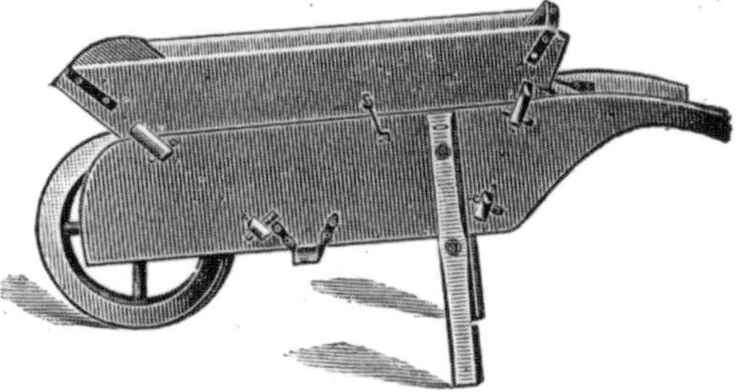

BOX GARDEN BARROW, C2. With wood wheel and shifting top boards; painted three coats 30/0

NOTE.—Nos. S1 and C2 procured to order, about 5 days required. Sent direct from Work, carriage paid in London only.

For other patterns of Wheelbarrows, see page 55.

A selection of metal and wood wheelbarrows, two of the wood examples with extendable sides, 1913 catalogue

Attr. James Crawford Thom (1835-1898), 'In the Cart', oil on board. (Courtesy Sotheby's)

'The carnation, the ranunculus, and the auricula, have each their devotees . . .' From Rowlandson's England, by Robert Southey, *ed. John Steel, 1985*

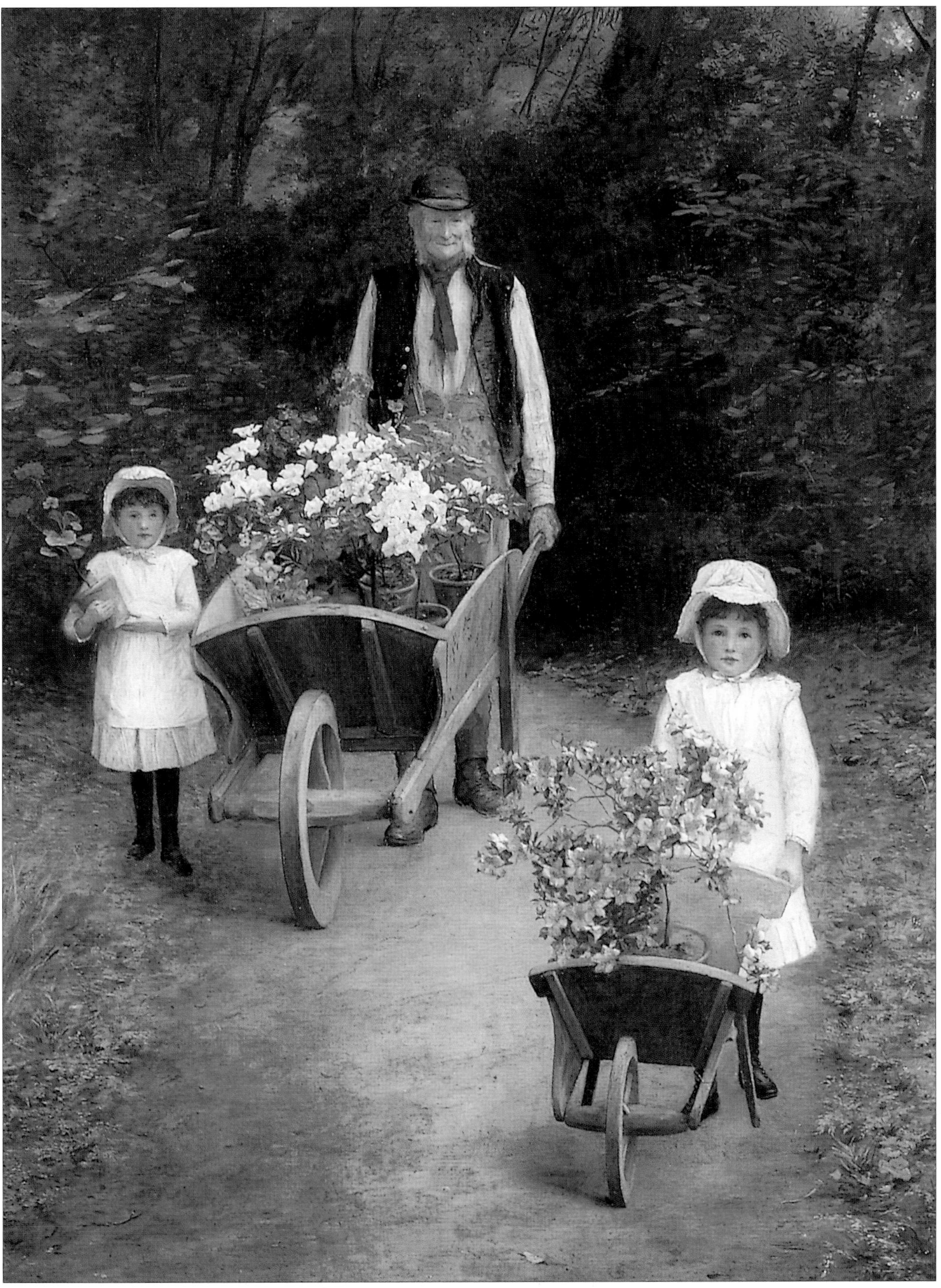

Mary Hayllar (fl.1880-1885), 'Helping Gardener', oil on canvas, 1884. (Courtesy Sotheby's)

EDGINGS

All manner of materials can be used for edging paths and flower borders. The most obvious and oldest is stone; later, wood and metal were used, as were sheep, horse and cattle knucklebones which seem to have been favoured in the seventeenth century. In the eighteenth century narrow plates of clay tile were used, sometimes with simple cut ornament. As we enter the nineteenth century cast iron was also used.

Mass production of relatively inexpensive earthenware edging tiles in the middle of the nineteenth century allowed Victorian gardeners to define pathways and borders with a variety of shapes, some of which are still produced and sold in larger garden centres.

As an alternative, or in addition to edging tiles, wire borders had been a popular choice since Regency times and a hundred years later (circa 1913) attractive wire borderings could still be easily obtained from mail order catalogues.

Another early nineteenth century delight was the iron wire basket edging which Loudon included in his *Encyclopedia of Gardening*, where he recorded 'Its use is to enclose dug spots on lawns, so that, when the flowers and shrubs cover the surface, they appear to grow from, or give some allusion to, a basket.' In addition Loudon noted that 'these articles [are] also formed in cast iron, and are used as edgings to beds and plots in plant stores and conservatories.' Basket edgings have been making a comeback.

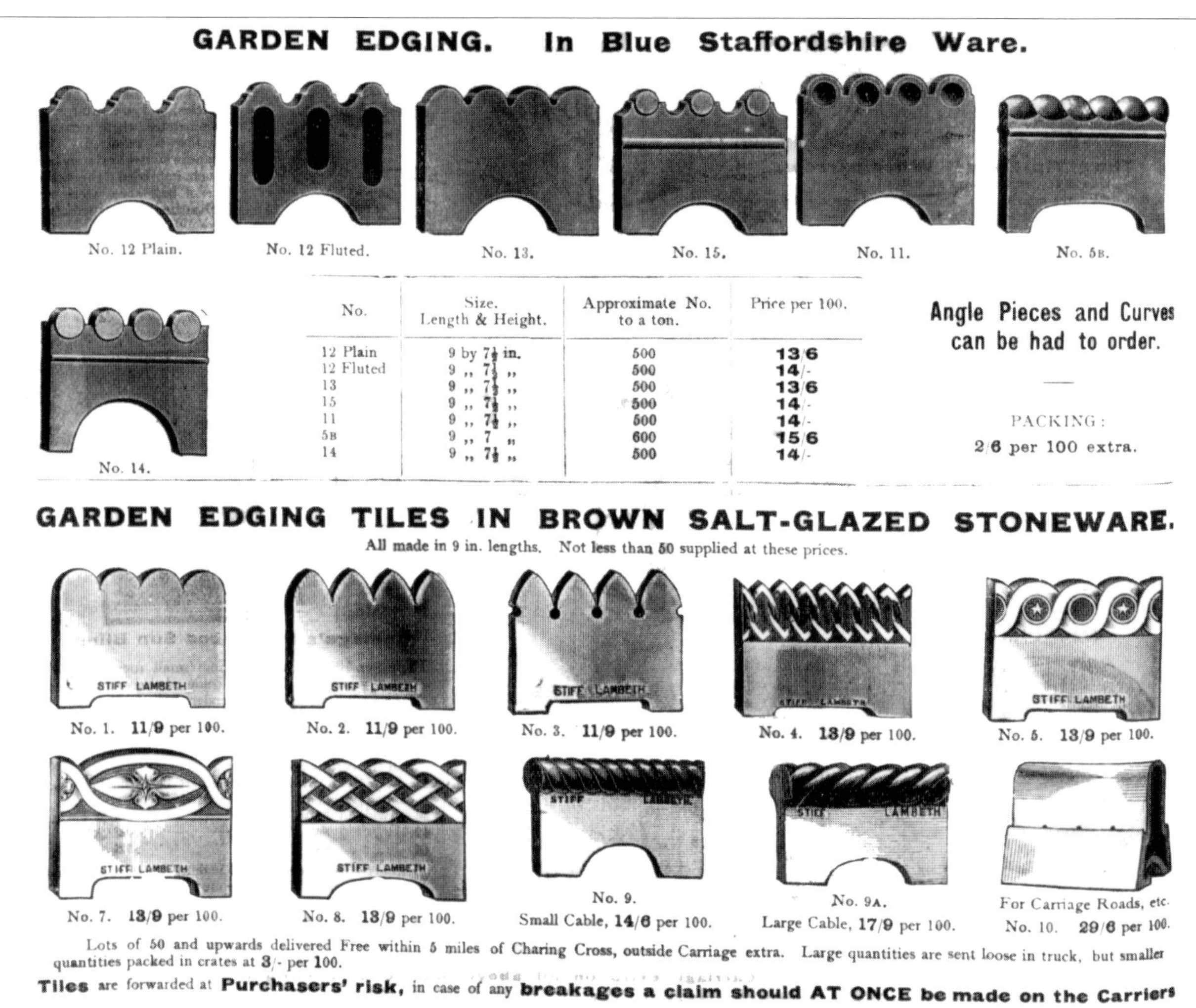

GARDEN EDGING. In Blue Staffordshire Ware.

No. 12 Plain. No. 12 Fluted. No. 13. No. 15. No. 11. No. 5B. No. 14.

No.	Size. Length & Height.	Approximate No. to a ton.	Price per 100.
12 Plain	9 by 7½ in.	500	13/6
12 Fluted	9 ,, 7½ ,,	500	14/-
13	9 ,, 7½ ,,	500	13/6
15	9 ,, 7½ ,,	500	14/-
11	9 ,, 7½ ,,	500	14/-
5B	9 ,, 7 ,,	600	15/6
14	9 ,, 7½ ,,	500	14/-

Angle Pieces and Curves can be had to order.

PACKING: 2/6 per 100 extra.

GARDEN EDGING TILES IN BROWN SALT-GLAZED STONEWARE.

All made in 9 in. lengths. Not less than 50 supplied at these prices.

No. 1. 11/9 per 100. No. 2. 11/9 per 100. No. 3. 11/9 per 100. No. 4. 13/9 per 100. No. 5. 13/9 per 100.

No. 7. 13/9 per 100. No. 8. 13/9 per 100. No. 9. Small Cable, 14/6 per 100. No. 9A. Large Cable, 17/9 per 100. For Carriage Roads, etc. No. 10. 29/6 per 100.

Lots of 50 and upwards delivered Free within 5 miles of Charing Cross, outside Carriage extra. Large quantities are sent loose in truck, but smaller quantities packed in crates at 3/- per 100.

Tiles are forwarded at Purchasers' risk, in case of any breakages a claim should AT ONCE be made on the Carriers

A catalogue selection of early twentieth century tiles: at the top, Staffordshire products; below a selection of London wares manufactured by Stiff. James Stiff had worked for Doulton & Watts before starting his own company which was sold to Doulton in 1913

Variations of earthenware edging tiles including three types of cable or rope design and a deeper, squarer tile, the top decorated with roundels centred by star motifs. 25cm.: 10ins. high. Tiles of very similar style are still made today

An elaborate arrangement of edging tiles in glazed earthenware, probably late nineteenth century. The border tile, with three arched panels centred with flowering plants, is shown with two matching uprights. Tile 30cm.: 12ins. wide

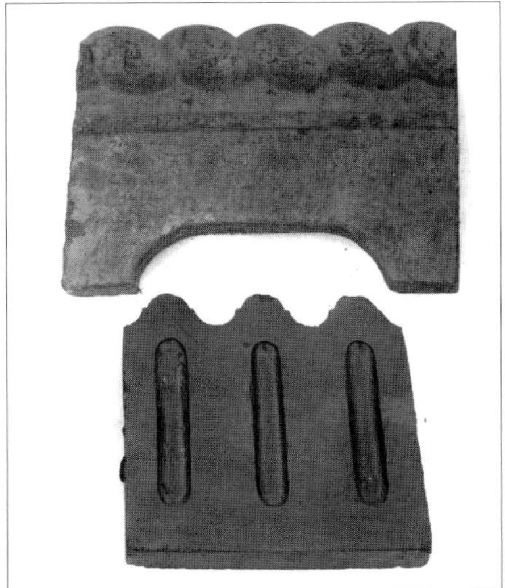

Two examples similar to the Staffordshire products of the early twentieth century (opposite), the cable or rope top being a popular design

BORDER ARCHES, No. 197.

Made of spiral iron, galvanized.
Easily fixed to any shaped lawn or flower beds.

Each arch .... 9 in.......	12 in.	15 in. wide.
1/10	2/3	2/8 per doz

GALVANIZED WIRE GARDEN BORDERINGS.

Strong quality. Made of Hard Wire Lattice.

No. 200A.

In 3 ft. lengths, ¾ in. mesh, including spikes for fixing.

6 in.	9 in.	12 in.	15 in. high.
0/7	0/9	0/11	1/1 each.
6/9	8/3	9/9	11/9 per doz.

No. 204A.

In 3 ft. lengths, 1 in. mesh, strong, including spikes for fixing.

6 in.	9 in.	12 in.........	15 in. high.
0/8	0/10	1/0	1/3 each.
7/9	9/6	11/6	14/0 per doz.

Extra Spikes, Galvanized.

For 6 in.	9 in.	12 in.	15 in. Borderings.
0/9	0/11	1/4	1/10 per doz.

WIRE BASKET WITH HANDLE.

No. 670.

A catalogue selection of wirework: border arches, borderings, and a wonderful 'wire basket with handle' available to almost any diameter. Circa 1913

Inspired by a drawing in Humphry Repton's Red Book for Brighton Pavilion, wrought iron flowerbed surrounds of arcaded form with rope twist base

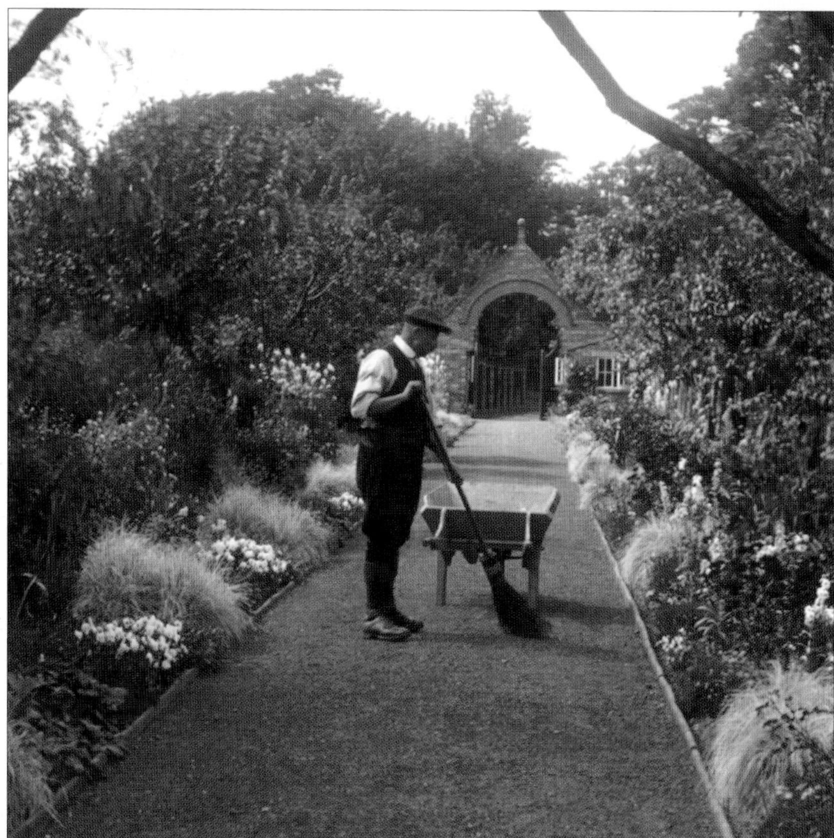

The New Kitchen Garden. From Vale Royal Abbey, Cheshire, 1915 album

Humphry Repton (1752-1818) and J. Adey Repton, 'Sunshine After Rain', watercolour

Joseph Kirkpatrick (b.1872), 'The Cottage Garden'

Based on a design by Humphry Repton, which he intended for the Brighton Pavilion, this is a modern interpretation in bronze of basket edging. The basket, of oval form with latticework arcaded sides and rope twist handle, has a zinc liner. 165cm.: 65ins. wide

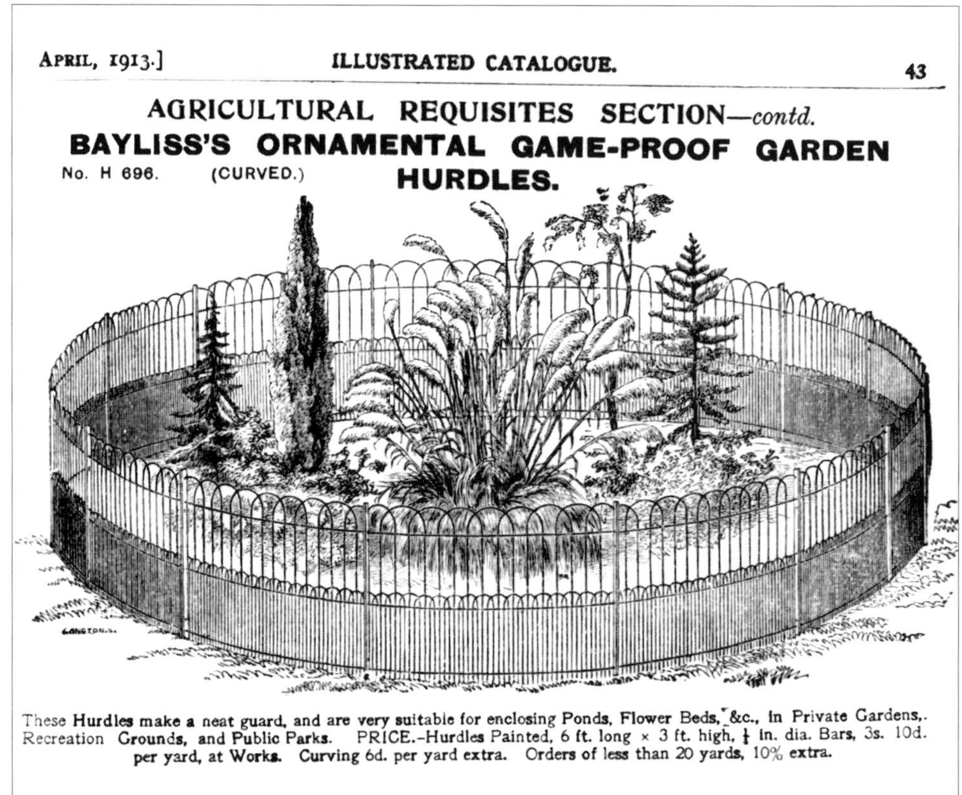

APRIL, 1913.] ILLUSTRATED CATALOGUE. 43

AGRICULTURAL REQUISITES SECTION—*contd.*

BAYLISS'S ORNAMENTAL GAME-PROOF GARDEN HURDLES.

No. H 696. (CURVED.)

These **Hurdles make a neat guard, and are very suitable for enclosing Ponds, Flower Beds, &c., in Private Gardens,** Recreation **Grounds, and Public Parks.** PRICE.-Hurdles Painted, 6 ft. long × 3 ft. high, ¼ in. dia. Bars, 3s. 10d. **per yard, at Works. Curving 6d. per yard extra. Orders of less than 20 yards, 10% extra.**

Catalogue illustration showing curved hurdles. Sold by the yard, these would have been particularly useful in recreation grounds and parks for protecting plants or enclosing ponds. Circa 1913

Recreation, Novelties and Awards

GARDEN TOYS

Toys of a gardening nature are a natural way of introducing children to the adult world, and probably the earliest garden-related toys would have been child-size spades and rakes, or a toy wooden village or farm of the type made in the Black Forest area of Germany in the middle of the nineteenth century. The most outstanding twentieth century contribution was that offered by Britains Ltd., whose metal 'Miniature Gardening' series was certainly comprehensive. Britains' competitors, notably Hill & Co. and Pixyland-Kew, also produced a limited range of garden related die-cast toys. There are also a few garden-related toys by other leading makers such as Dinky and Lines Brothers, but generally speaking pre-1960s' products are scarce.

The toy company Britains is internationally known for its toy soldiers, but amongst their extensive range they also produced the delightful 'Miniature Gardening' series in the 1930s, of which the prize piece is probably the greenhouse

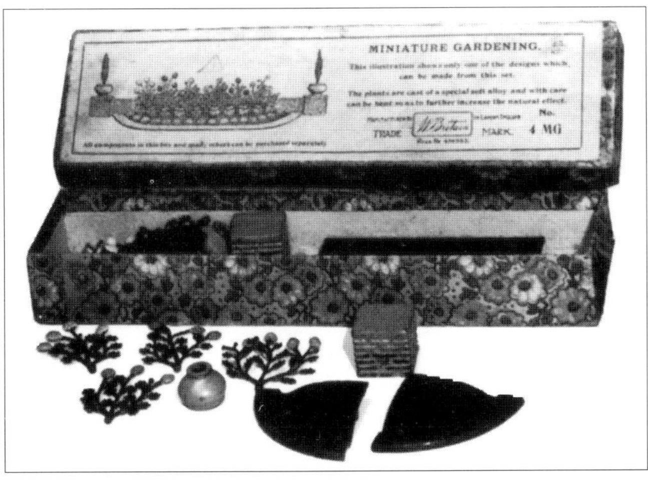

From Britains' 'Miniature Gardening' series (4MG), a selection which included walling, border with flowers and garden pots. Circa 1935

Bill (or is it Ben?) from the Sacul Company, a die-cast metal figure generated by the highly popular television series 'The Flowerpot Men'. Sold as a set with two flowerpot men, two terracotta flowerpots and Weed. Now a scarce collector's item. Circa 1951. 8cm.: 3ins. high

Britains' 'Miniature Gardening' range included a greenhouse, a cold frame, flowers and vegetables, paving, sundial, garden bench, fencing and rockeries. It was wonderful toy for both children and adults, and the firm even recommended the series to those planning a new garden layout or design. Circa 1930-40

Terracotta gnome, probably South German or Austrian. Circa 1910. 71cm.: 28ins. high

GNOMES

For the Garden or for Decorative Use

Illustrations actual size

No.	Each. d.	
169b	2	Gnome, $2\frac{3}{4}''$ high (standing, hands in pockets).
170b	2	Gnome, 2″ high (sitting, hands on knees).
171b	2	Gnome, 2″ high (sitting, cross-legged).
241b	6	Gnome, $5\frac{5}{8}''$ high (standing position).
242b	$4\frac{1}{2}$	Gnome, $3\frac{3}{4}''$ long (lying position).
243b	2	Gnome, $2\frac{1}{2}''$ long (lying position).

These models are very brightly and attractively finished.

No. 169b

No. 170b

No. 171b

No. 241b

No. 243b

No. 242b

Manufactured By W. Britain in London England

Trade Mark

Regd. No. 459993

Britains also produced a range of die-cast metal gnomes for garden or decorative use. Circa 1940

Toys which advertise garden products are very scarce. Atco motor mowers attracted some free advertising when their name appeared on one of the '28' series of Dinky Toy delivery vans. Circa 1935

Another van advertising Atco motor mowers is this tin-plate clockwork 'Mimic' van produced by Tri-ang. Circa 1950

Produced in the 1950s, this lawnmower was totally out of scale compared to other models in the Dinky Toy range. The toy has rotating blades and detachable grass box

In the early twentieth century, a number of biscuit manufacturers recognised the marketing advantages of offering their products in a novelty tin. A number of these tins have a garden-related interest. Left, a scarce 'lawnmower' biscuit tin by Barringer, Wallis & Manners, hinged top lid, lithographed details. Circa 1913. 10cm.: 4ins. high by 23cm.: 9ins. long with extending handle. Right, a rare Huntley & Palmers 'garden roller' biscuit tin, with hinged flap to cylinder and shaped handle. Circa 1913. 18cm.: 7ins. high

Above, Thomas Davidson (fl. 1863-1893), 'The Winning Stroke'. (Courtesy Sotheby's)

Above right, English School, detail from 'The Gibson Children in the Garden of the House at Southall, Middlesex', showing two young boys carrying a cricket bat, stumps and ball *(see p. 10)*

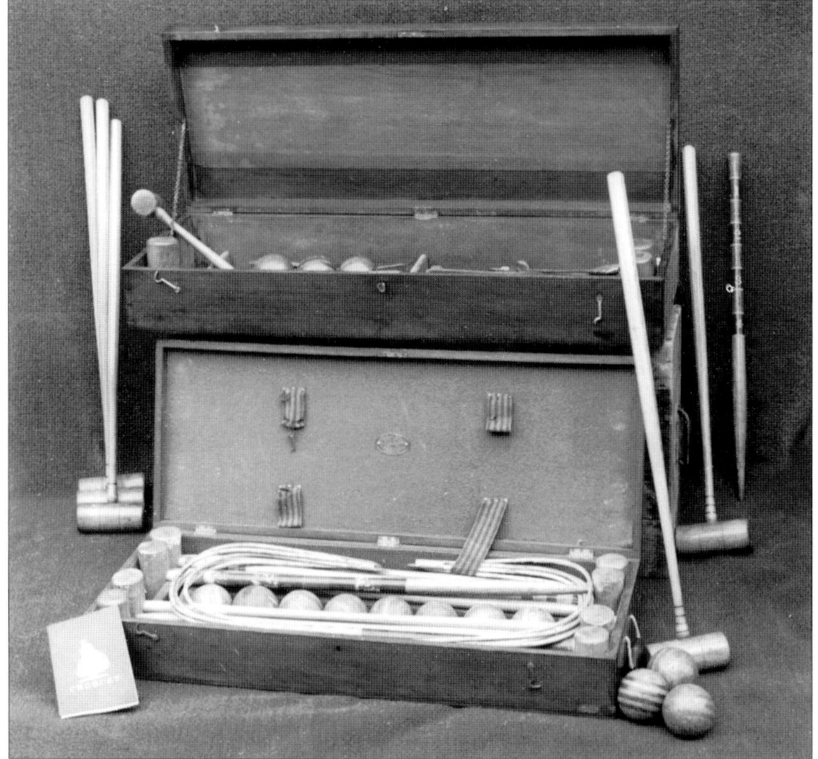

Two Jaques croquet sets, with mallets, balls, marking poles, hoops, marking flags and clips, in their mahogany storage cases. Mid-twentieth century

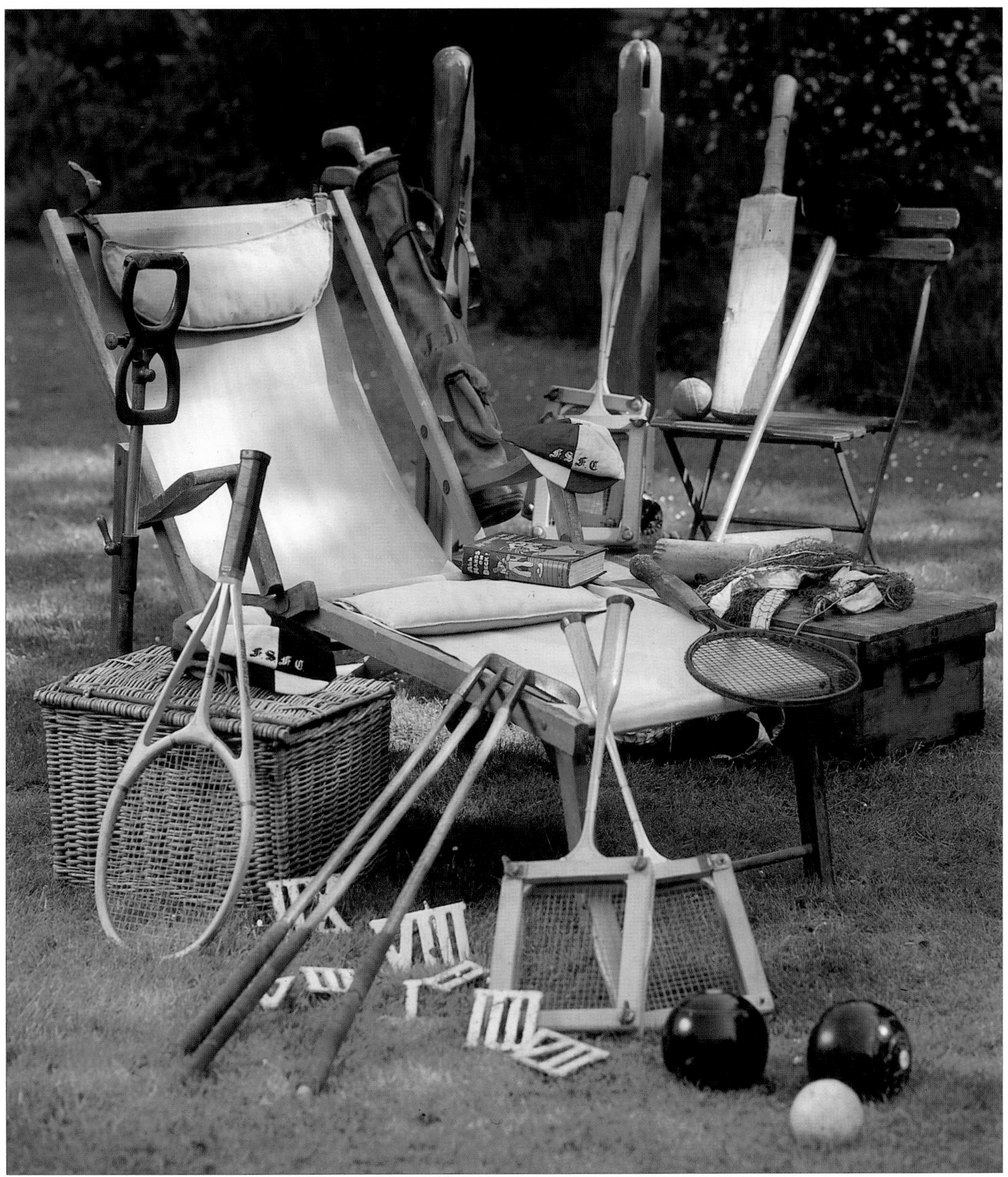

A selection of games and accessories, including an Edwardian deck lounge chair, with heavy green canvas cloth seat detachable head pillow, leg pad and leg rest, circa 1910; a green standard wrought iron frame folding chair, circa 1915; games equipment including Army & Navy badminton set in wooden storage box, circa 1910-20; F.H. Ayres Championship Tennis Posts, circa 1930; Hazells' 'Streamline' tennis racket, circa 1935 (this unusual racket was favoured by Bunny Austin in the 1930s); the metal-framed racket lying on the deck chair was an early attempt to use steel for both frame and strings, circa 1930; clock golf numerals in cast iron, circa 1910; three hickory shafted putters, circa 1900-20; Mills patent aluminium telescopic stick seat, circa 1914 (Mills, a company based in Sunderland, produced a range of products in aluminium including aluminium headed golf clubs, one of which can just be seen in the child's size canvas golf bag hanging on the deck chair. The company was also responsible for the famous Mills bomb); also shown are bowls, cricket bat and ball, badminton net and rackets

GAMES AND LEISURE

Probably the oldest sport or pastime related to the garden is archery. In the sixteenth century, the game of bowls became highly popular, and bowling greens were to be found incorporated in many larger gardens of the seventeenth and eighteenth centuries. Naturally, the grass needed to be cut short and be well maintained, which required skilled work with a scythe.

In the nineteenth century, the greater recreational time available to a wider middle class coincided with the introduction of the domestic lawnmower, enabling more people to have suitably cut lawns for garden games. The range of such games broadened immediately. Appreciating that nearly all games have some ancient lineage using a ball or a ball and stick, 'new' games such as croquet appeared in the 1850s. Its praises were sung in *Cassell's Book of Sports and Pastimes*, circa 1900: 'Croquet then, in its origin and early history, is entitled to be numbered amongst numerous athletic games which have been introduced with so much energy and with such immense benefit during the last forty years. It was productive of what may be almost called a revolution in the social life of the country; for from the time of its recognition as a national game, garden parties, which had hitherto been very dull and monotonous affairs, became the most common and popular of all entertainments in country places'.

In addition, there was lawn tennis, the outdoor version of the old indoor game, and badminton (which in spite of its English name had its origins in India), and lawn billiards. If these games were too serious or energetic, there was a host of novelty lawn games – a number of which were related to golf, as well as obstacle putting games, quoits and a game of tennis – 'Tonette' – which could be played on a small lawn.

On the left F.H. Ayres double croquet set with four large and four small mallets, eight balls, hoops, markers and accessories, shown with pine storage box, circa 1918. Ayres produced a range of sporting equipment around the turn of the century, including golf clubs and tennis rackets. On the right a Jaques boxed croquet set including mallets with brass bound heads and shown with pine box with maker's label

GAMAGES OF HOLBORN. — 124 — BENETFINKS OF CHEAPSIDE.

CROQUET SUNDRIES.

The Little Gripper Croquet Stand and Carrier.

This Stand is designed to hold a Croquet Set for 4 players, it is made in japanned steel with mahogany handle.
Very compact and neat in appearance.
Price .. .. **6 6** Carriage extra.

The Tournament Set, as illustration, picked Boxwood Balls, well painted and seasoned, correct size and weight, packed in polished wood box with brass handle, lock and key. Price per set, **12/6**

The **Holborn Set**, correct weight and size, selected Boxwood, in cardboard box,
Price **10/-** per set.

Cheaper quality do., per set of 4 .. **7/6**
Do. do. 8 to order **14/6**
Carriage extra under 10/-

Croquet Balls to match Sets 1 to 8.

	Nos. 1.	2	3	4
Set of 8 ..	3 in.	3⅜ in.	3⅝ in.	3⅞ in.
Price ..	**2/9**	**3/6**	**4/6**	**5/3**
		Nos. 5	7	8
Set of 8, Boxwood ..		3⅛ in.	3⅝ in.	3¼ in.
Price		**7/-**	**11/9**	**13/9**

Carriage extra under 10/-

The Midget Composition Clips

Actual size of illustration, very light and dyed the same colour throughout.

Packed in neat box,

Price **1/9** per set
Postage 2d.

Clips.

Enamelled Metal Spring Clips, as illustration.
1/3 per set of 4. Postage 2d.

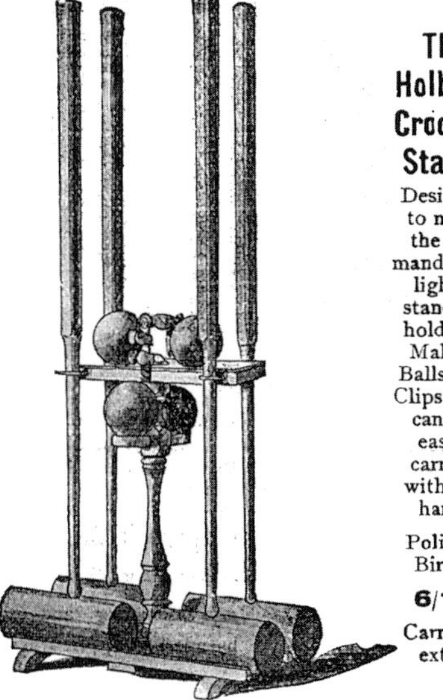

The Holborn Croquet Stand.

Designed to meet the demand for a lighter stand to hold the Mallet, Balls and Clips. It can be easily carried with one hand.

Polished Birch, **6/11**

Carriage extra.

The "G.B." Croquet Stand.

To hold 4 Mallets, set of Balls and Clips.
Polished birch with brass fittings .. **8/11**
Carriage extra.

Polished Walnut Carrier.

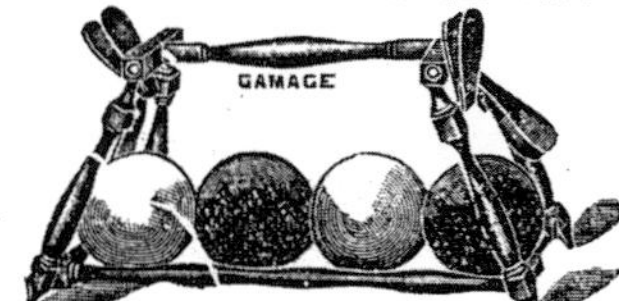

To hold 4 balls and 4 clips.
Price .. **3/4** each. Carriage extra.

Waterproof Mallet Case.

Price .. **3/3**

Post 4d.

Made from brown mail canvas, bound with leather, and leather handle.

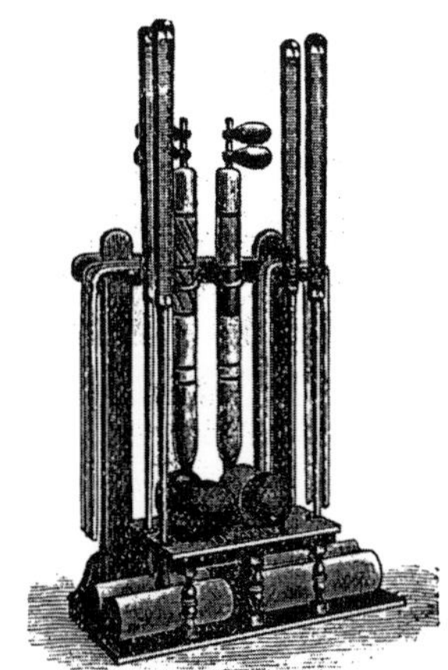

Slazenger's New Hall Croquet Stand.

A very compact and serviceable article.. **10/-**
Carriage extra.

"Excelite" Croquet Balls.

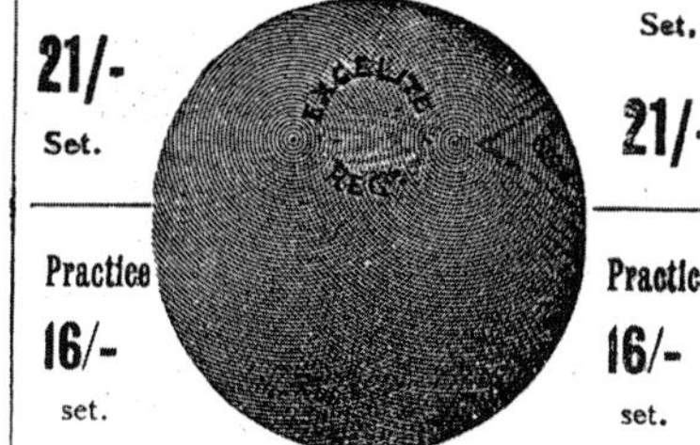

21/- Set. Set. **21/-**

Practice **16/-** set. Practice **16/-** set.

Four-ball Sets.

These Croquet Balls are correct Regulation weight and size, and will be found a great improvement on the Boxwood Ball. They will not chip, and are not affected by wet weather. Each set packet in neat box. Carriage free.

Slazenger's Stadium Composite Croquet Ball.

Used at many leading Tournaments.
Price **17/9** per set of 4.
Carriage paid.

Wire Netting for Croquet Borders.

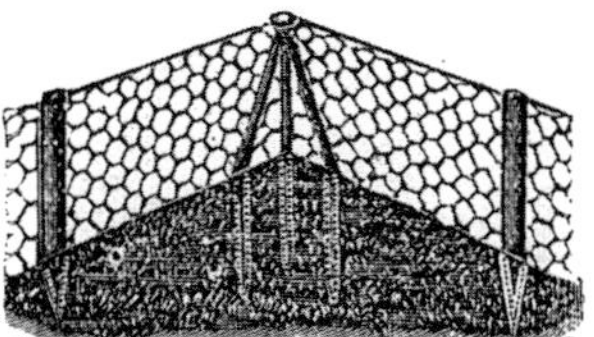

Wire Netting, consisting of 2 29-yd. lengths, 2 36-yd. lengths, 4 corner supports, 65 spikes
Netting 6 in. high.
Price **55/-**

Netting in Rolls of 50 yards, including spikes, **8/9** per roll.

Netting in 3 ft. lengths, including spikes, **3/6** per doz. Carriage extra.

The Gamages catalogue of circa 1914 included a wide variety of croquet accessories. Not shown here were turning posts, a ball painting compendium, and five varieties of hoop

34

THE HERTFORD DESIGN.

Length between arms	3 ft. 7 in.
Total length	4 ft. 0 in.
Width of seat	1 ft. 7 in.
Deal, painted green or white	£2 18 6
Dark Oak, varnished	£4 12 6
Teak, oiled	£5 0 0

Lock 2/6 extra.

THE HARLINGTON DESIGN.

Length between arms	6 ft. 0 in.
Total length	6 ft. 5 in.
Width of seat	1 ft. 7 in.
Deal, painted green or white	£3 15 0
Dark Oak, varnished	£5 7 6
Teak, oiled	£6 0 0

Locks 5/- extra.

GARDEN SEATS FOR CROQUET LAWNS.

These seats are made with boxes under the seats to contain croquet mallets, balls etc. The lockers are quite water-tight and the water runs off the back of the seats which are solid.

Any of the seats illustrated in catalogue can be made with lockers similar to the two illustrated on this page at an extra cost of 5/- per foot for deal seat, 7/6 for oak, and 8/6 for teak; thus to fit an ordinary 6ft. deal seat with locker would cost 30/-, oak 45/-, or teak 51/-.

Extract from "Country Life," June 3rd, 1905.

Everyone knows what a nuisance it is, having decided to spend the next two hours over a game of croquet, to be obliged to go back to the house and bring out armfuls of mallets, balls, and clips, which insist on dropping and rolling away down the path, and which necessitate a great deal more exercise than is compatible with keeping cool. It makes just all the difference to find everything ready to the hand on the lawn, and the garden seat with box should appeal to the laziness, the legitimate laziness, of everyone on a hot July day. At other times, too, when a storm comes on, everything can easily be put under cover, and altogether Messrs. J. P. White, of the Pyghtle Works, Bedford, are to be congratulated on the new designs shewn here.

The popularity of croquet in Edwardian times required appropriate garden furniture. J.P. White offered these garden seats especially for croquet lawns, with their practical 'water tight' lockers. Note the endorsement from Country Life

George Charles Haité (1855-1924), 'The Flower Show', 1898

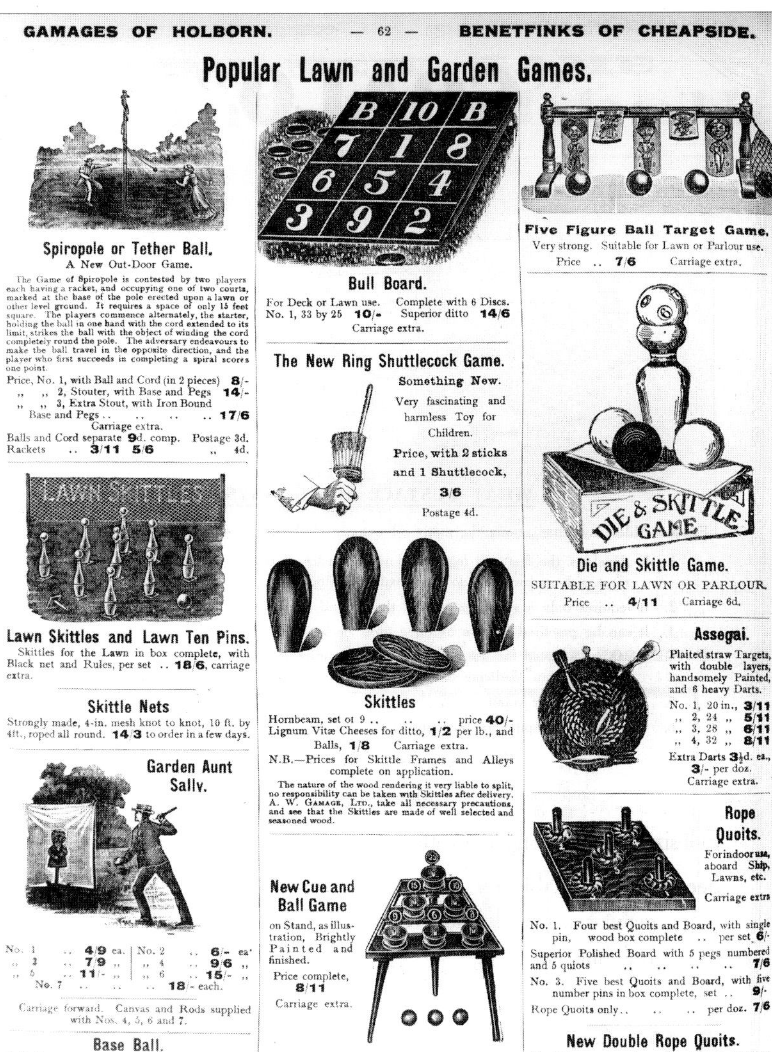

GAMAGES OF HOLBORN. — 62 — BENETFINKS OF CHEAPSIDE.

Popular Lawn and Garden Games.

Spiropole or Tether Ball.
A New Out-Door Game.

The Game of Spiropole is contested by two players each having a racket, and occupying one of two courts, marked at the base of the pole erected upon a lawn or other level ground. It requires a space of only 15 feet square. The players commence alternately, the starter, holding the ball in one hand with the cord extended to its limit, strikes the ball with the object of winding the cord completely round the pole. The adversary endeavours to make the ball travel in the opposite direction, and the player who first succeeds in completing a spiral scores one point.

Price, No. 1, with Ball and Cord (in 2 pieces) **8/-**
,, ,, 2, Stouter, with Base and Pegs **14/-**
,, ,, 3, Extra Stout, with Iron Bound Base and Pegs **17/6**
Carriage extra.
Balls and Cord separate **9**d. comp. Postage 3d.
Rackets .. **3/11** **5/6** ,, 4d.

Lawn Skittles and Lawn Ten Pins.
Skittles for the Lawn in box complete, with Black net and Rules, per set .. **18/6**, carriage extra.

Skittle Nets
Strongly made, 4-in. mesh knot to knot, 10 ft. by 4ft., roped all round. **14/3** to order in a few days.

Garden Aunt Sally.

No. 1 .. **4/9** ea. | No. 2 .. **6/-** ea.
,, 3 .. **7/9** ,, | ,, 4 .. **9/6** ,,
,, 5 .. **11/-** ,, | ,, 6 .. **15/-** ,,
No. 7 .. .. .. **18/-** each.

Carriage forward. Canvas and Rods supplied with Nos. 4, 5, 6 and 7.

Base Ball.
Balls **4/-** and **5/-** each, carriage 3d. Sticks from **1/-** each, carriage 5d. Outfits to order. Other qualities to order. Particulars on application

Bull Board.
For Deck or Lawn use. Complete with 6 Discs.
No. 1, 33 by 25 **10/-** Superior ditto **14/6**
Carriage extra.

The New Ring Shuttlecock Game.
Something New.
Very fascinating and harmless Toy for Children.
Price, with 2 sticks and 1 Shuttlecock, **3/6**
Postage 4d.

Skittles
Hornbeam, set of 9 .. .. .. price **40/-**
Lignum Vitæ Cheeses for ditto, **1/2** per lb., and Balls, **1/8** Carriage extra.
N.B.—Prices for Skittle Frames and Alleys complete on application.

The nature of the wood rendering it very liable to split, no responsibility can be taken with Skittles after delivery. A. W. Gamage, Ltd., take all necessary precautions, and see that the Skittles are made of well selected and seasoned wood.

New Cue and Ball Game
on Stand, as illustration, Brightly Painted and finished.
Price complete, **8/11**
Carriage extra.

"**Ringolf**" is the latest Lawn Golf Game. Try It! .. . page 58.

Five Figure Ball Target Game.
Very strong. Suitable for Lawn or Parlour use.
Price .. **7/6** Carriage extra.

Die and Skittle Game.
SUITABLE FOR LAWN OR PARLOUR.
Price .. **4/11** Carriage 6d.

Assegai.
Plaited straw Targets, with double layers, handsomely Painted, and 6 heavy Darts.
No. 1, 20 in., **3/11**
,, 2, 24 ,, **5/11**
,, 3, 28 ,, **6/11**
,, 4, 32 ,, **8/11**
Extra Darts **3½**d. ea., **3/-** per doz.
Carriage extra.

Rope Quoits.
For indoor use, aboard Ship, Lawns, etc.
Carriage extra

No. 1. Four best Quoits and Board, with single pin, wood box complete .. per set **6/-**
Superior Polished Board with 5 pegs numbered and 5 quiots **7/6**
No. 3. Five best Quoits and Board, with five number pins in box complete, set .. **9/-**
Rope Quoits only.. .. .. per doz. **7/6**

New Double Rope Quoits.
Consisting of two 5-peg Boards and five rope Quoits, forming box when closed, **10/6**
Carriage extra outside London carrier radius.

It seems endless garden games were available at the beginning of the twentieth century, although perhaps using the word 'garden' was just a marketing technique, since most of the games shown in this Gamages selection of circa 1914 could be played indoors

The Parachute Captive Golf Ball.
1/3 1/6 and **2/-** each. Post 3d.

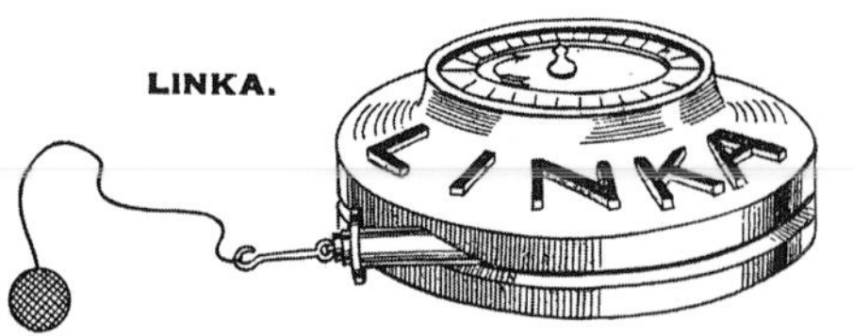

This ingenious instrument will automatically registered with accuracy the distance that would be reached when playing a free ball. It affords most excellent practice with an club. Price **21/-** Carriage paid

The "Ion" Golf Ball Trainer.
A capital device far indoor use or any limited space when the favourite game can be practised without fear of lost ball or any damage being done.
Price **3/3** each. Post 4d.

Gamages also offered a selection of 'Golf Lawn Games and Sundries' including the Parachute Captive Golf Ball, the Linka (which automatically registered the distance reached if playing with a free ball), and the 'Ion' Golf Ball Trainer

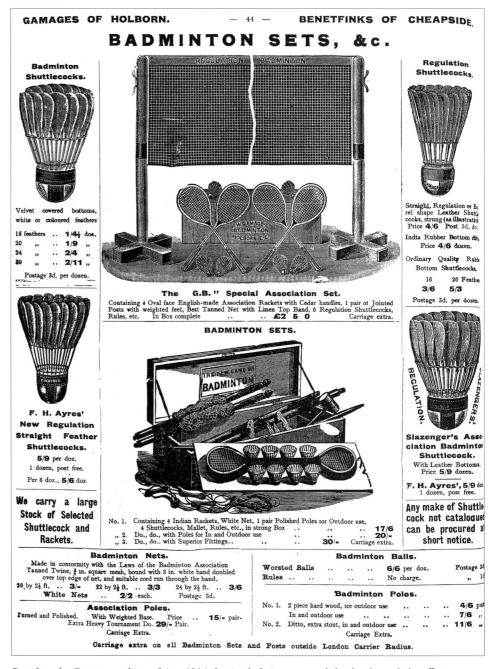

GAMAGES OF HOLBORN. — 44 — **BENETFINKS OF CHEAPSIDE.**

BADMINTON SETS, &c.

Badminton Shuttlecocks.

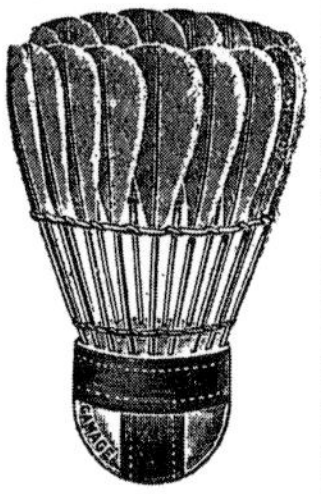

Velvet covered bottoms, white or coloured feathers

16 feathers .. **1/4½** doz.
20 " .. **1/9** "
24 " .. **2/4** "
30 " .. **2/11** "

Postage 3d. per dozen.

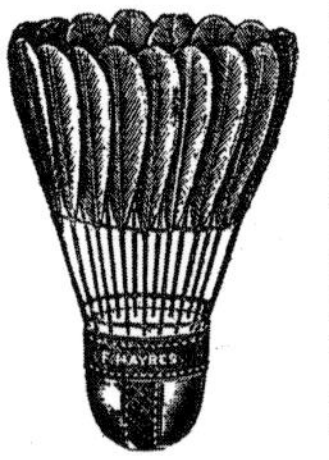

F. H. Ayres' New Regulation Straight Feather Shuttlecocks.
5/9 per doz.
1 dozen, post free.
Per 6 doz., **5/6** doz

We carry a large Stock of Selected Shuttlecock and Rackets.

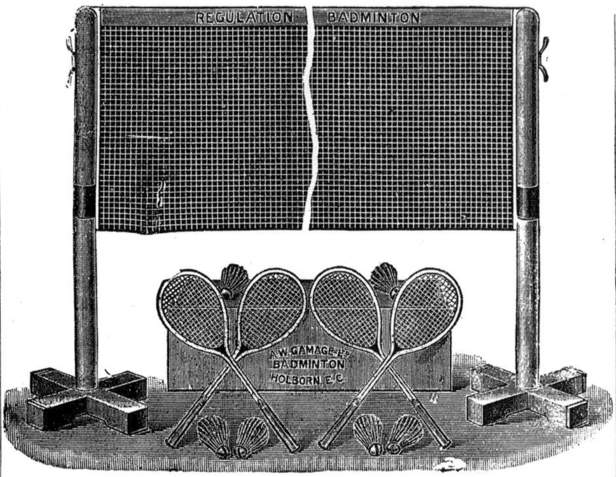

REGULATION BADMINTON

A. W. GAMAGE LTD BADMINTON HOLBORN, E.C.

The G.B." Special Association Set.
Containing 4 Oval face English-made Association Rackets with Cedar handles, 1 pair of Jointed Posts with weighted feet, Best Tanned Net with Linen Top Band, 6 Regulation Shuttlecocks, Rules, etc. In Box complete .. .. **£2 5 0** Carriage extra.

BADMINTON SETS.

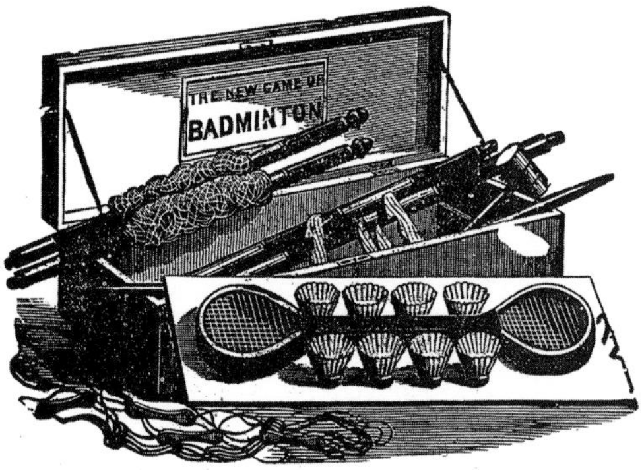

THE NEW GAME OF BADMINTON

No. 1. Containing 4 Indian Rackets, White Net, 1 pair Polished Poles for Outdoor use, 4 Shuttlecocks, Mallet, Rules, etc., in strong Box **17/6**
" 2. Do., do., with Poles for In and Outdoor use **20/-**
" 3. Do., do.. with Superior Fittings.. .. .. **30/-** Carriage extra.

Regulation Shuttlecocks.

Straight, Regulation or Barrel shape Leather Shuttlecocks, strung (as illustration) Price **4/6** Post 3d. doz.
India Rubber Bottom ditto Price **4/6** dozen.
Ordinary Quality Rubber Bottom Shuttlecocks.
16 20 Feathers
3/6 **5/3**
Postage 3d. per dozen.

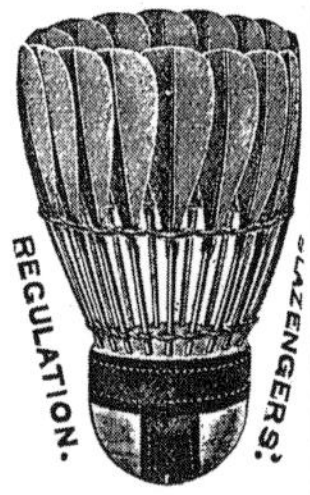

REGULATION. SLAZENGERS.

Slazenger's Association Badminton Shuttlecock.
With Leather Bottoms. Price **5/9** dozen.

F. H. Ayres', 5/9 doz
1 dozen, post free.

Any make of Shuttlecock not catalogued can be procured at short notice.

Badminton Nets.
Made in conformity with the Laws of the Badminton Association Tanned Twine, ¾ in. square mesh, bound with 3 in. white band doubled over top edge of net, and suitable cord run through the band.
20 by 2¼ ft. .. **3/-** 22 by 2¼ ft. .. **3/3** 24 by 2¼ ft. .. **3/6**
White Nets .. **2/2** each. Postage 3d.

Association Poles.
Turned and Polished. With Weighted Base. Price .. **15/-** pair.
Extra Heavy Tournament Do. **29/-** Pair.
Carriage Extra.

Badminton Balls.
Worsted Balls .. .. .. **6/6** per doz. Postage 3d
Rules .. .. No charge. " 1d

Badminton Poles.
No. 1. 2 piece hard wood, for outdoor use .. .. .. **4/6** pair
In and outdoor use .. .. **7/6** "
No. 2. Ditto, extra stout, in and outdoor use .. .. .. **11/6** "
Carriage Extra.

Carriage extra on all Badminton Sets and Posts outside London Carrier Radius.

Page from the Gamages catalogue of circa 1914 showing badminton sets and shuttlecocks, and also offering badminton nets, balls and poles

A wide variety of garden tents, bathing tents and other forms of shelter was available from Gamages in the early years of the twentieth century. Shown here are the 'Ideal' Lawn Tent or Shelter which was erected without guy ropes, and the 'Tokio' Garden House

The ingenious 'Flexion' folding picnic table with four seats. Of steel and compressed board construction, the top doubles as a carrying case, making it a convenient portable accessory for the garden. English. Circa 1940. Similar sets are available today though these are of plastic construction

You need to be a little careful as you get in and out of this unusual swinging and reclining deckchair. Wrought iron frame and canvas cover and canopy. Late nineteenth/early twentieth century

EPHEMERA, NOVELTIES, AWARDS

A number of items associated with garden decoration or use fail to fit neatly into defined categories. They may be unique items or particular to a very limited use, and in some cases they will be ephemeral. Collecting gardening ephemera can be a fascinating collecting field in its own right. Apart from the interesting and attractive headed paper illustrated opposite, the subject extends to all manner of disposable advertising and promotional material, from seed packets to postcards, tickets, photographs, labels, instructions, booklets, magazines, etc., and even sets of gardening related cigarette cards or horticultural prize certificates.

Although awards for horticulture were given in the early nineteenth century, the popularity of flower and vegetable growing in the second half of the century through to the First World War has left us a legacy of interesting small collectables commemorating and celebrating all types of produce from championship pineapples to prize chrysanthemums. Many were given by seedsmen or guano manufacturers, or by local horticultural societies and national institutions. Many of the earlier awards are attractive, some designed by leading nineteenth century medallists such as Wyon, and are usually found in silver or bronze.

A very interesting early nineteenth century painted wood sign or picture, the standing gentleman gardener with spade bears a remarkable likeness to the frontispiece illustration of Abercrombie's Every Man His Own Gardener, *1800, depicting a garden scene and John Abercrombie at the age of seventy-two*

At a time when all seeds were packeted by hand, seed spoons would be required to measure quantities. The Liverpool company of Blake & Mackenzie produced this brass seed bowl stamped 'The Perfect', together with graduated measuring ladles. Circa 1900

A selection of headed paper from seedsmen and gardeners, circa 1855 to 1892, and a landscape gardener's leaflet which highlights the vogue for croquet, tennis and bowling greens in the 1880s and 1890s

Wooden Labels. 3-inch, 4d.; 4-inch, 6d.; 5-inch, 7d.; 6-inch, 8d.; 7-inch, 10d.; 8-inch, 1s. per 100.
Silver Sand, for potting purposes, per cwt. 4s.
London Peat, for potting purposes, per cwt. 7s.

Flower Bouquet.

Bouquet Making Material, &c.

Camellia Wire, in 7-inch lengths. Per lb., 3s.
Bouquet Wire, on ¼-lb. Reels. Per lb., 3s.
Bouquet Holders, in glazed card, 3s. per doz.
Bouquet Holders, in wicker, 6d. each.
Bouquet Papers, various patterns, 1s. to 3s. per doz.
Bouquets of Everlasting Flowers and Grasses, in great variety, 9d. to 1s. 6d. each.
Loose Gnaphaliums, assorted colours, in bunches, 6d. each.

Table Decoration.

WREATHS.

Cape Flowers on Green Moss, from 2s.
Cape Flowers, with Lily of the Valley, Forget-me-not, Pansy, &c., 2s. 3d., 3s. 6d., and 5s.

THE PATENT VERMIN ASPHYXIATOR,

FOR DESTROYING—Rats, Rabbits, Moles, Snakes, Reptiles, Insects, &c.
FOR DISINFECTING—Hospitals, Vessels, Drains, Rooms, Bedding, Clothes.
FOR FUMIGATING—Greenhouse Plants, &c.
FOR PERFUMING—Apartments, Halls, &c.

Price of each Machine complete, including Two Feet of Flexible Tubing with Tin Nozzles and Rose attached, Two Wrenches, Packing Charges and Carriage, £2 15s.

Extra Lengths of Flexible Tubing at 1s. 6d. per foot.

Sulphur Paper,	0s. 6d.	per lb.
Smoke Paper,	0s. 4d.	,,
Tobacco Paper, for Greenhouses,	1s. 3d.	,,
Insect Destroying Compound, for do.	1s. 3d.	,,
Snake and Reptile Destroying Compound (in 3-lb Tins)	1s. 0d.	,,

98

Above, catalogues and advertisements are useful in identifying the products of early manufacturers. A broadsheet illustration of a range of artificial stone garden ornament offered for sale by Ransome & Parsons, Ipswich. Circa 1840

Above right, Benjamin Reid & Co. of Aberdeen catalogue advertisement for a selection of garden related items, including a 'Patent vermin asphyxiator'. Circa 1875

A Yates seed display vending box flanked by two seed despatch boxes. Circa 1900

A Sutton & Sons tin transportation seed box. Circa 1935

Royal ceremonial spades are more often found with silver plated blades and an ivory bar to the grip. However this is a much used spade with a steel blade stamped 'I. Black Ford, Forge 2', circa 1900, the ebonised handle and shaft with twelve applied silver shields inscribed as follows, on the front: 'Her Most Gracious Majesty Queen Victoria, 24th April 1900'; 'Her Royal Highness Princess Henry of Battenberg, 24th April 1900'; 'Their Royal Highnesses Alexander Leopold and Maurice of Battenberg, 24th April 1900'; 'Her Royal Highness Princess Christian of Schleswig Holstein, 26th April 1900'; 'His Royal Highness the Duke of Connaught KG, 21st April 1904'; 'Her Royal Highness the Duchess of Connaught, 21st April 1904'; 'Her Royal Highness Princess Margaret of Connaught, 21st April, 1904'; on the reverse: 'His Most Gracious Majesty King Edward VII, April 30th 1904' and 'Her Most Gracious Majesty Queen Alexandra, April 30th May 1904'; 'Her Royal Highness the Princess Victoria, 30th April, 1904'; 'Her Royal Highness Princess Patricia of Connaught, 21st April 1904'; 'His Royal Highness Prince Arthur of Connaught KG, 4th May 1904'. This is a fascinating record of British and European continental royalty at the turn of the century and a real collector's item

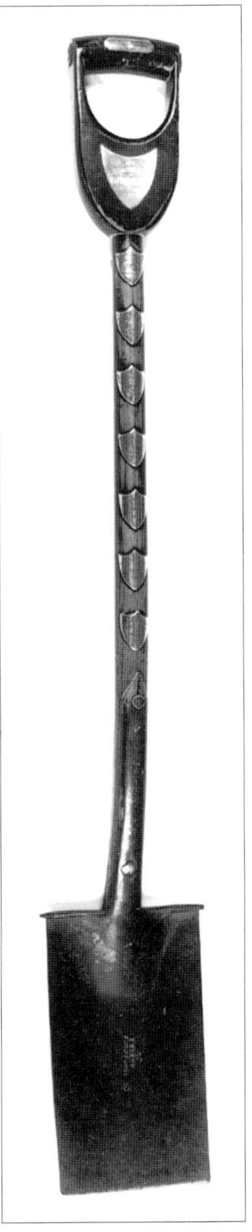

A rare Gardeners' Friendly Society ceremonial wooden axe, the head painted with crossed spade, fork and rake, and the initials 'HL' and 'No 1'. Parcel gilt shaft with arrowhead and slitted cup. Circa 1835. 60cm.: 35½ins. long

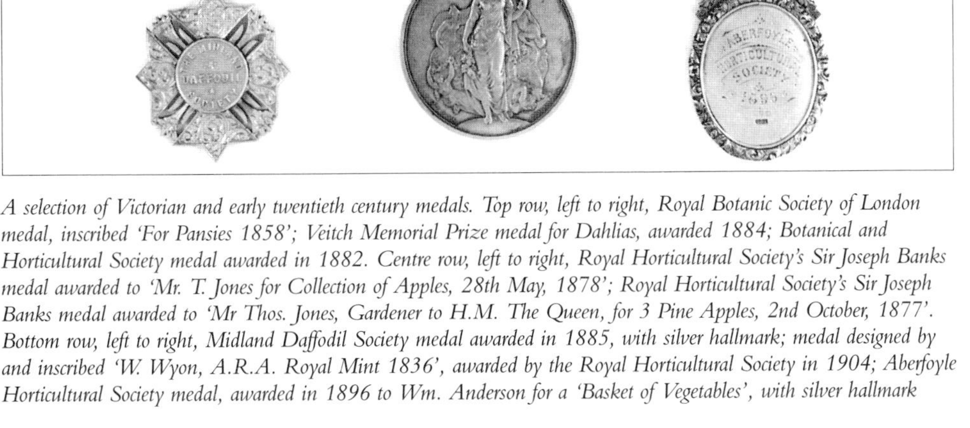

A selection of Victorian and early twentieth century medals. Top row, left to right, Royal Botanic Society of London medal, inscribed 'For Pansies 1858'; Veitch Memorial Prize medal for Dahlias, awarded 1884; Botanical and Horticultural Society medal awarded in 1882. Centre row, left to right, Royal Horticultural Society's Sir Joseph Banks medal awarded to 'Mr. T. Jones for Collection of Apples, 28th May, 1878'; Royal Horticultural Society's Sir Joseph Banks medal awarded to 'Mr Thos. Jones, Gardener to H.M. The Queen, for 3 Pine Apples, 2nd October, 1877'. Bottom row, left to right, Midland Daffodil Society medal awarded in 1885, with silver hallmark; medal designed by and inscribed 'W. Wyon, A.R.A. Royal Mint 1836', awarded by the Royal Horticultural Society in 1904; Aberfoyle Horticultural Society medal, awarded in 1896 to Wm. Anderson for a 'Basket of Vegetables', with silver hallmark

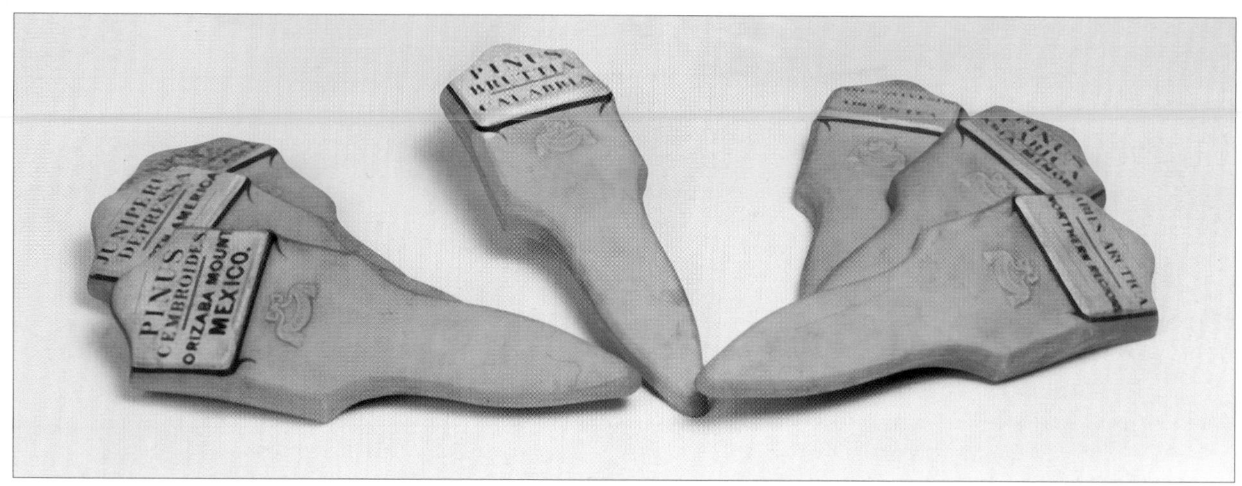

Ceramic tallies or plant labels, stamped 'Bourne' and fitted with name labels in Latin and the country of origin. Tallies appear in wood and metal, but these are probably some of the most attractive. Early nineteenth century. 30cm.: 11ins. long

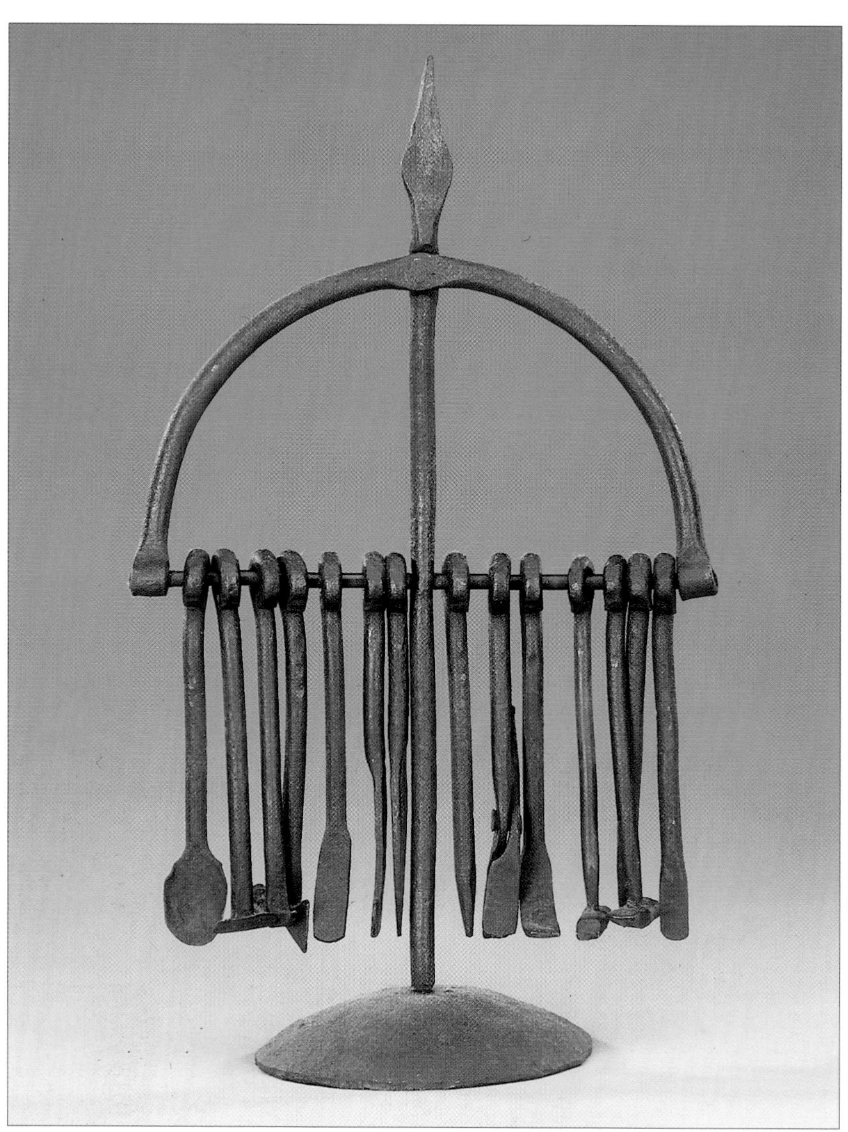

A rare eighteenth century tradesman's sample of miniature iron implements including spade, axe, pick and billhook with stand, reputedly a method of indicating the variety of tools available from a local blacksmith or specialist manufacturer. 23.5cm.: 9¼ins high

EVERY REQUISITE
SUPPLIED FOR
THE FARM
THE GARDEN
AND
THE FOREST

The
Queen's Seedsmen.

Ben. Reid & Co.
Aberdeen,
Scotland.

The Queen's Seedsmen, Benjamin Reid & Co. of Aberdeen, produced this extensive catalogue which includes not only seeds but also a selection of garden implements and general accessories. Circa 1875

A brooch suitable for a lady gardener, complete with basket and rake. Circa 1900

Three early horticultural medals, left to right, Loyal and Independent Gardeners medal, possibly in paktong, with grapes to suspension loop, circa 1840, 6.5mm.: 2½ins. wide; an attractive oval prize award in silver, issued by the Dumfries and Galloway Horticultural Society and inscribed to 'Mr Jas. Bogie for the Best Tulips, 1813', pierced for suspension; Royal Horticultural Society medal in silver inscribed 'Presented to Mr George Washington Jones, July 14th 1823'

An interesting bronze presentation plaque designed by H. Thornycroft, R.A., awarded by Toogood & Sons of Southampton. Circa 1910. 16cm. 6ins. wide. The female figure flanked by trees with a pair of cupids above is a charming period concept

Toogood & Sons. of Southampton Championship Shields, one bronze, one silver, mounted on stands. Circa 1912

Bibliography

BOOKS

Beeton, S.O., *Beeton's Garden Management*, London n.d. circa 1871.
Beeton, *New Dictionary of Everyday Gardening*, London n.d. circa 1895.
Burton, Elizabeth, *The Georgians at Home*, London 1967, 1973.
Cassell's Book of Sports and Pastimes, n.d. circa 1900.
Davies, Jennifer, *The Victorian Kitchen Garden*, London 1987.
Davis, John, *Antique Garden Ornament*, Woodbridge 1991.
Hadfield, Miles, *A History of British Gardening*, London 1978, 1983.
Halford, David G., *Old Lawn Mowers*, Princes Risborough 1982, 1993.
Hunt, Peter (ed.), *The Shell Gardens Book*, London 1964.
Huxley, Anthony, *An Illustrated History of Gardening*, London 1978, 1983.
Jekyll, Gertrude, *Garden Ornament*, London 1918, reprinted Woodbridge 1982.
Jellicoe, G. and S., Good, P., and Lancaster, M., *The Oxford Companion to Gardens*, London 1986.
Loudon, John Claudius, *Encyclopedia of Gardening*, London 1822, 1834, 1878.
Pilcher, Donald, *The Regency Style*, London 1947.
Plumtre, G., Garnock, J., and Rylands, J., *Garden Ornament*, London 1989.
Robertson E.G. and J., *Cast Iron Decoration*, 1977.
Rose, Graham, *The Traditional Garden Book*, London 1989.
Sanecki, Kay N., *Old Garden Tools*, Princes Risborough 1979, 1987.
Symes, Michael, *A Glossary of Garden History*, Princes Risborough 1993.
Thacker, Christopher, *Historic Garden Tools*, London 1990.
Triggs, H. Inigo, *Formal Gardens in England and Scotland*, London 1902, reprinted Woodbridge 1988.
Weaver, Lawrence, *English Leadwork*, 1909, reprinted 1972.

CATALOGUES

Army & Navy Auxiliary Catalogue, 1913.
Army & Navy General Catalogue, 1935-36.
Joseph Bentley Ltd. Catalogue, 1937-38.
Blanchard & Co. Illustrated Catalogue, London circa 1856.
Coalbrookdale Company Catalogue, 1875.
William Cooper, *The Gardeners' and Poultry Keepers' Guide and Illustrated Catalogue*, London circa 1910.
Gamages General Catalogue, 1911, 1914.
William Hunt & Sons, The Brades Ltd. Catalogue, 1941.
Richard Melhuish, Garden Tools Catalogue, 1936.
Pearson Page & Co. General Catalogue, Birmingham/London circa 1920.
Benjamin Reid & Co. Catalogue, Aberdeen circa 1875.
C.T. Skelton & Co. Catalogue, Sheffield circa 1885.
C.T. Skelton & Co. Illustrated Catalogue of Tools, Sheffield 1927.
Robert Sorby & Sons Catalogue, Sheffield 1854.
Sotheby's, *Glory of the Garden*, Loan Exhibition, London 1987.
Walter Thornhill Catalogue, London circa 1860.
C.W. & R. Vaughan Bros. Catalogue, Birmingham, 1870.
J.P. White, *Garden Furniture & Ornament*, 1910, reprinted 1987.
William Wood & Son Catalogue, 1938.
John Wright Co. Catalogue, Birmingham circa 1872.

Places to Visit

British Lawnmower Museum, 106–114 Shakespeare Street, Southport PR8 5AJ.
Halford Lawnmower Collection, Trerice Manor, nr. Newquay, Cornwall TR8 4PG.
Ironbridge Gorge Museum, Ironbridge, Telford, Shropshire TF8 7AW.
Museum of English Rural Life, University of Reading, Whiteknights, Reading, Berkshire RG6 2AG.
Museum of Garden History, St. Mary's at Lambeth, Lambeth Palace Road, London SE1 7JU.
Museum of London, London Wall, London EC2 5HN.
Walled Kitchen Garden Exhibition, Clumber Park, Worksop, Nottinghamshire S80 3AZ

PLEASE
KEEP OFF THE GRA